Baseball's
BRIEF LIVES

*Player Stories Inspired by
the Infinite Inning*

Steven Goldman

Also by Steven Goldman

Forging Genius:
The Making of Casey Stengel

Baseball's Brief Lives: Player Stories Inspired by the Infinite Inning
Copyright © 2022 Steven Goldman

All rights reserved. This book or any portion thereof may not be reproduced or used in any manner whatsoever without the express written permission of the publisher except for the use of brief quotations in a book review.

ISBN: 979-8-9867609-0-2 (paperback)
ISBN: 979-8-9867609-1-9 (eBook)

Cover and Interior Design by KUHN Design Group | kuhndesigngroup.com
Images via the Library of Congress

First Edition: August 2022

Published 2022 by Steven Goldman and FTG Publishing
sgoldman@baseballprospectus.com

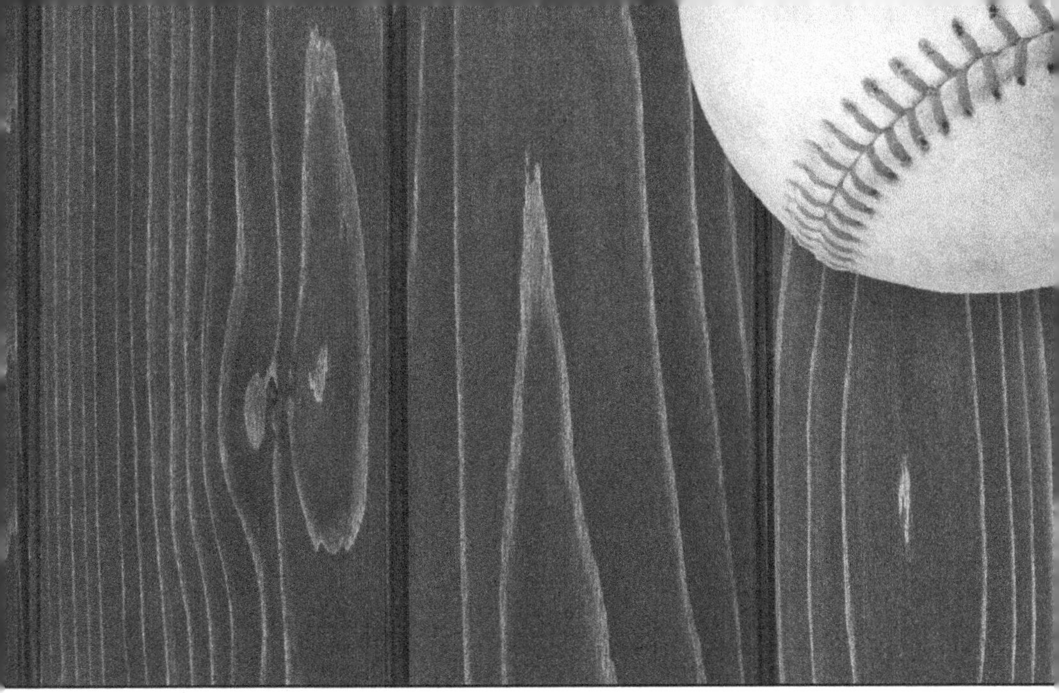

For Sarah and Clemens

*Somehow stories like these awakened me to life;
may you find the stories that illuminate yours.*

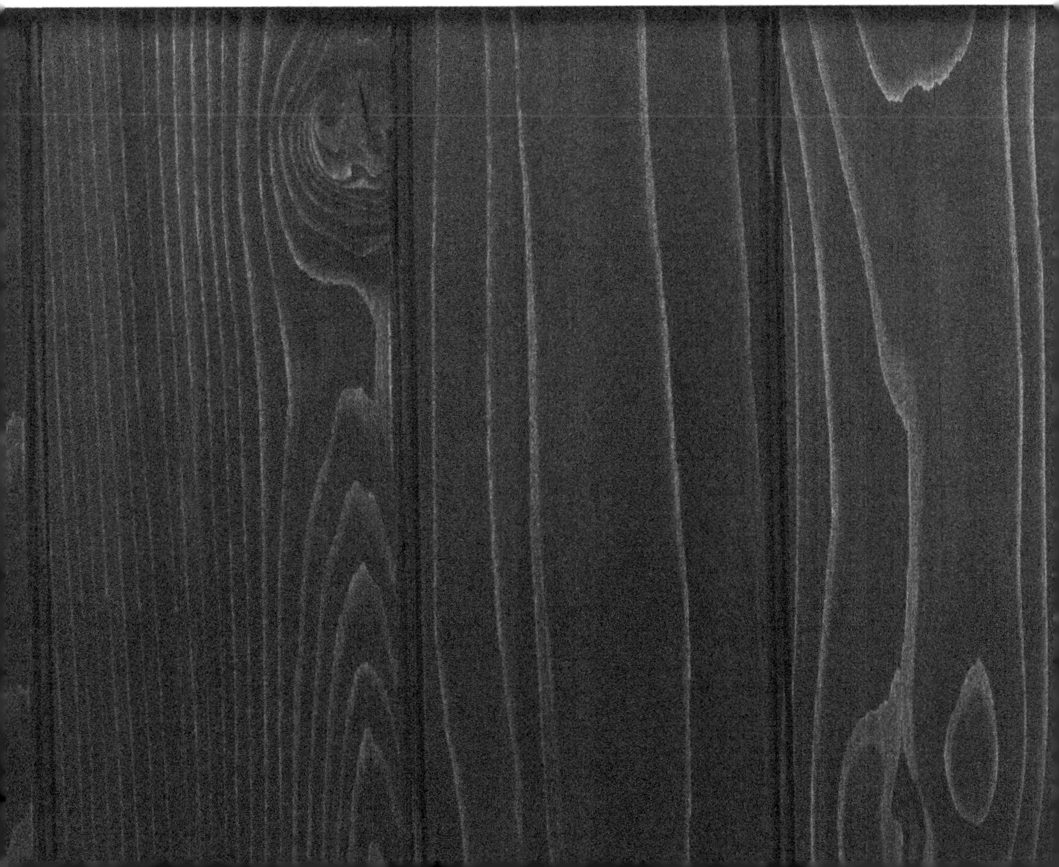

CONTENTS

Contents 7
Foreword 11
Introduction: Harold Baines and the Process of Re-enchantment 17

Chapter One: Team of Greats 27
   Biz Mackey, C 27
   Jim Bottomley, 1B 31
   Billy Herman, 2B 33
   Bill Madlock, 3B 36
   Joe Sewell, SS 38
   Charlie Keller, OF 40
   Tris Speaker, OF 42
   Andre Dawson, OF 45
   Brian Downing, DH/OF 48
   Don Drysdale, RHP 49

Chapter Two: Names 53
   Bubbles Hargrave, C 53
   Kitty Bransfield, 1B 55
   Bip Roberts, 2B/OF 57
   Battleship Gremminger, 3B 58
   Pee-Wee Wanninger, SS 60
   Wildfire Schulte, OF 62
   Birdie Cree, OF 63
   Nemo Leibold, OF 64
   Preacher Roe, LHP 65

Chapter Three: Yankees of Varying Quality 69
   Elston Howard, C/OF 69
   Tino Martinez, 1B 73
   Horace Clarke, 2B 75
   Gil McDougald, IF 77
   Frankie Crosetti, SS 80
   Ping Bodie, OF 83

Whitey Witt, OF/SS	84
Roberto Kelly, OF	85
Don Baylor, DH/OF	88
Jeff Weaver, RHP	91
Grant Jackson, LHP	93

Chapter Four: On the Fringes ... 95

Tim Blackwell, C	95
Tony Muser, 1B	96
Pete Coscarart, 2B	98
John Vukovich, 3B/IF	101
Billy Hunter, SS	104
Rollie Zeider, IF	107
Eddie "Mongoose" Lukon, OF	110
Eddie Brown, OF	110
Sumpter Clarke, OF	112
Jimmy Stewart, PH	114
Kent Greenfield, RHP	116

Chapter Five: The Too-Short Peak ... 121

Bill Schroeder, C	121
Wally Joyner, 1B	123
Delino DeShields, 2B	124
Bob Horner, 3B	127
Nomar Garciaparra, SS	128
Ben Grieve, OF	130
Dan Gladden, OF	132
Tracy Jones, OF	134
Sam Horn, DH	136
Sloppy Thurston, RHP	138
Bill Caudill, RHP	140

Chapter Six: Team of Greats II ... 145

Rick Ferrell, C	145
Bill Terry, 1B	147
Nellie Fox, 2B	152
Ron Santo, 3B	154
Pee Wee Reese, SS	156
Henry Aaron, OF	158

Al Simmons, OF	161
Mel Ott, OF/3B	164
Pedro Martinez, RHP	165
Ellis Kinder, RHP	167

Chapter Seven: More Yankees of Varying Quality ... 171

Ron Hassey, C	171
Chris Chambliss, 1B	173
Steve Sax, 2B	175
Red Rolfe, 3B	177
Álvaro Espinosa, SS	180
Gene Woodling, OF	181
Gerald Williams, OF	186
George Selkirk, OF	188
Bob Porterfield, RHP	191
Bob Shirley, LHP	194

Chapter Eight: Getting On Base ... 197

Frank Fernandez, C	197
Elbie Fletcher, 1B	200
Max Bishop, 2B	202
Harlond Clift, 3B	203
Willie Wells, SS	204
George Burns, OF	208
Roy Thomas, OF	209
Bobby Abreu, OF	212
Andre Thornton, DH/1B	215
Sugar Cain, RHP	216

Chapter Nine: The Abandoned ... 219

Wally Schang, C	219
Joe Kuhel, 1B	224
Ski Melillo, 2B	226
Art Devlin, 3B	232
Cecil Travis, SS	238
Chuck Hinton, OF/UT	239
Hi Myers, OF	241
Tommy Holmes, OF	244
Dutch Leonard, RHP	249

Chapter Ten: It's Complicated ... 251
    Spud Davis, C ... 251
    Rudy York, 1B ... 254
    Gary Sutherland, 2B ... 257
    Red Smith, 3B ... 258
    Bill Dahlen, SS ... 260
    Rico Carty, OF ... 264
    Dusty Cooke, OF ... 267
    Matty McIntyre, OF ... 270
    Pete Rose, OF/1B/3B/2B ... 272
    Pascual Perez, RHP ... 274

Acknowledgements ... 277

Notes ... 281

FOREWORD
by David Roth

Given how much of it there is, it can be frustrating how little baseball does with its history. It's not that all that history is somehow shoved out of frame, or is even ever anything but heavily palpable; it is always, always there, to the point where the games that happen on the field this summer and every other can sometimes come to feel crowded by the insistent glowering presence of the past. The issue, when it comes to baseball and the history it alternately drags along or rides triumphantly astride, is more about how—and specifically how punitively—it tends to be used.

Baseball, both institutionally and constitutionally, is hardly alone in instrumentalizing history to make whatever point seems worth making at that moment. This is more or less how history has been used and abused forever by people with some interest in using or abusing it. For all practical and ideological purposes, up to and including society-shaping Supreme Court rulings, this is what the American past has been for, and the version of it that is most useful in the present is the one that tends to be the one that wins. The calculated political abuse of history tends to reside at the darker, deeper end of this spectrum—because those efforts can do more damage to more people, and because these teetering Jenga constructions of isolated factoids and crabby memetics and desperate, decontextualized self-justifications require so much more work. The purpose of all that labor is to make sure that the quantum of human suffering in the future isn't too much smaller than the past's, and, while it's important to note that it's lazy and recursive and stupid, it is more important that it's cruel.

In baseball, at the moment, the past isn't treated with much more respect or care, but that misuse tends toward a similarly grumpy but much less ambitious end. The logical end point and only barely unstated goal of all that history abuse in our politics is that people get hurt; in baseball, it mostly just leaves fans feeling scolded and bored. The purpose of the past, from one idle gripe or sour bit of time-filling color commentary to the next, is to demonstrate that It's a Lot Different Now, and that the game is cheaper, softer, less meaningful, and otherwise worse than it used to be. The avalanche of acronyms for new statistics, the players that look and play and act differently than the ones that came before, all the new ways of understanding the game, and the new things to enjoy about it all somehow resolve into the same old way of not understanding and not enjoying it—*it's not what it was*.

You have probably noticed by now, due to my masterfully subtle shadings of language and extremely long sentences, that I think this specific instrumentalization sucks. There is no way that it could not suck. For starters, it exists to make people appreciate the things that they enjoy *less*. It is one thing to say that It Used to Be Different, but not an especially meaningful thing. *Everything* used to be different, because, even in a sport as habitually hidebound and literally rule-bound as baseball, things change. There is no more reason to believe that baseball used to be better at some past moment When It Was Different than there is to believe that the practice of medicine somehow had more integrity when it was built around leeches and saws and straps on which patients were supposed to bite down during the application of one or the other. Things change, at least living things do. This is how we know that they are still alive.

More than that, using what baseball has been to diminish or dismiss what it is *now* is such a needless, shameful waste. The game changes as it has always changed, and the people playing it change along with it. If you care about baseball, it is impossible not to care about this, because baseball is just the people that play it—the seasons are the sum of their labors and the story that work makes, but the people that make up baseball are what brings the bigger thing to life. What baseball is, in this last and most essential sense, is still and will always be what it was, which is a game played by, and also a story told by, people—living and breathing, variously flawed or flagrantly fucked-up, transcendent in their athletic genius or merely workmanlike in it, all working together in the ways that people work together, and all working against the various systems and biases and structures that working people always work against.

In this sense, the game is not unchanging, not ever, but also fundamentally the same as it has always been. The idea that baseball not only could but *should* be different, and its companion, that somehow the state of affairs is getting worse, is mostly an abstraction. It's not remotely a new one, either. "We don't like [ballplayers] as much as we once did," Roger Angell wrote in *The New Yorker* back in 1992, "and we don't like ourselves as much, either." To understand the first bit, you've got to acknowledge the second. Those aforementioned systems and biases and structures have something to do with that, but there's also how the past always tends to look relative to the present. If it is harsher, or more stifling, or just more stubbornly stupid and backwards, it is at least legible and settled in a way that the current moment never is, mostly because the past has happened already. Anyway, all that cynicism and broader disgruntlement seems like a terrible thing to hang on baseball players, of all people.

A person does not need to love every baseball player to love baseball, of course. There are a not-insignificant number of wholly irredeemable turds among the 100 players whose stories Steven Goldman tells in the pages following this one, and it is perfectly possible—it is, in fact, necessary—to love this game and the story it continues to tell without sparing any sympathy for Hal Chase or Pete Rose, or even forgiving Preacher Roe his spitballs or Bob Horner his perm or Jeff Weaver the portion of his career that he spent in Yankees pinstripes. They are all just who they are, and they are all characters in the ongoing, unhurried story that baseball continues to tell every summer, every day. It is baseball's way and human nature to plug these players into statistical hierarchies and file them under various types and taxonomies, but while some of their careers were more successful or lucrative or otherwise memorable than others, none of them were really insignificant if you have made the decision to understand baseball's long story as significant in itself.

Their variously notable comings and goings are, in the context of that longer story, as or *more* important than the winning or losing. To understand baseball in the way that Steven does is both to understand it and know it in a way that very few people ever have and to understand it in a way that has always seemed, to me, uniquely humane and joyful. Not because he always finds the best in every player's life in the game—sometimes there just isn't much good to find there—but because of how he connects those lives to each other and to the greater, longer life of the sport. The challenge that he set himself in *Baseball's Brief Lives* is not one that many writers would choose, and one that I think only he could accomplish nearly as astutely or lovingly or well.

I should say here that I don't think there's any story about the game that Steven *couldn't* tell, because he knows so much and understands so much about the game, and because he understands how and where baseball's past and the present connect with and inform each other. He has done this for as long as I have known him, over drinks and in editorial suggestions tucked into the margins of drafts, suggestions that, when unfolded, expand those stories' reach and grasp exponentially, and, more recently, through *The Infinite Inning* podcast. It is masterful without ever being overbearing, both apparently and earnestly just one recent incident in the long story of baseball reminding him of another less-recent one, and then there you are, not just learning about the cosmic-scale shit luck of George "Twinkletoes" Selkirk, but somehow feeling something about it—about what that luck (and the brutal, stupid systems that forced it upon him) cost him, and also feeling some modicum of pride at what he won despite that, many decades before you were born. The story is not always about George "Twinkletoes" Selkirk, I should note. But it doesn't have to be. That's the point.

This book is not an attempt to tell The Story of Baseball In 100 Brief Baseball Lives, even though that might have been a grabbier elevator pitch. It is, I think, something much more difficult, and more honest, and more suited to Steven's unique suite of skills. It is, when all these disparate and different and variously difficult baseball lives are taken altogether, 100 Brief Baseball Lives Telling the Story of Baseball. Not the *whole* story, of course, and not telling it in a way that turns all this unruly and unlikely human stuff into the sort of just-so sludge that baseball history tends, in its weaponized sense, to become. These parts don't fit together into a complete whole, but they couldn't—there is no selection of 100 baseball lives, let alone the random 100 that Steven takes on here, that could tell the entire story of a game that has been alive for as long as this one has.

More to the point, in the worldview of *The Infinite Inning*—"forever adrift and forever becoming," as Steven puts it, in the space before a third and final out that might never arrive—"the whole story" is just not an option. The whole of baseball is not known to us just yet, and it is not knowable, because the game is still growing, day by day, through the force of the people pushing it outward. This is the real waste in baseball's history being reduced to a sour counterpoint to baseball's present—what has happened before cannot, and should not, be seen as the opposite or enemy of what is happening now, not merely because using it that way is so shortsighted and petulant, but because it is *all the same story*. All these things, all this time, all these lives add up to baseball. All the stories flow from and disappear into the same current. It is probably true that the broader story of the game could be told as well through any other 100 baseball lives, although I think Steven does a beautiful job telling it here, through these. Anyway, there's a sequel if he wants it.

Introduction

HAROLD BAINES AND THE PROCESS OF RE-ENCHANTMENT

Harold Baines was inducted into the National Baseball Hall of Fame in 2019, an Eras [né Veterans] Committee decision that was widely derided as watering down the Hall's standards. That reaction was the kind that revealed more about its advocates than its subject, demonstrating an ossified mindset that insists on trying to place boundaries on something inherently subjective and amorphous. This has always been the problem with the Hall of Fame; it is, as Bill James has written, a self-defining institution. Yet, even self-definition has been an elusive target. Inflexible standards are too limiting, but without them the idea of establishing a coherent pantheon becomes ridiculous, because the potential membership is unlimited. The elevation of Baines, a longtime designated hitter with good-not-great statistics, heightened those contradictions until they simply floated away on the wind like dandelion seeds.

This is not an essay on the Hall of Fame—not really. The Hall's gallery of plaques is a gaudy irrelevancy. This is an essay on values.

Baines' plaque says:

> Respected and clutch left-handed hitter whose professional approach and humble demeanor made him one of the most consistent and reliable players of the 1980s and 1990s. Right fielder

and heart of lineup for 1983 A.L. West champion White Sox. Persevered through knee injuries to earn outstanding designated hitter of the year award in his first two seasons at the position, 1987 and 1988. Six-time All-Star and first overall selection in 1977 MLB draft. Totaled 2,866 hits and drove in 1,628 runs, retiring 21st on the all-time RBI list.

If "consistent and reliable" sounds less than Ruthian, that's because Baines was that kind of player. He was good—there are no bad players in the Hall of Fame—but he was by no means great. As a right fielder with bad knees, he had little defensive value (he was playable when healthy, but he was never Roberto Clemente). Even if you rank him on career offensive value alone, he was only the 268th-best player of the modern era (1901–present). The list of players more accomplished than him in this regard who are *not* in the Hall of Fame (not including players in various states of disgrace, such as Pete Rose and Joe Jackson or the many performance-enhancing-drug cases) includes second basemen Lou Whitaker and Bobby Grich and center fielder Bernie Williams towards the top and third baseman Carney Lansford, right fielder Tim Salmon, and left fielder Roy White well down the list, closer to (but still above) Baines.

At this point, you might want to argue that we are talking about a Hall of Statistical Accomplishments and not a Hall of *Fame*. It could be that, or it could be the Hall of Players with Two Arms and Two Legs, or anything else that you might want to assert, because "fame," which we take to mean "popularity," is such a vague term. That a player must pass certain statistical requirements, whether old school or modern sabermetric, to be legitimate is a kind of folkway that grew up around the annual Hall voting argument, a way of framing a problem that resisted coherence. When you already have a picture, a carefully chosen frame can accentuate its beauty, but when you are using that frame to try to corral the ineffable, the result is merely reductive.

The cliché about statistics being used like a drunkard utilizes a lamppost, for support rather than illumination, applies here. If greatness is reducible to a set of statistics, then there can be no debate about a player's qualities, because the necessity for critical thinking has been obviated by whatever numerical threshold you've selected. At present, there are 269 former players in the Hall. Imagine we were to restart the Hall with statistical qualifiers in place: For batters, 3,000 hits and/or 500 home runs and/or a batting average greater than

.310 over a career of at least 10 years. Baines disappears in a puff of smoke, as do Barry Larkin, Ron Santo, Ivan Rodriguez, Tim Raines, and a host of others. Players fall away going back beyond Tinker, Evers, and Chance. So too do the 35 Negro Leaguers, who lack full statistics; no more Satchel Paige, Josh Gibson, Pop Lloyd, and the rest.

Wait a minute, you might say. Satchel Paige isn't on the wall in Cooperstown because of statistics. He's there in spite of their absence. That's exactly the point: We have values other than statistics. There has always been a conflict between what Robert Pirsig, the author of *Zen and the Art of Motorcycle Maintenance*, called classical and romantic values:

> A classical understanding sees the world primarily as underlying form itself. A romantic understanding sees the world primarily in terms of immediate appearance.... The romantic mode is primarily inspirational, imaginative, creative, intuitive. Feelings rather than facts predominate. "Art" when it is opposed to "Science" is often romantic. It does not proceed by reason or by laws. It proceeds by feeling, intuition, and esthetic conscience.... The classic mode, by contrast, proceeds by reason and by laws—which are themselves underlying forms of thought and behavior.... Persons tend to think and feel exclusively in one mode or the other and in doing so tend to misunderstand and underestimate what the other mode is all about.

Baines represents Pirsig's dichotomy. The Hall of Fame, which was initially conceived as a statue around the plinth of which would be carved the name of memorable players, came to be "The Hall of Players Approved of by Classical Thinking." The player eligible via romantic thinking is only reluctantly permitted, if at all, because classical thinkers say it will water down the honor. That is only true if you believe it is, but we could easily disbelieve it, as well.

Phil Rizzuto, the longtime Yankees shortstop and broadcaster, is a good example of a romantic-thinking Hall of Famer. He was an outstanding defensive player who, but for his 1950 MVP season, was generally a slightly below-average offensive performer (by the standards of his contemporaries at his position, he was stronger; from 1940–60, major-league shortstops averaged .258/.326/.355, while Rizzuto hit .273/.351/.355). He missed three prime seasons due to service in the Navy during World War II, which meant he didn't reach any of the big, round statistical milestones that allow classical-Hall gatekeepers to avoid the labor of thinking, but he probably wouldn't have reached any of them even if the threat of a world conquered by fascism had not intervened. A career Yankee, Rizzuto played on nine pennant-winning teams and won seven championship rings. When he retired, he went directly into the Yankees' broadcast booth, where he remained for 40 years. An eccentric announcer who would sometimes comment on cannoli as often as the game, he endeared himself to generations of fans. He was on the Baseball Writers Association of America ballot until 1976, well into his career as a broadcaster. In short, he had all the fame but none of the numbers. That was enough to deny him entry until 1994, when the Veterans Committee finally capitulated to years of campaigning.

We need not be so limited in our imaginations. *There is more than one way to be great, to be important, to be of value to posterity.* No one has ever held a hit in his hands, whether the total is one or 3,000. They don't exist except as hashmarks on a page. For those of us who love baseball statistics, they are wonderfully evocative, but so is a story about a player that makes us understand something about the human condition. To deny this and insist on a purely quantitative definition of "fame"—of one's worthiness to be remembered—is an act of self-deprivation. We have, depending on attribution, 15 paintings by Leonardo da Vinci and more than 10 times that number by Pablo Picasso, but that doesn't mean that the latter was "better" or more important. We don't even have a way of expressing that kind of comparison in definitive terms. It becomes an argument about aesthetics, and therefore, to a large extent, subjective. However we might choose to begin that discussion, it wouldn't be that Picasso's works are better simply because they are more *numerous*—but that's how we're expected to appreciate ballplayers.

This is one reason why players who are the subjects of extended Hall of Fame debates disappear once they're enshrined. As long as Bert Blyleven and Tim Raines weren't in, their careers hadn't ended. They were ongoing due to being unresolved. Once they received their bas-relief ticket to Valhalla, they vanished. That's a shame, because we can learn so much more about them by talking about *anything* other than what's on their plaques. Blyleven's notes that he was a "fun-loving Dutchman" but doesn't specify all those dugout hotfoots (hotfeet?). Raines' is crowded with information but can't convey how thrilling he could be, the way he reappeared at Shea Stadium on May 2, 1987, collusion having robbed him of spring training and the first month of the season, and went 4-for-5 with a stolen base against the Mets, hitting a game-winning grand slam in the top of the 10th. We can't dispense with what they did—what they did is what brought them to our attention—but it's the *how* of it that makes them worth remembering. Once we realize that *any* player is a potential Raines or Blyleven, provided they have left us stories to tell, the world becomes a larger, more-colorful place.

As with every player, we can find many stories about what Baines did and the memorable games in which he played. One for the greatest-hits album came on May 8, 1984. Baines' White Sox hosted the Milwaukee Brewers. The game was full of future Hall of Famers beyond Baines, including Don Sutton, Robin Yount, Ted Simmons, and Rollie Fingers for the Brewers, and Carlton Fisk and, eventually, Tom Seaver, for the White Sox. The game was tied 3–3 after nine innings. It stayed that way for nearly 24 hours. The Brewers got Jim Gantner to second with one out in the 13th, but he was picked off. The White Sox loaded the bases with one out in the 14th, but the Sox' roster was thin that year, so they had to use hitters like Marc Hill and Dave Stegman in such situations. They both made outs, and the game limped on. At one point it snowed, but the players and umpires persevered.

There was room in the schedule for curfews in those days, and the umpires stopped the game after 17 innings. They resumed the next day. In the top of the 21st, Brewers outfielder Ben Oglivie hit a three-run home run. No matter; in the bottom of the inning, the Sox scored three runs of their own. The White Sox nearly won it in the top of the 23rd after a leadoff single by Stegman, but, as he rounded third on a subsequent hit by Tom Paciorek, Stegman was called out for interference when he ran directly into his own third-base coach, Jim Leyland. In the top of the 25th, Sox manager Tony La Russa brought in Tom Seaver, who was the scheduled starter for that day's game. Finally, *finally*, in the bottom of the 25th, after Stegman had struck out by bunting foul with two strikes, Baines stepped in against Brewers righty Chuck Porter (now in his eighth inning and clearly taking one for the team) and parked one over the center-field fence to end, at eight hours and six minutes, the longest game in American League history. Seaver, credited with the win, stuck around and won the second game—he was already loose.

That's a fun story, but it tells us nothing about Harold Baines. We can glean a little more about Baines from the fact that he had five extra-inning walk-off home runs in his career, as many as George Brett, Hank Aaron, and Willie Mays had. At that point, we may start to sense why he was seen as "professional," as well as "consistent and reliable," but to see Baines for who he really was, we have to switch from statistics to biography—which is to say, from the classical to the romantic mode of thinking. On June 5, 1983, just as he was achieving stardom, he discussed his father, Linwood Baines, a mason:

> He's my idol more than anybody else.... He went out of his way to do what he could for his kids. He worked six days a week and he even had a bleeding ulcer once. It's not like we were ever a very rich family. We had to struggle. We never had much, but we survived.... He knew what he had do in life. And no matter what happened, he always came out on top. We always had clean clothes on our back and food on our table...He doesn't dwell on the past.

Therein we begin to sense the value of Harold Baines, not as a player, but as an example to us—we who, like our ancestor-worshipping forebears (from whom we are not as different as we like to pretend we are), try to find meaning in an uncertain and seemingly purposeless world by walking in the shoes of those who have gone before. The distance from the early Christian cult of the saints to the Hall of Fame is short. The inscription on the tomb of Martin of Tours (316–397) reads:

> *Hic conditus est sanctae memoriae Martinus episcopus*
> *Cuius anima in manu Dei est, sed hic totus est Praesens manifestus*
> *omni gratia virtutum.*

> Here lies Martin the bishop, of holy memory, whose soul is in the hands of God; but he is fully here, present and made plain in miracles of every kind.

Now that's a plaque. The only difference between the saints of old (and the household gods who preceded them) and baseball's saints is that the earlier elections were more democratic. Who decided which skulls had value, which finger bones?

These are purely romantic notions, which the classical mind can only overcomplicate by butting in. Trying to rationalize an inherently emotional system is insane. It's like trying to reorder the human body so that the organs are placed more efficiently, even if the patient dies in the process. In Bill James' 1995 book *Whatever Happened to the Hall of Fame?* he gnaws on the enshrinement (*shrine*, noun: a place regarded as holy because of its associations with a divinity or a sacred person or relic, marked by a building or other construction) of 1960s Dodgers pitcher Don Drysdale and, in the process, refutes his own argument:

> Don Drysdale isn't in the Hall of Fame because of his strikeouts; he's in the Hall of Fame because of his charisma. He was a big handsome-as-hell blond boy from Van Nuys, and he pitched in L.A., so Hollywood loved him and Hollywood made him a star. They would have made a star out of Wes Parker if he could have hit .270. Baseball isn't about charisma, it's about *winning*. Drysdale's won-lost log, in the context of his team, is one of the poorest ever for a Hall of Famer.

"Baseball" may not be about charisma, but "fame" is, and fame is what matters, not base notoriety but renown, approbation, esteem—these are also powerful reasons for putting a player in a place of eminence so that they will be remembered. "Winning" is momentary, but heroes are forever. To deny that foments a cognitive dissonance that can even damage its subjects. In 1978, Brooklyn Dodgers great Pee Wee Reese failed on his 16th trial before the voters of the Baseball Writers Association of America. In all those elections, spanning 1964 through '78, he had never received even half of the vote. The snub had him questioning his entire career:

> "If I had to do it over again," he said, "I would try to be a more aggressive hitter. I got in a jam trying to get on base for the Sniders, Campanellas, Hodges and Robinsons. Walked 1200, 1300 times. And, you know, none of them was given to me…. Numbers," he sighed. "I played 2000 games and had 2000 hits. But the numbers don't tell it all."

"Numbers" indeed. Baseball statistics, as James first observed 40 years ago, have a unique power to tell stories, but they aren't dispositive of a player's value. The stories are, for, in the realm of the senses, impressions matter. Consider Yankees scout Bill Skiff's evaluation of Reese:

> He's the best player Brooklyn's got…. Pee Wee is the most dangerous of the Dodgers. Pee Wee can beat you so many ways. He is a

superb fielder, everybody knows that. But also, he'll take a base on balls if the pitcher gets careless. He'll steal a base if his team needs it. He'll get a base hit. And all the time he'll look so innocent.

"He'll look so innocent" is the hint that we need to look further to understand what it was about Reese that caused Skiff to marvel but Hall of Fame voters to yawn.

Baseball's Brief Lives is dedicated to that investigation. It was initially inspired by my long run as a writer and editor of the Baseball Prospectus annual. Each new edition contains hundreds of "comments" on contemporary players, brief, pithy evaluations of their recent past and possible future. These were great fun to write, but I wanted to provide the same contextualization for the players of the past. I first attempted this sort of project with a sporadic feature at the BP site, which I called (with black humor) "Dead Player of the Day." I've revived it from time to time since, including for Patreon supporters of the *Infinite Inning* podcast. Many (though not all) of these comments first appeared there in a different form.

Whether the subject is films, music, or ballplayers, there is an art to the capsule review. In the right hands, a pithy encapsulation can provide as much pleasure as a monograph on the same topic. This was demonstrated in baseball by Bill James, whose historical player comments provided the bulk of the pleasure and the re-readability of *The Bill James Historical Baseball Abstract*. James' approach in that book greatly influenced mine here (specifically in the illustrative block quotes that accompany many of the comments), with one notable exception: This collection contains examples of all sorts of players, from the best in history to those who made the briefest of cameos. James limited himself to a list of the top-100 players at each position (ca. 2000). This project, like the podcast from which it derived, is infinite. It is not concerned with any kind of rubric which limits its potential subjects. To do so would be to elevate statistics above story, and, as we've seen, quality is not bounded by one's number of 100-RBI seasons. It's there to be found where you look for it.

To further prove that point, the vast majority players were not selected by me but rather via a virtual roll of the dice. Baseball-Reference (without which this project would have been very difficult, if not impossible) allows the user to initiate a "random" search of the site. I have used that feature to pick the players, accepting whoever it returned and relying on their lives and careers rather than their "fame" to provide a subject of interest. The goal was never to say everything about a given player; it's just not possible in this format. Rather, it is to paint an evocative picture. Should that picture pique the reader's interest, they are encouraged to venture further, where possible, into full-on biography.

Indeed, a few players so captured my imagination that their comments border on biographical essay (a few of James' did, too). In that sense, this book has gone far afield from its source of inspiration; those *BP Annual* comments have to top out around 200 or 300 words, or the book would become unpublishable due to its size. Under no pressure to cover any particular set of players, I was free to tell a fuller story when the capsule format proved to be inadequate. For this presentation, the subjects are sorted into thematic "teams." Though these players span nearly 150 years of real time, humanity is consistent in its foibles and finds ways to stage old dramas in modern dress. Thus, it was not difficult to group like with like.

None of the foregoing is to say that there are no statistics in the book. There are many, mostly used to place a player in some sort of context (including the end points of their careers, total number of games played, and wins above replacement, per Baseball-Reference's formula, atop each entry). At some point, we began to pretend that the numbers generated themselves, but they didn't. Behind those performances were living human beings, their adventures, their highs and lows. Their statistics remain an essential means to an end, but they are not the end in itself. Here, the story is the thing.

When I began the *Infinite Inning* podcast, I explained that the title signified an emotional state of unbounded possibility. If the third out never arrives, then we are forever adrift but also forever becoming. There is potential for unending rapture or unending melancholy. As we travel through that inning, our mission is to cope with all the emotions with which permanent uncertainty might challenge us. (If you think the foregoing sounds like a metaphor, you're right.) In the 100 player stories within this book, I have endeavored to put back on display some of the details that have, over time, been obscured by the back of the baseball card, so that we might put aside for a few minutes the question of who is deserving of one wholly ancillary honor, or even who is better than whom, and re-enchant ourselves by reveling in the magic of what they did and who they were. Baines himself put it best when he, once again, recalled his father during his Hall of Fame induction speech. "When you ask me why I never have been outspoken or said very much, think of my dad and the lessons he passed onto me many years ago, often as we were playing catch in the yard. As he told me, 'Words are easy, deeds are hard. Words can be empty, deeds speak loudest, and sometimes they echo forever.'" I hope that, in the pages that follow, you'll hear those echoes.

Chapter One

TEAM OF GREATS

> Just as you don't need a weatherman to know which way the wind blows, you don't need a plaque to tell you who was good. Seven of the 10 players in this chapter are in the Hall of Fame, but the only difference between those seven and the other three is a matter of perception.

BIZ MACKEY, C
894 G, 1920–29, '33–41, '45–47
.328/.390/.469 (132 OPS+), 25.7 WAR

Mackey was one of the players most victimized by segregation. The Negro Leagues great was wounded not just by the constriction of opportunity or the outright abuse and inequality countenanced by Jim Crow, but in his legacy—you had to be there to get the whole effect, and his audience had been artificially limited. All Negro Leagues players suffered in this regard due to the inconsistent coverage and haphazard record-keeping of their games compared to that accorded to the white leagues, but the damage to Mackey was greater than most.

Whereas we are able say, with almost perfect accuracy, that on May 12, 1923, Babe Ruth went 1-for-4 with a home run against Detroit, and on May 13 he went 0-for-4 against that same team, striking out once, and so on, it's nearly impossible to do that for the Negro Leaguers except for some special occasions. In some cases, we know what Ruth said before, after, and during his games, and what the white players' managers and general managers were thinking about what they did, as well. Whereas with the Negro Leaguers, a good portion of what we know about how the best players in the game played, carried themselves, thought, and spoke comes from reminiscences recorded by historians years after the fact.

Some of those players had such distinctive, vivid images that we can compensate for this lack of in-the-moment documentation. Such is the case with Mackey's fellow catcher Josh Gibson. We know what a massive power hitter looks like, even if we've never experienced one who precisely emulated Gibson's outsized achievements while performing in the National or American Leagues. Mackey was less easily defined. A switch-hitting, line-drive-smashing catcher who was so athletic he could play a good shortstop, Mackey was rated the best defensive catcher in Negro Leagues history. He was an expert handler of pitchers. His arm was so strong he was able to throw out baserunners from his crouch, sometimes having to wait for an infielder to cover the bag on steal attempts because he was ready so quickly. In 1937, Cum Posey, then secretary of the Negro National League, said, "Mackey has probably caught more men off-base than any other catcher of modern times." Mackey sounds like a cross between Mickey Cochrane (the main point of comparison in his own time) and Yadier Molina, and *that* combination of traits we haven't seen.

> Oooh, my goodness, I didn't know he was such a catcher!...I've pitched to some great catchers, but my goodness that Mackey was to my idea the best one I pitched to. The way he handled you, the way he just got you built up, believing in yourself. He was marvelous! He caught me that day and I just—ooh. I was just on *edge*, and it looked like all my stuff was working. Had the hitters looking like they didn't know what to do. Mackey told me, "I don't see how in the world you *ever* lose a game!"

—Hilton Smith

James Raleigh "Biz" Mackey of Texas peaked (per the available statistics) with a .423/.456/.588 season with the Hilldale Club of the Eastern Colored League in 1923, but what makes him a fascinating and endearing character is that he wasn't just a player, however great, but a teacher and ambassador. In the former category, he tutored a teenaged Roy Campanella when both were with the Baltimore Elite Giants in 1938 and '39. Players who saw both Mackey and Campanella play said that the future three-time NL MVP became a virtual clone of Mackey in his defensive movements. To the extent that Campy tutored subsequent Dodgers catchers—and, despite his paralysis, he was still giving tips as late as Mike Piazza—Mackey's legacy lasts nearly down to the present day.

In the 1940s, Mackey managed the Newark Eagles for parts of five seasons, coaching the 1946 team to a seven-game Negro Leagues World Series win over the Kansas City Monarchs. Among his charges during this period were future integration pioneers Larry Doby, Monte Irvin, and Don Newcombe. "I probably learned more baseball from him," wrote Irvin, "than from anybody else I've ever been around."

> More than once he said to me: "I know I am helping you take my job someday but I am getting old and you are coming on and I am going to do all I can for you."
>
> I did take his job, too. When they thought I was good enough, they let him go and I was the first-string catcher. It made me feel bad that I had cost him his job but, like he said, that was the way it had to be.
>
> **—Roy Campanella**

In Rich Westcott's *Biz Mackey: A Giant Behind the Plate*, Irvin recalled, "He was a good storyteller. He was jovial, a fun-loving guy. He liked to laugh and tell jokes. When we were on the road, everyone would try to get a seat next to him on the bus, knowing they'd be in for a fun ride. Everyone wanted to sit next to him at dinner, too. Players always wanted to socialize with him off the field."

According to Mark Ribowsky's *A Complete History of the Negro Leagues*, Mackey's only weakness was drink. "Often he played while drunk and if opponents smelled whiskey on his breath when they came up to hit, then they knew they could challenge him on the bases. But even pie-eyed, Mackey could gun them down." It was said he frequently threw out Cool Papa Bell. For his part, Bell called Mackey "the best catcher that ever was."

There's a photo of Mackey from one of three barnstorming trips he made to Japan, the first of which was in 1927. He's standing next to a Japanese player who is perhaps two-thirds as tall as he is. The picture is reminiscent of latter-day shots of Aaron Judge with Jose Altuve. From Kazuo Sayama and Bill Staples Jr.'s *Gentle Black Giants: A History of the Negro Leaguers in Japan*:

In the game against the Tomon club of Waseda University, Mackey was hit by pitcher Wakahara. Mackey made a face. The pitcher felt small, and, taking his cap off his head, bowed politely to Biz Mackey. Mackey made a Japanese bow in the same polite way. A happy mood prevailed.

Sayama and Staples argue that early Negro Leaguers' trips to Japan left a greater legacy to Japanese baseball than the more celebrated visits by white major leaguers around the same time, because the latter tended to goof around and not take the Japanese players seriously. The Black players, perhaps used to not being taken seriously themselves, treated their counterparts as worthy opponents and colleagues.

There's a wonderful coda to Mackey's Pacific adventures: On his first trip to Japan, he met Lucille, the daughter of a Black father and a Japanese mother. Smitten, the two began a correspondence that lasted until the Second World War interrupted communications. After, Lucille moved to San Francisco, where Mackey caught up with her again. They soon married.

Mackey received a wonderful encomium from Campanella years after their professional association had ended. On May 7, 1959, the Dodgers held a benefit for Campanella at the Los Angeles Coliseum. Nearly 100,000 turned out to see the exhibition against the Yankees, and many thousands more had to be turned away. Mackey, long since out of baseball, lived in Los Angeles and attended the game. When Campanella addressed the crowd, he said, "This is the man that gave me all the techniques in my catching ability, that started me out at a young age." He had Mackey stand up and take a bow.

◆

Mackey's SABR bio says that he earned his nickname because of his talkativeness at the plate; he gave batters "the business." It seems far more likely that he just absorbed the *nom de sport* of Frank "Biz" Mackey, a white bantamweight who boxed professionally from 1901–16. That Biz Mackey fought 340 times, including against Abe Attell, who would later help arrange the 1919 World Series fix.

◆

You got to scold some, you got to flatter some, you go to bribe some, you go to think for some and you've got to mother them all.... If you can do all those things son, you'll be the biggest man in the league.

—**Biz Mackey to Roy Campanella**, on pitchers

Mr. Horace Stoneham, President,
New York Giants Baseball Club
Polo Grounds, New York City

Dear Mr. Stoneham:

...What your club needs is more potential batting power and more COLOR. And the men we're about to recommend have that, and plenty of it. So, without further ado, we're submitting a roster of stars and a bit of star-dust which could make your finest dreams come true:

CATCHERS—

JOSH GIBSON...one of the hardest hitters in baseball...once hit a ball father than Babe Ruth's longest in the Yankee Stadium...hit over 60 home runs during the past season...batted .644 in three East-West all-star games...good receiver...has strong throwing arm. BIZ MACKEY...as smart and cagey as catchers come...a hard hitter...throws a ball like a shot from a cannon.

—**Chester Washington**, *Pittsburgh Courier*, 1937

JIM BOTTOMLEY, 1B
1991 G, 1922-37
.310/.369/.500 (125 OPS+), 35.8 WAR

When Bottomley is discussed today, it's usually to deride him because he was one of the "I'm good to my friends," Frankie Frisch–era Veterans Committee picks for the Hall of Fame. Ironically, once Bottomley was enshrined, he completely disappeared from view. He could no longer be assessed purely for who he was: a very good player and occasionally a great one. He now existed purely as a comparison point for other Hall of Famers, almost all of whom were superior players on a career basis.

At the risk of belaboring the point, to discuss Bottomley only in terms of how he compares to Lou Gehrig and Jimmie Foxx is to (a) lose sight of Bottomley himself, (b) put the focus on the feckless Veterans Committee rather than on the player, and (c) needlessly and nonsensically insult Bottomley by arguing that a very fine player didn't deserve a career-achievement award simply because there were other players who were better for longer (although he felt no pain, having been dead for 15 years by the time the VC tabbed him). Bottomley wasn't a bad player by any means, but he also wasn't any better than, say, Mark Teixeira. He also wasn't any *worse* than Teixeira. Bottomley won an MVP award and played on four pennant winners. He came to the majors because Branch Rickey believed he was a great prospect. In short, Bottomley is a worthy part of the tapestry. Whether that should entitle him to a plaque or not is entirely in the eye of the beholder.

◆

Bottomley's career suggests one solution to our present-day dilemma regarding a ball that makes home runs too cheap: Push back the fences. When Sunny Jim's career kicked off in the early 1920s, the Lords of Baseball hadn't fully accepted the Ruthian era, which had replaced the deadball game of "inside baseball." Some parks at that time were configured with tiny dimensions because only so many deep fly balls were hit. Counterintuitively to us today, others had distant fences to *promote* power—if the ball wasn't going to go over the fence, huge spaces in the outfield allowed for higher batting averages, as well as doubles, triples, and even inside-the-park home runs. Bottomley averaged 38 doubles, 12 triples, and 18 home runs per 162 games played. That wasn't because he was the kind of power-speed combination that genetics so rarely seems to put into one body, but because the parks made it possible. Imagine how exciting today's game would be if the full menu was on order each time a hitter came to the plate. In 1928, Bottomley hit .325/.402/.628 with 42 doubles, 20 triples, and 31 home runs. Even Mike Trout can't do *that*; balls that would have been triples then leave the building today.

On September 16, 1924, in Brooklyn, Bottomley had one of the all-time great games, going 6-for-6 with a double, two home runs, three runs scored, and 12 RBIs. One of the home runs was a grand slam, which was set up when Dodgers manager Wilbert Robinson intentionally passed Rogers Hornsby to pitch to Bottomley. Bottomley's record of a dozen RBIs in one game has been tied (by fellow Cardinal Mark Whiten on September 7, 1993) but never broken. The previous one-game RBI record had belonged to Robinson himself, and he was none too pleased to have aided in, as he put it, being chased right out of the record books.

Bottomley had an off-year in 1930, hitting .304/.368/.493. At first glance, that would seem to be a good season, but the National League's batting average was .303. Bottomley was 30 that year, and the season marked the beginning of his decline phase. He tried to pass it off as an outcome of the national economic and environmental malaise. "I'm starting 1931 as though there hadn't been any 1930," he said. "You know a good many people have tried to figure out things about 1930. The hunters are wondering what happened to the quail, and a good many people wondered what in the world happened to me. Well, I've just figured it out that the Big Drouth and the General Depression got me. So, let it go at that."

BILLY HERMAN, 2B
1922 G, 1931–43, '46–47
.304/.367/.407 (112 OPS+), 57.3 WAR

It would be blinkered thinking to insist that the way of life William Jennings Bryan Herman experienced in early twentieth-century Indiana no longer applies to present-day Americans. Somewhere in this great land of ours, a child has been born to a family of farmers and named D. J. T. Smith. At 16, he will drop out of high school to work a low-level industrial job. At 17, he'll marry the girl he took to the junior prom, knock out a kid, and… Well, it gets harder from there. Still, it seems exceedingly unlikely that anyone is going to be signed off of the local church team in 2038, as Herman was back in 1928.

Another aspect of Herman's life that no longer applies is his skill at "bat-handling," which is to say he was reputed to be the best hit-and-run man in the game. Intriguingly, he only once finished in the top 10 in at-bats per strikeouts. It seems fair to infer that, when he got the hit-and-run sign, he was able to cut down his swing and make contact, and that he was a little more free-swinging the rest of the time.

> By that late in the [1941] training season, I was able to tell Larry we had a hell of a ball club there. "This is a *good* ball club," I told him. "We could win the whole thing with one other player.
>
> And who was that? he wanted to know.
>
> "Billy Herman," I said.
>
> Billy Herman had been the premier second-baseman in the National League for nine years. He had become universally accepted as the classic #2 hitter in baseball, an absolute master at hitting behind the runner.
>
> —**Leo Durocher**, *Nice Guys Finish Last*

Larry MacPhail was able to get Herman from the Cubs in May 1941 because Herman had been passed over as manager, and either he was embittered, or the player who was chosen, catcher Jimmie Wilson, felt threatened by him. The Cubs got outfield prospect Charlie Gilbert, utility infielder Johnny Hudson, and $65,000, which is to say a couple of so-so prospects and a ton of money MacPhail borrowed from the bank. The Dodgers jumped from 88–65 and second place to 100–54 and the World Series. "Herman will help us more than you expect," Durocher said after the second baseman's first game with Brooklyn. "He'll steady the kid [Pee Wee Reese] at shortstop. He'll take charge of the infield. And he gives us sustained power on attack. Anywhere along the line right down to the pitcher we're likely to blast."

As home runs have increased in frequency over the last couple of decades, and the optimal batting order has been rethought, it's no longer shocking to see a power hitter batting behind the leadoff man. In Herman's time, though, the idea of having a "bat-handler" who could hit and run in the number-two slot still reigned. Through 1940, the most home runs ever hit by a second-place hitter was 21 (Cy Williams in 1923 and Lefty O'Doul in 1929). Only Harlond Clift had drawn 100 walks from the position. Eddie Matthews hit

46 home runs batting second for the 1959 Braves, but that remained an outlier into the early 1980s, when Dwight Evans twice reached 30 homers while hitting behind Wade Boggs. Ryne Sandberg became the second number-two hitter to hit 40 homers in 1990.

Herman was the epitome of the old-school number-two hitter, but unlike many other players who managers believed fit the bill (see Gary Sutherland in Chapter Ten), he was good at getting on base. Until managers figured out that on-base percentage should be the goal, they tended to waste the spot on players who could control the stick the way Herman could but lacked his ability to hit—there have been a couple hundred seasons of players like Larry Bowa hitting .275/.298/.338 while sandwiched between better hitters (it's a miracle Mike Schmidt drove in 116 runs in 1974).

> It's going to be fun playing here in Brooklyn. The fans get so worked up over the game it's like playing a World Series every day.... One thing's sure. There'll be no chance to relax here. Those fans see to it a fellow keeps on his toes.
>
> —**Billy Herman,** May 6, 1941

♦

> Casey Stengel, the phrase-coiner, always referred to Herman as "John the Baptist." Old Case was not being sacrilegious but merely descriptive. "His head is always on the plate," he insisted. Billy has always had the annoying habit—at least enemy pitchers thought so—of leaning over the plate, dropping his shoulders and breaking his knees so that the umpires have a tendency to call a ball on a perfect strike.
>
> —**Arthur Daley,** *The New York Times.*

♦

> Finally they wrote a deal on paper. It was me and a few other players, none of whom had great stature, for Bob Elliott and another player. [Pirates owner Frank] McKinney handed me the piece of paper and asked me what I thought of the deal....

"Mr. McKinney," I said, "that's a terrible deal."

"You think it is? He asked.

"I sure do," I said. "I'm over the hill as a player and these other fellows you're getting aren't going to help you very much. You can't give up Bob Elliott for us."

He thought it over for a few moments, and then said, "Well, I don't care. I want you to manage the ball club, so that's the deal."... You know who was the Most Valuable Player in the league the next year, don't you? Bob Elliott.

—Billy Herman

BILL MADLOCK, 3B
1806 G, 1973–87
.305/.365/.442 (123 OPS+), 38.2 WAR

Writing about Madlock in his 1985 *Baseball Abstract*, Bill James listed, "Hitting for average, line-drive power," under "strengths," and under "weaknesses," wrote, "Sour cream, fudge, desserts of all kinds." Just in case one missed the point, he added, "Probably the one largest reason for the Pirates' dismal season." In this, Madlock anticipated Pablo Sandoval, with the key difference that, whereas Sandoval peaked at 24, Madlock was such a talented hitter that he was able to persevere regardless of his conditioning.

James made a fair point. Madlock did fall off hard after the last of his four batting titles in 1983, hitting just .253/.297/.323 (75 OPS+) the following season. Yet, inflated figure/deflated offense shouldn't be the defining image of Madlock; 1984 was the only full season of his career in which he didn't produce at better than a league-average level. He was in his mid-thirties at that point, and he never did get back on the beam, hitting an unremarkable .273/.340/.414 over the remaining three years of his career. It wasn't *bad*, but his fielding made him a break-even proposition compared with a player with a weaker bat but better glove. Madlock did have his moments, though. For example, he hit .333 with three home runs for the Dodgers in the six games of the 1985 NLCS.

Madlock was traded twice early in his career, once sensibly, once dubiously.

After hitting .351 in a cup of coffee with the Rangers in 1973, he was dealt to the Cubs with utility prospect Vic Harris in return for pitcher Fergie Jenkins. That, at least, was defensible from the Rangers' point of view, but when the Cubs traded Madlock to the Giants over a then-big contract ask—he reportedly wanted $1.5 million over five years, about double what he had been making—that was penny-wise and pound-foolish. For decades, the Cubs had refused to value hitters who could get on base. Wrigley Field has always been a good home-run park. If, in any given game, both teams are likely to hit a home run, then the team which hits theirs with men on is going to win. In three seasons at Wrigley Field, Madlock had hit .336/.397/.475 (139 OPS+) and won two batting titles.

To this day, only eight Cubs have ever drawn 100 walks in a season. Madlock didn't walk much, but he did hit his way on base. In the long dry period between the Cubs' 1945 and 2016 pennants, they had just 16 seasons in which a player posted a .400 on-base percentage (minimum 400 PA), by far the fewest such seasons among the 16 teams active since the beginning of the twentieth century. Madlock had two of them, but excellence costs, so the Cubs opted for an aging Bobby Murcer instead. "We can't stay in business paying that kind of money," Cubs general manager Bob Kennedy complained. "They're trying to make me the scapegoat," Madlock said, "Whatever the Giants sign me for, the Cubs could have had me for less."

CUBS WITH .400 OBP SEASONS, 1946-2015		
Player	#	Years
Mark Grace	3	1989, 1997, 1998
Derrek Lee	2	2005, 2007
Sammy Sosa	2	2000, 2001
Bill Madlock	2	1975, 1976
Gary Matthews	1	1984
Andre Thornton	1	1975
Jim Hickman	1	1970
Ron Santo	1	1966
Richie Ashburn	1	1960
Phil Cavarretta	1	1946
Stan Hack	1	1946

After he struck out on a checked swing against the Expos on May 1, 1980, Madlock, then with the Pirates, picked up his fielder's glove and thrice biffed plate umpire Jerry Crawford on the nose with it. "What I said was between the umpire and me," Madlock told reporters after the game. "I never talk about that." It wasn't what he had *said*, of course, and when the National League was slow in issuing a suspension, the crew for the Pirates' next game had to be talked into officiating by manager Chuck Tanner. "What about the safety of the umpires?" said crew chief John Kibler. "Suppose Madlock gets angry again and comes at one of us with a bat?" When NL President Chub Feeney denied Madlock's appeal, Madlock turned to the commissioner, arguing that the umpires had pressured him into the ruling. Finally, after more than a month of argument, Pirates ownership pressured Madlock into dropping the appeal for the good of the game. "Everything has been said that can be said," Madlock shrugged. "I'd just like to forget the whole thing."

JOE SEWELL, SS
1903 G, 1920–33
.312/.391/.413 (109 OPS+), 54.7 WAR

In 1989, Texas Rangers manager Bobby Valentine batted second baseman Julio Franco fifth. As Bill James noted at the time, "The traditional number-five hitter is a low-average power hitter who doesn't run well, like Danny Tartabull, Gary Carter, or Jeffery Leonard, while Franco is a high-average hitter who runs very well. The man on the Rangers who fits the image of the number-five hitter is [low-average strikeout-machine Pete] Incaviglia.... With a runner on second and first base empty, which is the basic 'protection' setup, a single scores the run most of the time, so you're going to be more afraid of Franco's .320 batting average than Incaviglia's 25 home runs."

Tris Speaker, who managed Cleveland in the 1920s before he was swept out due to a game-fixing scandal, came to this same conclusion with regard to Joe Sewell, except Speaker batted Sewell fourth. Sewell was the bat-control guy's bat-control guy, striking out an average of nine times per 154 games over the course of his career. The tradeoff, naturally, was that he averaged even fewer home runs per season, just four. Nevertheless, Sewell batted fourth in almost 40 percent of his games with Cleveland. His time as a cleanup hitter ended when he signed with the Yankees in 1931. They had Lou Gehrig in that spot, *thankyouverymuch*.

Speaker seems to have figured out the benefits of having a high-contact, high-on-base hitter in the cleanup spot by process of elimination. He began the 1923 season with first baseman Lou Guisto in that role. Guisto was a minor-league slugger whose career was interrupted, and probably derailed, by the First World War, although, at this great distance, it's hard to see a promising player just from his minor-league stats. His major-league stats were disastrous: In 156 games and 513 plate appearances spread out over five seasons, Guisto hit .196/.277/.252 (47 OPS+) with 19 doubles, 3 triples, and no home runs. This was Speaker's Opening Day cleanup man. Speaker subsequently tried another first baseman in the cleanup spot. Frank "Turkeyfoot" Brower wasn't a bad hitter, but he was briefly injured just when he might have established himself as a key part of the offense. After trying a couple of other players, including himself, Speaker finally elevated Sewell, who had been batting sixth despite his .336 average.

Sewell had only two 100-RBI seasons in his career, both coming when he acted as Cleveland's cleanup hitter. The first was 1923, the best season of his career, when he hit .353/.456/.479 with 41 doubles, 10 triples, and 3 home runs. The second came the following year, when he wasn't quite as spectacular (.316/.388/.429, although he led the league with 45 doubles). However, spending almost the entire season batting fourth behind leadoff man/left fielder Charlie Jamieson (a combined .351/.415/.452 in 1923 and '24) and number-three hitter Speaker (.363/.453/.564 in those two seasons) meant plenty of opportunities for Sewell to advance runners just by indulging his ability to put the ball in play. We can also assume a downside, that he must have hit into plenty of double plays for the same reason, but the statistics are incomplete.

We love power and are distracted by speed, but the lesson is that offense in baseball is about one thing: not making outs. There are different methods of going about this, but put runners on in front of a good hitter and you're going to score, even if said hitter only hits three or four homers all year. With a top-100 career batting average (67th all-time in the modern era, min. 3000 PAs) and on-base percentage (81st), Sewell was just as qualified to drive in runs as he was to score them.

◆

Sewell famously got his chance to break into the majors with Cleveland due to the fatal skulling of Ray Chapman by Carl Mays. Chapman's death was unlikely on its own. That a great shortstop happened to be waiting in the wings as well stretches the story into God-playing-dice-with-the-universe territory. If you want to throw a third coincidence in there, it's that said shortstop turned out to be the best contact hitter in history, with just one strikeout every 63 at-bats and 75 fewer in his career than Eugenio Suárez had in 2019 alone.

> Playing for the Yankees the next season, Sewell recalls that in one game he was again batting against George Blaeholder, who was supposed to have invented the slider. "Bill McGowan was the umpire and the count was 3 and 2. The next pitch was a fast ball right even with my cap bill. McGowan hollered 'Strike three—Oh my God I missed it.' All this in one breath. I looked at him but did not say a word. The next day he came over before the game and apologized for missing the third strike in the previous game. He was a good umpire, very capable, and I never held it against him."
>
> —*The Baseball Research Journal*

CHARLIE KELLER, OF
1170 G, 1939-43, '45-52
.286/.410/.518 (152 OPS+), 43.8 WAR

"King Kong" Keller wasn't a big guy, but he was strong and had the heavy brow of a primitive man. Teammate Lefty Gomez said Keller wasn't scouted, he was *trapped*. Once he got to New York in 1939, he joined with Joe DiMaggio and Tommy Henrich to form one of the all-time great outfields. Greatness is a fragile, high-energy state abhorred by nature: It took a few years for the unit to coalesce (George Selkirk had to succumb to injuries first), and, almost as soon as it came together, World War II intervened. The trio only made it through one more full season together after the peace.

Keller was an almost perfect hitter—he hit to all fields with power, had tremendous plate judgement, and didn't need to be platooned—but being a Yankee was bad for him in certain ways, costing him time and perverting his approach in ways that might have been deleterious. He got to the Yankees' top farm team at Newark at 20 and hit .353 for the great 1937 Bears team. He was ready. The Yankees, even though their corner-outfield situation was unsettled at the time, weren't convinced and didn't even invite him to major-league camp. Keller went back to lovely Newark for another full season. He hit .365 with 22 home runs in 150 games. He finally got his chance in 1939 and was one of a couple of reasons (the other being second-year second baseman Joe Gordon) that the team was able to absorb the rapid decline and departure of Lou Gehrig and still win 106 games and the World Series.

Keller hit .334/.447/.500 in 111 games in 1939, but that wasn't enough for manager Joe McCarthy. McCarthy is hard for us to see properly at this great remove because so much of what he did was about setting expectations. He excelled at that. The more obvious, results-based aspects of his coaching can be more equivocal. He wasn't necessarily a great tactician, and, like all managers, even the great ones, he made some spectacular misjudgments. His handling of Keller was arguably among them. McCarthy told Keller that, as a left-handed hitter playing in Yankee Stadium, he would have to stop trying to hit the ball where it was pitched and learn to pull the ball for home runs.

Keller loved McCarthy, but he didn't like that. As a young player, he had no choice but to go along with it. New-style Keller was still a great player. A left fielder who could hit .298/.416/.580 with 24 doubles, 10 triples, 33 home runs, and 102 walks, as Keller did in 1941, could write his own contract. There was a cost, though we can't prove the causality: Back problems effectively ended Keller's career in 1946 at the age of 29.

He stuck around for parts of another six seasons (if you pile them all together, he hit .260/.390/.455 in 765 PAs), but he just couldn't keep his back limber enough to play every day. The human spine is complex and sometimes goes wrong on its own, whether subject to repetitive stress or not, but Keller's story seems like an antecedent to Don Mattingly's: excessive torque leading to degeneration. Perhaps in some alternate universe, Keller signed with a different club, made it to the majors at 20, and retired with a .320 average. It would be presumptuous of us to insist that Keller's life be rewritten—he seems to have liked his lot well enough—but, unlike a lot of other players who wrung every drop of value out of their limited talents, circumstances seem to have combined to shortchange him on his.

TRIS SPEAKER, OF
2789 G, 1907-28
.345/.428/.500 (158 OPS+), 134.8 WAR

Speaker was, obviously, one of the great players of his day. Baseball-Reference credits him with 17 seasons of between 5.2 and 10.1 WAR. Ty Cobb had 18 between 5.4 and 11.3. Cobb was probably 10 percent better, but that's all, and if you were 90 percent of Ty Cobb, well, you must have been a very talented fellow. Insofar as Cooperstown bragging rights went (were it not dangerous to brag to Cobb), Cobb went to three World Series and lost them all, whereas Speaker went to three and won each time. Speaker was the definitive defensive outfielder of his time, and Cobb and Joe Jackson were his only competitors with the bat in the pastures. Writing for *Baseball Magazine* in 1913, F. C. Lane argued that Speaker, who had hit .383 in 1912, wasn't quite their offensive equal, but allowed, "If Speaker continues to bat as he did last season, he may be compared with either of the others, for as a fielder pure and simple he excels them both. There is not a better fielder in the game than Speaker.... Speaker's specialty is to play well behind second base.... It is almost impossible to force a Texas leaguer between him and the infield. He is able to play as far in as he does because of his phenomenal ability to run back flies.... He has a wonderful throwing arm. It is almost impossible to score on an outfield fly that reaches Speaker's glove."

Speaker had to revise his approach when the lively ball came in—one didn't stand behind second base when Babe Ruth was at the plate—but, in general, his theory was that an outfielder should begin the game with his back scraping the wall, then gradually walk forward until he was as far in as he could be without risking being beaten by a fly ball over his head. You might have the odd triple get past you, he reasoned, but that was a rare occurrence compared to the number of singles you'd prevent. On at least a few occasions, he saved runs by allowing those same singles. In April 1918, Speaker twice turned an unassisted double play by letting a pop fly to shallow center drop in front of him with runners on first and second, then running in and tagging the runner who was forced to hold at second and the second-base bag. Usually this is written up as him playing in so close that he caught a liner on the fly and then ran in to double off the runner. He executed that version at other times, such as in the ninth inning of Game 7 of the 1912 World Series. The Giants' Art Wilson was on second base in the top of the ninth, when shortstop Art Fletcher lined to Speaker. Wilson had apparently misread the ball and was well down the line, so Speaker had time to jog in and tag the bag himself. It's hard to know if this play was as great as it was later made out to be; the Red Sox were being blown out 11–4, with the Giants having pummeled ace Smoky Joe Wood, so no one took much note of it at the time.

What's more interesting than Speaker's on-field accomplishments is the way he was and was not divisive. Speaker's career took place during one of America's great racist and nativist flowerings (in truth, that particular plant is budding more often than not, but we like to pretend that, between the *really* bad eruptions, we put out the welcome mat). One of the reasons Speaker's very successful Red Sox team had to be broken up (this is even before the foibles of Harry Frazee) is that the clubhouse was split between Catholics and Protestant bigots. Speaker was among the latter and might have been a Ku Klux Klan member—the Klan was almost a mainstream party at that point and captured the government of the state of Indiana before their inherent stupidity, cupidity, and corruption dragged them down. Flash forward thirty years or so: Speaker was engaged by Bill Veeck to help transform Larry Doby, the first African-American player in the American League, from a second baseman into an outfielder. For the rest of his life, Doby talked about how supportive Speaker was. Had Speaker changed, or did he simply understand what he had to do to get paid? If the former, we could treat the Doby-Speaker experience as a story of redemption. Unfortunately, we'll never know.

Similarly, when Cleveland shortstop Ray Chapman was killed by a Carl Mays pitch in 1920, Speaker raged against Chapman having a Catholic burial to the point that he got into a physical altercation with two of his teammates. Five years later, Speaker married Mary Frances Cudahy of Cleveland. As his biographer Timothy M. Gay notes, Speaker, "prickly son of the Confederacy, was married in a Catholic ceremony in a Catholic dwelling in the presence of not one but two monsignors of Irish descent." Did he back off his earlier biases, or did he only acquiesce to the conditions necessary to get Ms. Cudahy down the aisle? That, too, will forever remain a mystery.

No human being is all one thing, even those we might want to judge for severe failings, like bigotry. Whatever the hatreds that possessed Speaker, he was affable—terse, but friendly. He was no Cobb; people liked him, and he seems to have mellowed as he aged. Although writers sometimes tried to lure him into making the old ballplayer's rote condemnation of his successors, he kept his comments limited and specific. He didn't succumb to saying, "We did it better in our day," but rather praised stars like Joe DiMaggio and

Willie Mays. He also created a moment at the intersection of filial love and the game that should be an indelible part of baseball history but is rarely spoken of. There are even pictures, but somehow it hasn't left much of an impression.

When young Speaker wanted to go into baseball, his widowed mother, Jenny, objected. She wanted him to finish college and make a reliable income rather than be "sold into slavery." She didn't get her way, but her disapproval seems to have weighed on Speaker. On October 12, 1920, Cleveland beat Brooklyn in Game 7 of the World Series to win the championship. As the players celebrated, Speaker, the player-manager, did not join in the dogpile, but ran from center field to the infield, dodging former spectators who had swarmed onto the field, and worked his way through the first of box seats along the foul line to the owner's box. Jenny was there. Speaker threw himself across the railing and embraced his mother, crying, "This is why I had to go away and play ball." "The embrace and kiss awed the crowd into a moment of silence," the *Cleveland Plain Dealer* reported, "and then a cheer went up. All over the stands women were standing on tiptoe or leaning across the railings, many of them with glistening eyes."

> I never let him know how much I admired him when we were playing against each other. I was out to win and so was he and for 20 years we fought it out as baseball enemies. It was only after we finally became teammates and then retired that I could tell Tris Speaker of the great underlying respect I had for him.
>
> **—Ty Cobb,** on the occasion of Speaker's passing in 1958

◆

> That morning, as thousands gathered at St. John's Roman Catholic Cathedral for the funeral services, [Cleveland outfielder Jack] Graney and Speaker were conspicuously absent. It was reported that Graney was too distraught to attend.... Speaker remained in bed.... reportedly under the care of a physician after suffering a nervous breakdown. But among themselves, the Cleveland ballplayers were telling a far different story. There had been a disagreement over where Chapman's funeral services should be held.... [Second baseman Bill Wambsganss] said it was common knowledge on the

team that Speaker fought with Graney and [catcher Steve] O'Neill over the funeral arrangements.

"Speaker was a very bigoted man at the time," Wamby recalled. "He was a 32nd degree Mason of the South. And he couldn't see the idea of Chapman being buried in the Cathedral. I think there was quite an argument about it between him and Graney and O'Neill. And they really knocked the hell out of him."

—from Mike Sowell, *The Pitch That Killed*

ANDRE DAWSON, OF
2627 G, 1976–96
.279/.323/.482 (119 OPS+), 64.8 WAR

Dawson was the 1977 NL Rookie of the Year, the 1987 NL MVP, an eight-time Gold Glove winner, and an eight-time All-Star. Nevertheless, the Hall of Fame electorate rejected him in eight elections before accepting him on the ninth try. He'd been retired for 14 years at that point; nothing had changed.

The MVP award invites contemplation on the difference between objective and subjective reality. Before we even get to the statistics, we have to acknowledge that Dawson made for a terrific story: Desperate to get away from Montréal's artificial turf, which had further damaged a knee which had been problematic going back to his amateur days, Dawson was caught in the web of collusion that would have remanded him right back into Expos custody. Rather than submit, he gave the Cubs a blank contract and said he would sign for any amount. They gave him $500,000 plus the opportunity to meet various bonus thresholds. He ended up with $700,000, a huge cut from the $1.05 million he'd earned with the Expos in 1986. "I just wanted to play ball and be happy again," Dawson said. Taking massive advantage of Wrigley Field's cozy dimensions and often-friendly winds (as well as 1987's juiced baseball), Dawson won two legs of the Triple Crown with 49 home runs and 137 RBI. He also made highlight reels with his terrific arm.

And yet, it wasn't that good a season. For those early converts to the Church of On-Base Percentage, this was clear from Dawson's lack of walks. Impatience was the only real flaw in his game. On his career, he averaged 36 walks a season, nine of them intentional. In 1987, he drew only 32 passes, resulting in a .328 OBP. That OBP ranked 42nd in the league, landing between such lesser lights as Gerald Perry and Johnny Ray. WAR still lay in the future, but its backwards-looking eye confirms that Dawson was not one of the very best players in the league—he was tied with Milt Thompson at 18th in wins above replacement. According to Baseball-Reference's WAR formulation, there were three NLers over 7.0 WAR that year: Tony Gwynn (8.6), Eric Davis (7.9), and Dale Murphy (7.7). Tim Raines (6.7) prevented by collusion from playing a full season. Ozzie Smith (6.4), who played amazing defense at short for the pennant-winning Cardinals while having one of his best offensive seasons, also ranked towards the top. Dawson's total was 4.0.

Much of this was clear at the time, even if it couldn't be described in modern technical terms. Dawson won the award anyway, edging Smith 11–9 in first-place votes. Gwynn, Davis, and Murphy finished eighth, ninth, and eleventh, respectively. No doubt home runs and RBI still held sway as a shorthand for productivity—most newspapers still reported hitting statistics each Sunday in a long column containing only batting average, home runs, and RBI—but it also seems fair to say that Dawson's season caught the popular imagination, and the narrative won over reality. When this happens in governance, politics, or medicine, it's a dangerous thing. In sports, where Babe Ruth's called shot is a harmless tall tale, it can be a valid way of going about things. After all, Dawson wasn't a *bad* player in 1987, and just because we don't have a stat for "story" doesn't mean narrative doesn't have huge value to the sport.

You might recall the infamous 2004 comment attributed to a "senior advisor" to President George W. Bush, widely assumed to be Bush consigliere Karl Rove, that condemned critics of the administration as, "in what we call the reality-based community…. We're an empire now, and when we act, we create our own reality. And while you're studying that reality—judiciously, as you will—we'll act again, creating other new realities…. We're history's actors…and you, all of you, will be left to just study what we do."

This was a terribly arrogant thing to say. The essence of folly is to behave according to how we wish things to be rather than how they are. Rove (or whoever it was) was correct about the United States' massive strength, but, as we've seen from the Korean War to Afghanistan, where there are structural issues that constrain that strength (and there almost always are), a country's offensive potential is irrelevant to its functional ability to act. Over the roughly 150 years of organized baseball in America, teams have gradually learned that, if they ignore a reality-based approach to team-building, they won't be competitive. To cite just one example, from 2000–19 there were 20 teams that drew fewer than 400 walks in a full season. Their average record was 73–89, and just two of them—the sustained outlier that was the 2014–15 Kansas City Royals—made the postseason. Thus, as much as a front office or a fanbase might like to "create new realities" with impatient players like Dawson, it's self-defeating to have too many of them.

Awards, though, are different, because they contain an aesthetic component. When it comes to an entertainment, in the final analysis, accuracy partisans are making an argument that comes down to rigidity as a category error. When deciding to go to war, persuading enough people that there are values higher than "this feels good to me" is literally a matter of life and death. For the consumers of entertainment, it's not clear that they need to be receptive to that argument, and it might even be disrespectful of something valuable to insist that they must be.

DAWSON WITH THE EXPOS				
	AVG	OBP	SLG	HR
Home	.267	.322	.448	95
Road	.292	.329	.503	130

DAWSON WITH THE CUBS				
	AVG	OBP	SLG	HR
Home	.302	.349	.543	94
Road	.268	.305	.473	80

We've shaken Andre's hand so much lately, we decided to wait 'til the next time.

—**Cubs catcher Jody Davis,** on not congratulating Dawson after a home run

BRIAN DOWNING, DH/OF
2344 G, 1973-92
.267/.370/.425 (122 OPS+), 51.5 WAR

One of the weird beliefs that possessed even the great baseball minds for well over 120 years was the idea that, in the absence of a leadoff hitter who was both patient and fast, you'd be better off emphasizing the latter skill than the former. Thus were dozens of speedy middle infielders (Luis Aparicio, Maury Wills, Horace Clark, Bert Campaneris) and outfielders (Otis Nixon, Vince Coleman, Juan Pierre), who had no particular skill at getting on base, chosen to receive more playing time (in the form of plate appearances) than any other hitter on their teams. All along, though, there were cases that disproved their utility: slow hitters with patience. This was particularly true in the 1980s, when Wade Boggs and Brian Downing led off for the Red Sox and Angels, respectively. No doubt they were overlooked as exemplary leadoff hitters because they were contemporaries of Rickey Henderson and Tim Raines, who had the full package of leadoff skills.

Downing's career had two distinct halves. First signed by the White Sox as an undrafted amateur, he reached the majors as a soft-bodied catcher without much punch. He always had a good eye at the plate, so he contributed *something*, but he was by no means a slugger, hitting .243/.351/.344 in five years with the team. In December 1977, he was traded to the Angels in a six-player deal centered around Bobby Bonds that brought long-term rewards to each team—pitcher Richard Dotson was a solid contributor to the White Sox for most of 10 years, while Downing spent 13 years in Anaheim. Realizing he wasn't a great defensive catcher (Nolan Ryan and Frank Tanana preferred not to throw to him) and taking criticism of his production to heart, he started lifting weights. "I accomplished some things in the weight room that changed my life, really," he told John Weyler of the *Los Angeles Times* in 1990. "I never had much self-confidence and I made some numerical goals that year [1978; his first of intense training] that gave me some real self-esteem. There are a lot of parallels between the weight room and life.... I've never been able to master the idea of body leverage, and without weight training, I couldn't hit the ball within 20 feet of the warning track."

Simultaneously, he adopted a new, open batting stance in which he faced the pitcher to get a better look at the ball. Jim Murray called it a stance "right off a mustache cup or a Cap Anson tintype," noting that Downing's manager had chastised him for squaring up when he hadn't been given the bunt sign.

Even when sac-happy Gene Mauch was his manager in Anaheim, Downing didn't bunt much; it was just that the unorthodox position gave him a better chance to hit the ball the other way. In 1979, he hit .326/.418/.462, but with only 12 home runs. In the ensuing years, he made another adjustment, sacrificing some of his batting average for power. He would hit up to 29 in a season, typically with a batting average in the .270s and 75 or more walks. An ankle-shattering collision with Rickey Henderson early in the 10th game of the 1980 season more or less ended his catching career for good. From then on, he was a left fielder and designated hitter. Downing was no gazelle as an outfielder, but he set two records for consecutive errorless games, going more than a season and a half between miscues each time.

In 1982, Downing hit .281/.368/.482 for the AL West–winning Angels, scoring 109 runs as the team's primary leadoff hitter. He made only three stolen base attempts all year. There were many leadoff hitters who checked off the "speedy" box that year, but few who could get on base as well as Downing could: Only Henderson and Willie Randolph had higher OBPs, only Henderson and Paul Molitor scored more runs.

"If I played 10 more years," Downing said in 1990, when he was 39, "it still wouldn't wash away that pain," of the Angels' postseason losses of 1979, '82, and '86. Of the 1986 season, he said, "There's a permanent scar and I'll never be able to come to grips with it." He played until he was 41 and was still a vital hitter when he retired. He never did get the ring that might have put some of those nightmares to rest.

DON DRYSDALE, RHP
518 G, 1956–69
209–166, 2.95 ERA (121 ERA+), 67.1 WAR

Imagine dying in an Edward Hopper painting. Hopper's most famous piece is *Nighthawks*, his depiction of a noirish nighttime diner, but he often painted people alone, whether on trains, in apartments, restaurants, hotel rooms, or even a movie theater. Sometimes there is more than one person in the painting, but it's clear they're alone together, not connecting. Some of the solitary occupants of these rooms are men, and some are women. They vary in states of dress and undress, but the nudity isn't erotic or an expression of freedom, it's a concession to loneliness: If no one sees you, you have nothing to conceal. Occasionally, as in his *Macomb's Dam Bridge* or *House by the Railroad*, even buildings are alienated. The bridge depicted in the former is adjacent to Yankee Stadium (old and new), but Hopper chose an angle that didn't include that welcoming edifice. Not every Hopper painting conforms to this theme, and the painter himself liked to deny there was a theme at all, but the bulk of his work exists in the penumbra of human warmth.

After Don Drysdale retired in 1969, he stayed in the game as a broadcaster, bouncing through Montréal, Texas, Anaheim, and Chicago before finally landing back in Los Angeles. He had a wife and four children but nevertheless pursued a peripatetic life. That life no doubt had its comforts and amenities, but the vagabond's existence has certain risks, whether one sleeps in a suite or on a park bench. On July 3, 1993, Drysdale suffered a fatal heart attack while alone in a Montréal hotel room. He was less than three weeks away from his 57th birthday.

> I did a pre-game interview with him recently and I remember thinking how good he looked. How healthy and strong. I guess you never know what's going on inside a person.
>
> **—Dusty Baker.**

There are no further details to give, because the ex-pitcher was alone when he died; Drysdale had had some heart problems, and they caught up with him at a moment when aid was impossible. He saw the Dodgers beat the Expos, probably had dinner, then retired for the night. Fans take for granted the high status enjoyed by ballplayers and the other participants in major-league baseball and often use that to claim that the players owe them something—say, not striking for better pay or improved conditions, or playing through a pandemic. Never let it be forgotten that baseball is a grind, and it can exact a price from all involved, whether players, front office members, or broadcasters. They sacrifice home and family for your entertainment, and every once in a rare while, the last thing they see on this earth is the hotel minibar or the thin comfort of an alien pillow.

Drysdale still holds the modern NL record for hitting batters, with 154. "The pitcher has to find out if the hitter is timid," Drysdale told Dave Anderson of *The New York Times* in 1979. "And if the hitter is timid, he has to remind the hitter he's timid." He picked up the philosophy from veteran pitcher Sal "The Barber" Maglie, who was with the Dodgers when Maglie was 40 and Drysdale was 19. Maglie only hit a few batters per season, though; his point was about intimidation, pushing the batter off the plate so he could drop a curve on the outside corner. Drysdale took it to an extreme, hitting up to 20 batters a season. A number of pitchers have since hit more batters than Drysdale (the closest active pitcher, Charlie Morton, has 148 (through mid-season 2022) and may pass Drysdale's total in less than half as many innings), but few of them were criticized for being headhunters, because they didn't proselytize on behalf of intimidation like he did.

> Drysdale led us in wins that year [1957]. He threw hard and he threw sidearm and he was mean enough to knock people down, but the big guy was just a kid at the time and wasn't a smart pitcher or sure of himself.... Driz, as I called him [was] a very volatile guy. He had a hair-trigger temper. He was a good guy, but he could be as mean as [Koufax] was clean.
>
> **—John Roseboro**

Chapter Two

NAMES

This team wouldn't win the pennant, but it would lead the league in colorful appellations.

BUBBLES HARGRAVE, C
852 G, 1913–15, '21–28, '30
.310/.372/.452 (118 OPS+), 16.6 WAR

One of the small difficulties the baseball historian must endure is keeping the Brothers Hargrave straight in his mind. One of them won a batting title, the other did not. Was it Eugene Franklin "Bubbles" Hargrave or William McKinley "Pinky" Hargraves? It would normally help to remember that it was the catcher who hit .353 to lead the NL in 1926, but they were both catchers. As Casey Stengel said, you could look it up: Bubbles was the one who got credit for the title. Today he wouldn't have; he had only 366 plate appearances. Paul Waner led qualified hitters at .336; it would have been his third batting title.

Is Hargrave the most obscure winner of a batting title? While the answer is subjective, he's a good candidate. Of the 236 batting titles from 1901 to present (excluding active players), 125 have been won by future Hall of Famers. Another dozen or so player won a batting title and an MVP award and, though they haven't made the Hall of Fame (Pete Rose and Barry Bonds among them), they could hardly be called obscure. That leaves 43 players who won a single batting title and never received another major award. A few of them are still eligible for election to the Hall of Fame, so the number may change slightly; most of them aren't going anywhere. There are players who are well-remembered for reasons of association—they were part of historic moments for the Dodgers (Pete Reiser, Dixie Walker, Carl Furillo) or Yankees (Bernie Williams, Paul O'Neill)—as well as some who are in some sense infamous (Hal Chase and Bill Buckner, albeit for *very* different reasons). That leaves Hargrave and a few other prime candidates:

- **Ginger Beaumont, 1902:** Pirates outfielder who played on the losing side in two World Series and was the first batter in modern World Series history.

- **Cy Seymour, 1905:** Early Reds outfielder killed it with a 182 OPS+; was also a quality pitcher in the 1890s.

- **George Stone, 1905:** You might think this St. Louis Browns player, with his anodyne name and affiliation to a defunct team, is obscure, but here it is nearly 120 years later, and we're talking about him, whereas there are few reasons to try to come up with the leading figures of, say, the 59th Congress, which kicked off that same March. Nor could many of you reading this claim to have also read the year's best-selling novel, *The Marriage of William Ashe* by Mary Augusta Ward. The continuity of baseball keeps the players alive. Stone was a little guy who posted a 193 OPS+ in his big year and was pretty good in most other seasons, as well. He seems to have had the skills of a Hall of Famer, but he made to the majors at a relatively advanced age and was quickly gone.

- **Lew Fonseca, 1929:** A second baseman who spent half his time at first (that was a thing in the 1920s and '30s), Fonseca was a .300 career hitter because he played at a time when it was easy to do that. His .369 in 1929 was still an outlier. He stayed in baseball forever broadcasting and making promotional and World Series highlights films.

- **Debs Garms, 1940:** Everyday utility guy named for a great American socialist. Split most of his time between third base and left field. Controversially won with only 385 PAs.

- **Snuffy Stirnweiss, 1945:** Wartime star at second base for the Yankees, very ordinary the rest of the time. Died when his commuter train plunged off of an open drawbridge outside Newark, New Jersey.

- **Ralph Garr, 1974:** Slap-it-and-run corner outfielder who had to hit .320 to be productive; it happened three times in his eight seasons as a regular.

- **Freddy Sanchez, 2006:** A Red Sox infield prospect traded to Pittsburgh in a fairly miserable deal that brought righty starter Jeff Suppan to Beantown, Sanchez spent six years hitting .301 for a Pirates team going nowhere in a hurry.

As obscure as he is, Hargrave was, for many years, the partial answer to a trivia question: Name the only two catchers to win a batting title. Until 2006, the answer was Hargrave and Ernie Lombardi (the latter in 1938 and '42). They've since been joined by Joe Mauer (three times) and Buster Posey.

The origin of the nickname "Bubbles" is obscure, but some sources suggest it arose in mockery of Hargrave's stutter—he struggled to say words that began with the letter B. They further say that Hargrave did not like the name at all.

KITTY BRANSFIELD, 1B
1330 G, 1898, 1901-11
.270/.304/.353 (98 OPS+), 10.2 WAR

A big-eared glove-man who played for the Pirates and Phillies at the turn of the twentieth century and one of the first of the first basemen to detach themselves from the bag and play back on the grass, William Bransfield was an impatient hitter who needed to hit close to .300 to contribute offensively. He did so a few times, but he was inconsistent. From 1903 to '07, he hit .253/.288/.328. Deadball Era or not, that kind of production from a first baseman is egregious. With Honus Wagner around, the Pirates were so good they could live with it. In 1903, Bransfield played in the first World Series (he hit .207 in eight games). He was an avid trencherman who sometimes struggled to keep his weight down, so perhaps some of those disappointing performances were due to his being out of shape.

As mediocre as Bransfield's hitting could be, he was remembered fondly by Pittsburgh fans due to who came after: After the Pirates traded him to the Phillies (for journeymen Del Howard and Otis Clymer), it would be 16 years before the team had another first baseman who lasted more than a couple of seasons. Charlie Grimm, another glove-oriented first-sacker who only produced occasionally, was the starter from 1920 to '24. Almost 120 years after Bransfield's day ended, the Pirates still await their franchise first baseman.

A catcher as an amateur and in the minors, Bransfield was converted to first base by the Pirates. Kitty had his best season for the 1908 Phillies, hitting .304/.335/.395 (130 OPS+) with three home runs, but the true highlight of his Phillies stint came when a gambler tried to bribe him to throw a game. Bransfield heard him out, then threw him down the stairs.

Bransfield was a quiet man who enjoyed working crossword puzzles. After his playing career, he managed in the minors, scouted, and also returned to the majors as an umpire for a year. He made only two ejections that season, but both chased future Hall of Fame shortstops: Dave Bancroft and Rabbit Maranville. Bransfield was replaced after only one season. Per the *Poughkeepsie Eagle-News*, "Kitty did not prove to be as good an umpire as he was a first baseman, though he tried hard to make good, and it was necessary to replace him." There was also some suggestion he had been seriously injured while umpiring.

◆

Bransfield lost his wife and two of his children when he was in his forties, leaving him with only a daughter. He called her every day when his teams were on the road. "I just like to hear her voice," he said. "She's all I've got now if she does not hear from me she does not want to go to bed."

According to James Skipper, author of *Baseball Nicknames*, Bransfield was called "Kitty" because he had a feminine hairstyle. David W. Anderson, Bransfield's SABR biographer, says that Bransfield's original nickname was "Kid," but "a reporter with bad hearing heard it as 'Kitty' and the name stuck." Bransfield's version:

When I was a youngster in Worcester [Massachusetts], 'Billy the Kid' was the hero of all the kids. The boys started calling me 'Kiddie' and the name gradually drifted into what you have today, 'Kitty.' Which is one for the fairy books, if you care to believe it.

The owner of the Hartford Senators, who employed him as manager in 1927, called him "Catherine."

A baseball man whose devotion to the game can be likened to that of a crusader going forth to the wars will be at the throttle of the Hartford train when it pulls out of the Eastern League shed on its long pennant run next Wednesday. Baseball is "Kitty" Bransfield's religion and he defends it with the zeal of a Galahad.

—*Hartford Courant,* April 17, 1927

BIP ROBERTS, 2B/OF
1202 G, 1986, '88–98
.294/.358/.380 (100 OPS+), 20.5 WAR

A switch-hitting little guy (5-foot-7) who slapped singles and stole bases ("If I get a good jump, I'm gone. I don't care if it's Tony Peña, I'm safe"), Roberts was a 1980s St. Louis Cardinals–style player lost in the 1990s. One of the better Rule 5 draft picks, he was snatched from the Pirates by the Padres as a second-base flyer in the aftermath of Alan Wiggins' lapse into drug use. In spring training 1985, Roberts and Bobby Bonilla collided, resulting in a separated shoulder for Roberts and a broken ankle for Bonilla. Both players went on to have down years and were lost in the Rule 5 draft when the Pirates left them unprotected (Pittsburgh subsequently reacquired Bonilla via trade).

The Padres platooned Tim Flannery and Jerry Royster at the keystone in 1985 and got a .284 average and 82 walks from them, but general manager Jack McKeon couldn't leave well enough alone. They endured the miserable obligatory season from Roberts in 1986 (including an 0-for-20 to start his career), but from 1988 through the end of his career, Roberts hit .297. That's not to say that he was always valuable; as a player who didn't walk much and had very little power, he had to hit towards the top of his range to contribute offensively. He also got hurt a lot. "'Roberts 2B' was the name atop the

Reds' lineup for the second straight game," Tom Groeschen of *The Cincinnati Enquirer* wrote on April 8, 1993, "and 'Roberts 2B' is what it will say about 160 more times this season. [He] is anchored at second under new manager Tony Perez." Roberts made it into 83 games; a thumb injury was the culprit. Finally, he had some problems with the switch-hitting aspect of, well, switch-hitting—lefty pitchers gave him problems. When he was healthy, though, Roberts was excellent at the fundamental aspects of hitting. In September 1992, he tied an NL record by making 10 straight hits (he was helped by having an out rained out of the record books), and he hit in 23 straight games in 1994.

Roberts had a terrific work ethic, in part a reaction to his father, who was a drug addict.

> I guess I was embarrassed by it more than anything. I mean, you don't hear of too many people having a drug addict for a father. He tore our family apart. My whole family's been destroyed because of him. But he's my dad, man. My own dad. You think I'm going to stop loving my dad?
>
> —Leon Joseph "Bip" Roberts III

That makes it somewhat poignant that, when Roberts was a rookie, he was asked, "Bip, what question do you hear the most these days?" (a question about a question), and he answered, "Alan Wiggins questions. Alan Wiggins questions. Definitely." Wiggins had worn number 2. The Padres made Roberts wear it, as well.

BATTLESHIP GREMMINGER, 3B
383 G, 1895, 1902-04
.251/.301/.340 (92 OPS+), 5.5 WAR

If you watch a Great War documentary, such as Peter Jackson's *They Shall Not Grow Old*, you may be surprised at how short the military-aged males of a hundred years ago were. Some of the relative dwarfism of the Western Front is not due to our superior diet and medicines but their superior ability to run a generation of alpha males into the machine guns: The British suffered so many casualties that they kept revising the acceptable height for induction downwards. They *started* at a minimum of 5-foot-3, suggesting how height-challenged the times were, but had so many volunteers that they kicked the bar upward to 5-foot-6. Once they'd plowed all the taller fellows under, they began revising it downward again, until they got to 5-foot-2. Yet smaller men kept volunteering, so the War Office permitted the creation of "Bantam Divisions," armies of men who stood from 5-foot to 5-foot-3 (provided they had a robust, 34-inch chest).

This goes a long way towards explaining how Lorenzo Edward "Ed" Gremminger (born 1874), an unremarkable specimen by our standards at 6-foot-1 and 200 pounds, got the nickname "Battleship." He was a big guy for then, not now. It's a subject that deserves further exploration, because Americans and Europeans were, on average, taller prior to the industrial revolution. The shift from agrarian life to industrialized capitalism meant biological damage inflicted by subsistence wages and processed food. That Gremminger was a battleship is an indictment of his times.

Gremminger played from 1895 through 1912 (and, starting in 1908, managed) but spent most of that time in minor league towns like Buffalo, Rochester, and Montgomery. He had a cup of coffee with the NL's old Cleveland Spiders in 1895, then vanished back to the sticks until 1902, when the Braves (then going by "Beaneaters")—whose star third baseman, Jimmy Collins, had jumped across town to Boston's new American League entry the year before—gave him a two-year trial at the hot corner. They sold Gremminger to the Tigers prior to the 1904 season; he began that year as the team's starting third baseman but lost his job at midseason, thus also losing the chance to torment a teenaged Ty Cobb the next year. Gremminger was 30 by then and, battleship or not, there would be no more chances.

> A sensational story was yesterday sent out from the police to the effect that Gremminger, the third baseman of the Cleveland National League team who is under contract to the Bisons for 1896, and who has been on the sick list for some time had brutally assaulted a police officer named Cutting from No. 6 and that a warrant was out for his arrest. At same time it was insinuated that Gremminger and Sam Wise, the veteran second baseman of the Buffalo team, who is also home on sick leave, where under the influence of liquor.... Gremminger is not so well known here, but those who have formed his acquaintance claim that he is one of the best fellows today in baseball and as one fan said last night, "he has a heart as big as an ox."

"For weeks past Gremminger has been insulted repeatedly by a man unknown to him," [Wise said], "who has been applying the most vile epithets to him both in a game and out of it. As we went by these two men Gremminger thought he recognized in Cutting his enemy and his temper getting the worst of him he slapped the man's face, not punched him as stated by Cutting. I took hold of Gremminger and got him away and that was all I had to do with it.... We did everything to apologize when we found we were mistaken."

—*The Buffalo Enquirer*, July 23, 1896

Second Baseman Robert Lowe was to-day appointed captain of the Detroit American League baseball team. He succeeds Capt. Gremminger, who resigned after holding the position through three games. Gremminger succeeded Capt. Carr.

—*Louisville Courier-Journal*, June 18, 1904

PEE-WEE WANNINGER, SS
163 G, 1925, '27
.234/.266/.295 (45 OPS+), −2.1 WAR

Babe Ruth gets a lot of credit, sometimes too much, and he gets a lot of blame, sometimes too much. In 1925, Ruth collapsed as the Yankees traveled north from spring training. He subsequently underwent surgery for an intestinal abscess and missed the first two months of the season. When he came back, he was very good but not "Ruthian," hitting .290/.393/.543. The Yankees, who had finished a close second in 1924, never got going in '25 and finished seventh with a record of 69–85–2. They were only slightly better with the Babe than without him, suggesting that the club had problems for which even Ruth couldn't compensate.

Paul Louis "Pee-Wee" Wanninger was one of them. Going back to 1922, the Yankees' shortstop had been Everett Scott, a durable (he played in a record 1,307 consecutive games) glove man. He was an egregious hitter and, at 32, was visibly slowing defensively, so the Yankees benched him for Wanninger, a

22-year-old rookie they had pulled from the Sally League. "The first sight that [Yankees manager] Miller Huggins had of his young shortstop was dramatic," John Kieran reported in June 1925. "Somebody hit a groundball over second base. The youngster drifted over like a streak and flipped the ball from his shoe-tops to first base on a dead line. 'That's enough!' said Huggins. 'He's a groundhog. You can tell them a mile away. What a fielder he must be! Now, if he can only hit a little bit.'"

He couldn't. Wanninger posted .236/.256/.305 averages and also made 30 errors in 111 games at shortstop. He actually started out hot by his standards, hitting .291 through the end of June, but his bat resigned at that point; he hit .174 the rest of the way. By early September, the Yankees made another change, benching Wanninger for Mark Koenig. Koenig wasn't a great shortstop either and was only the team's regular for three years, but because of his association with the 1927 team he's better remembered than he otherwise would have been. That December, the Yankees released Wanninger to the St. Paul Saints as part of a trade for catcher Pat Collins, who would also play for the '27 edition.

♦

WORST SEASONS BY A YANKEES SHORTSTOP (100 G MIN.)									
Rk	Player	Year	G	BA	OBP	SLG	OPS	OPS+	WAR
1	P. Wanninger	1925	117	.236	.256	.305	.561	43	-1.8
2	Gene Michael	1970	134	.214	.292	.255	.548	56	-1.0
3	Gene Michael	1973	129	.225	.270	.278	.547	58	-0.9
4	Derek Jeter	2014	145	.256	.304	.313	.617	76	-0.7
5	Everett Scott	1924	153	.250	.278	.316	.593	53	-0.7
6	Rafael Santana	1988	148	.240	.289	.294	.583	65	-0.6
7	Wayne Tolleson	1987	121	.221	.306	.241	.547	49	-0.2
8	Frankie Crosetti	1940	145	.194	.299	.273	.572	52	-0.1
9	Ruben Amaro	1967	130	.223	.297	.259	.556	70	-0.1
10	Everett Scott	1923	152	.246	.266	.325	.591	54	0.0

RUTH'S HOMER FAILS AS TIGERS WIN, 7 TO 3…Wanninger's Error Lets in Winning Runs…The game was kicked sky-high just when the Yanks had it won by virtue of Babe Ruth's ninth home run of the season.… Fothergill was inserted to bat in place of Holloway, who had succeeded Stoner, and when he rolled a grounder to Wanninger, Pee Wee fumbled the ball and Blue and Woodall hoofed it home. It was a sad sight to behold and sadder to relate.

—*The New York Times,* July 19, 1925

The story of this particular Sabbath game, witnessed by some 12,000 sweltering fans, was one of fairly decent pitching efforts by the New York staff ruined by wretched fieldling. Pee Wee Wanninger made three foozles in the first two rounds and helped the Browns to four runs.

—*The New York Times,* August 31, 1925

WILDFIRE SCHULTE, OF
1806 G, 1904–18
.270/.332/.395 (115 OPS+), 23.7 WAR

Baseball statistics have certain predictable shapes: You don't expect to see Deadball Era players showing a lot of home-run power, players who combine speed and power are rare, and so on. That's one reason why Frank Schulte was so cool, even if it was for only one season. In 1911, he won the Chalmers sort-of-MVP award by hitting .300 with 30 doubles, 21 triples, and 21 home runs, the last of which led both leagues. He also drove in 107 runs, which led the NL, and scored 105. He also stole 23 bases, which we can pretend weren't accompanied by an equal number of caught stealings (that data is missing, but his success rate in the seasons for which we have it was close to 50 percent). Willie Mays had a season that was a bit like Schulte's in 1957. In 2007, Curtis Granderson and Jimmy Rollins has seasons that superficially resembled Schulte's; Rollins won the NL MVP that year, but neither outshone the league to the extent Schulte did. George Brett had this season a couple of times in the late 1970s, that's as close as we come.

None of them were asked to bunt as often as Schulte was. That's an artifact of the era we can't (and don't) hope to see duplicated. Schulte finished in the

NL's top 10 in bunts five times and had 31 sacrifices in his Chalmers season. He's still 17th in career sacrifice bunts with 279. He's safe there; only two active players, Clayton Kershaw and Elvis Andrus, have even 100.

As Schulte's career averages suggest, his big season was a fluke. Still, he was a great Cub and a great American story. A first-generation American (his parents came over from Germany), Schulte mastered the game and became a key player on a great team that went to four World Series.

> Frank is tired of chasing around the bases, so he made a resolution this morning to cease hitting them inside the grounds. When they sail over the wall he is entitled to an easy trial jaunt around the track with no opposition, and if there's anything Frank likes it is running as slowly as possible. His resolution has nothing to do with one base clouts, but he has decided it will be with him either singles or homers so high and far away that the opposing outfielders will not even give chase.
>
> —**Ring Lardner,** *Chicago Tribune,* May 19, 1909

Spoilers for when some millennial Orson Welles decides to make *Citizen Schulte*: "Wildfire" was his horse.

BIRDIE CREE, OF
742 G, 1908–15
.292/.368/.398 (125 OPS+), 15.4 WAR

It's a slight stretch to say that Cree was the greatest one-season wonder in New York Yankees history, because he had several good seasons. Still, it's not wholly unreasonable to say, because his career was short and marked by constant illnesses and injuries: In an eight-year major-league career, he had only three seasons in which he was able to stay in the lineup for bulk of the campaign. Of those three, 1911 stands well above the rest: He hit .348/.415/.513 (152 OPS+) in 137 games. He hit only four home runs, for which we can't fault him because of the dead ball; we can intuit his power from his 30 doubles and 22 triples. He also stole 48 bases, but we don't have caught stealing numbers for that period and, given the typically abysmal success rates back then, it's entirely possible he was caught 50 times. Cree was worth 5.5 WAR that year.

Sticking with the one-season wonder idea, how many Yankees position players have had a season of 5.5 WAR or greater and never had another at that level? This is one of those questions the search engine at Baseball-Reference makes fairly easy to answer (if you enjoy doing this kind of spelunking, it's well worth the subscription price), though we have to be nuanced in our thinking here. The answer is both several players and no one. The most recent player on the list is Aaron Judge, but his story is still being told, so we'll cross him off as ineligible. There are several others who technically qualify: Ben Chapman, Earle Combs, Brett Gardner, Jason Giambi, Curtis Granderson, Gil McDougald, Roger Peckinpaugh, and Red Rolfe. If this were my game (and it is), I would eliminate them all: Every one of them had long careers in which they consistently delivered high value; it just happens that they had a Yankees peak a little above their norms. Cree was never *bad*, but he was only a star-level player for that one moment.

Cree taught eight grade before becoming a professional ballplayer. His real name was William, and I've read several different accounts of how he got to be "Birdie," including that he liked to sing in the postgame shower and/or he moonlighted as a musician. Cree himself said his fellow players bestowed the nom-de-baseball on him because of his high-energy style of play. The Occam's razor answer seems to be that, as an amateur, he played semi-pro games under the false name "Bill Burde," and somewhere along the line the surname was transposed and mispronounced.

NEMO LEIBOLD, OF
1268 G, 1913–25
.266/.357/.327 (91 OPS+), 10.8 WAR

Imagine a Zelig-like character who can be found lurking in the background of important historical events without ever figuring in the events themselves. Harry "Nemo" Leibold played on four World Series teams, including the 1919 White Sox, and yet he's a complete non-entity. He was the starting right fielder for the Black Sox, and he went 1-for-18 against the Reds in the Series, but no one has ever said he was part of the fix. No one has ever said *anything* about him. Nor does he figure in the lore of the 1917 White Sox or the 1924 and '25 Washington Senators, his other pennant-winners.

In the mid-1960s, Buffy Sainte-Marie wrote a protest song, "Universal Soldier." Donovan, who was better than people remember, got to number 53 with it:

> He's 5-foot-2, and he's 6-feet-4
> He fights with missiles and with spears
> He's all of 31, and he's only 17
> He's been a soldier for a thousand years…
> He's the universal solider, and he really is to blame…

Leibold was the universal fourth outfielder, and no one, apparently, blamed him for anything. He was only 5-foot-6. Maybe you had to be taller for Arnold Rothstein's minions to consider you worthy of corruption. He was Buck Weaver's roommate. Weaver failed to clue him in, which turned out to be a noble gesture given that even knowledge of the fix would have resulted in Leibold being the ninth man out. Leibold had no power at all, even for the Deadball Era, hitting just three home runs in his career. He had a long career as a minor-league manager, which is wonderful, but it's his status as a footnote that makes him immortal.

If Harry Loran Leibold's nickname inspires anyone to explore the Winsor McCay comic strip that inspired it, so much the better. Some of *Little Nemo in Slumberland* has dated badly due to racist caricatures, but McCay was an ingenious artist and, though it's difficult to overlook the way the conventional biases of the early twentieth century disfigured the work, the strip remains a tremendous feat of draftsmanship and imagination.

PREACHER ROE, LHP
333 G, 1938, '44-54
127-84, 3.43 ERA (116 ERA+), 29.6 WAR

Branch Rickey was the most important general manager of all time, but trades weren't his strong suit. He was focused on *sales* because (a) his creation of the farm system gave him a massive surplus of players, and acquiring more of them wouldn't have alleviated the problem; and (b) he got a cut of each transaction. That's not to say he never made a great deal. It's fitting that his best swap came as a consequence of his historic decision to sign Jackie Robinson.

Dixie Walker was a productive and popular outfielder known as "The People's Cherce." As his primary *nom du baseball* suggests, he was also a Stars 'n' Bars flyin' Southerner who lived down to one's worst expectations of bigotry, initiating a petition during spring training 1947 intended to pressure the Dodgers into abandoning the promotion of Robinson. This prompted the famous late-night meeting in which Dodgers manager Leo Durocher told the players that it didn't matter if Robinson was "black, white, or striped like a fucking zebra," because he was going to help them win, and that was what mattered. Walker asked to be traded. Rickey was fine with that, but he bided his time, getting one more good year out of Walker before fleecing the Pirates by sending Walker and two pitchers for Roe, third baseman Billy Cox (a weak hitter but with a sterling defensive reputation), and infield prospect Gene Mauch.

Walker was just about done, and the two pitchers didn't work out. Roe, who was going on 32, was coming off of a two-year period in which he had gone 7–23 with a 5.21 ERA (77 ERA+). Despite being a hard thrower, weak control had kept Roe buried in the Cardinals chain for most of his twenties. World War II manpower shortages and a questionable draft status made Roe attractive to the Pirates, who traded for him. He pitched well in 1944 and '45, but, after the 1947 season, the Pirates must have been tempted to write him off as a wartime-only player, as so many other 4-F players were. There should be a scouting award for whoever it was with the Dodgers—be it Branch, his son ("The Twig"), or some other perspicacious baseball mind—who was able to look at Roe and see that he had the capacity to be remade.

There were some mitigating factors: Roe had pitched through the aftereffects of a fractured skull in 1946 (a phys-ed teacher in the offseason, he protested a call while coaching a girls basketball team; the ref put him in the hospital). Coincidentally or not, Roe's velocity disappeared along with his cranial integrity. He compensated with off-speed stuff and one of the best spitballs of his time. It would be fascinating to know if the Dodgers were aware of the spitball at the time of the trade. Roe wondered that too, not the spitball part, but why Rickey bothered to acquire him at all.

"He said he figured I had had tough luck in the last three years," Roe quoted Rickey as saying in *For the Love of the Game*, "and I was gonna have a lot of good luck now and he wanted it to be with Brooklyn." Roe's stats suggest there was some truth to that, but maybe Rickey was talking less about poor defensive support and was thinking more of Roe's eight-inch skull fracture. Either way, the Dodgers got one of the best pitchers of the Brooklyn years:

Rk	Player	WAR	From	To	W	L	ERA	ERA+
1	Dazzy Vance	61.7	1922	1935	190	131	3.17	129
2	Nap Rucker	47.2	1907	1916	134	134	2.42	119
3	Jeff Pfeffer	33.0	1913	1921	113	80	2.31	125
4	Watty Clark	28.5	1927	1937	106	88	3.55	117
5	Burleigh Grimes	28.2	1918	1926	158	121	3.46	105
6	Van Mungo	27.6	1931	1941	102	99	3.41	114
7	Preacher Roe	25.1	1948	1954	93	37	3.26	124
8	Don Newcombe	23.6	1949	1957	123	60	3.42	119
9	Whit Wyatt	20.3	1939	1944	80	45	2.86	128
10	Leon Cadore	19.1	1915	1923	68	71	3.11	107

Roe's peak season, on a cosmetic basis, was 1951, when he went 22–3 with a 3.04 ERA. He won his first 10 decisions through June 21. Nine of the 10 were complete games. On July 20, he started another streak of 10 straight wins, which lasted almost through the end of the season. He really peaked in 1949, when he went 15–6 with a 2.79 ERA (fourth-best in the league), walking 44 and striking out 109 in 212 2/3 innings to lead the NL in strikeout-to-walk ratio.

The Dodgers played the Yankees in the 1949 World Series. In the bottom of the fourth inning of Game 2, left fielder Johnny Lindell of the Yankees hit a comebacker which smacked Roe in his pitching hand. Roe completed the 1–3 play to retire the side. In the dugout, a blood blister formed under one of his fingernails. The Dodgers trainer drilled a hole in the nail to relieve the pressure, and Roe went back to the mound and completed a six-hit shutout.

The guys on my team used to call it "your Beech-Nut curve."… That's because of the gum. On the bench, between innings, I'd dig into my pocket for a stick of it, and say: "I'm gonna get me a new batch of curve balls." I don't know why Beech-Nut was better. There seemed to be something in it that would make the ball slicker than any other gum. If this is a testimonial, then they can have it for free.… I found out something else about Beech-Nut. It was the only kind of gum that would make the ink on a ball fade, and I think that might have been what caused it to be the best.

—Preacher Roe, *Sports Illustrated*, July 4, 1955

As duplicitous as he was, there was one batter with whom Roe could do little: In 178 career plate appearances, Stan Musial hit .381/.441/.688 with 12 home runs against him. "I figure it's mostly up to Musial," Roe said in 1951. "Of course, I try to keep him off balance and cross him up and sometimes I get him out and start thinkin' I've found something. Then the next time I face him he knocks the same stuff I got him out on last time out of the park.... When he's gonna hit you he's gonna and there's nothing you're gonna do about it except refuse to throw the ball."

> I know one time I told Campanella that Stan's father was sick, and I told Campy to ask Stan how his father was. When the inning was over I said, "Well, did you ask Stan?" and Campy said, "Yeah, but before he could answer he was on third."

—Preacher Roe, *For the Love of the Game*

Chapter Three

YANKEES OF VARYING QUALITY

They weren't all good, but they were all Yankees, including two who deserve greater recognition.

ELSTON HOWARD, C/OF
1625 G, 1955–68
.274/.321/.427 (107 OPS+), 27.0 WAR

We can propose a number of counterfactuals about Howard's career, alternative-universe paths he might have taken in a world that wasn't so stacked against him. As a four-sport high school athlete in the mid-1940s who preferred to go pro right away instead of playing college ball, his baseball options were limited to the Negro Leagues. He was subsequently signed by the Yankees, who had no intention of integrating the major-league roster. His career in affiliated baseball had just begun when he was drafted and spent two years serving in Japan. He was already 24 years old by the time he started in earnest on his path to the white majors in 1953.

There had been pressure on the Yankees to integrate since Jackie Robinson broke the color line in 1947. They refused, hiding behind the excuse shared by all the racist baseball regimes of the time: *They would really, really like to integrate, but they just can't find the right guy.* Somehow Hank Aaron, Willie Mays, Ernie Banks (and on and on) were deficient in this mysterious quality that only Yankees (and Red Sox and Tigers and Phillies) scouts could perceive. This was as transparent an excuse then as it appears now. "The truth," general manager George Weiss told Roger Kahn in 1954, "is that our box seat customers don't want to sit with a lot of colored fans from Harlem."

The Yankees did sign some prospects of color, such as Howard, to try to prove they were sincere about the whole thing. It took six years for the Yankees—in spite of themselves—to develop a prospect who was good enough to call their bluff. That proved to be smooth-fielding first baseman Vic Power, a dark-skinned Puerto Rican. In 1953, Power hit .353 and won the American Association batting title. Since Lou Gehrig left the lineup in 1939, the Yankees had settled for a long series of good-not-great first basemen. There was every reason for Power to get a shot, so the organization assassinated him in the press as a dumb guy who chased white women, then traded him. Now the Yankees were exposed as the hypocrites they were. In 1954, as Power was becoming the first Black regular with the A's (pitcher Bob Trice had broken the team's color line with three starts the year before), Howard was with Triple-A Toronto, hitting .330/.380/.569 and winning the International League MVP award. The Yankees finally had no choice.

When Howard was called to the majors, he found himself playing behind Yogi Berra. Manager Casey Stengel, asked for the secret of his success, said, "I never play a game without my man," by which he meant Berra. Berra's backups so seldom played that one of Howard's predecessors, Charlie Silvera, was teased by friends that he persisted on the roster only because he was Stengel's bastard son. ("Maybe," Stengel told Silvera. "Was your mother ever in Kansas City?") One aspect of Howard's development that might have seemed negative now worked in his favor. No one could decide if he was best deployed as a catcher or an outfielder, and the team's decision to focus on the former seemed like another ploy to keep him out of the majors given Yogi's dwarfish-yet-looming stature. That indecision gave Howard the versatility to slip into the lineup in left field instead of wasting away on the bench. "Aw, listen," Howard said during the 1958 World Series, "I'm a better catcher than I am an outfielder, but I'll tell you this, if they want me to play the outfield, then I'm a better outfielder than I am a catcher."

Unlike most ballplayers, of whom we can say, "He was (talented/not talented) and came to the majors and (did/did not) play well," we're not yet finished with the list of obstacles in Howard's way. He was also a right-handed power hitter who was stuck in a version of Yankee Stadium with such distant fences in the left-field power alley that the ball needed to book passage on the *Millennium Falcon* to reach the stands. From 1955–66, Howard hit .278/.333/.419 with 51 home runs in 2,270 at-bats in the Bronx and .285/.323/.463 with 107 home runs in 2,574 at-bats everywhere else. Prorated to 500 at-bats, that the difference between 11 home runs and 21. When Howard retired in 1968, he had hit the eighth-most home runs of any player who was primarily a catcher. In a massively different alternative universe, in which he came up as soon as he could have and played in a friendlier park, he might have passed Roy Campanella for the second-most home runs by a catcher to that point (number one, of course, was Berra).

To the Yankees' credit, once Howard was in the big leagues, they never made him feel like a second-class citizen. He had particular praise for Phil Rizzuto, whom he jokingly called "The Great White Father" for befriending him. He also noted how the Yankees moved their spring training base from St. Petersburg to Ft. Lauderdale, because the former was segregated, and that Stengel insisted that team hotels in Chicago and Kansas City either serve Howard in their restaurants or the entire team would go elsewhere. Change wasn't wholly motivated by the white guys in power, though; in Jackie Robinson's *Baseball Has Done It*, Howard gave a great example of how community action forced teams to rethink their approach to spring training in Florida:

> All this came about because a Negro doctor in St. Petersburg, Dr. Ralph [Wimbish], spoke up. He used to board Negro ballplayers.... He announced he wasn't going to board ballplayers anymore and got the other Negro boardinghouse operators to refuse to take ballplayers in. He said it was about time the ballclubs did something about desegregating us. They did, with the result that the hotels are open to Negro players in St. Pete now.

Howard made the most of his opportunities, particularly once the aging Berra started to transition to the outfield corner Howard had previously occupied. An athletic catcher who was reputedly excellent at pitch presentation, Howard won Gold Gloves in 1963 and 1964. He won the 1963 AL MVP, becoming the first African American to claim that award. By then he was already in his mid-thirties, and, given the combination of age, injury, and an increasingly pitching-dominated era, he faded quickly. It's impossible to know if Howard would have been a Hall of Famer had all of those conditions not applied, but it's easy to like his chances. An honest Hall of Fame, which recognized great achievement in the face of adversity instead of rubber-stamping players based on statistical milestones, would have enshrined him decades ago.

Howard wanted to manage very badly. He remained with the Yankees after retirement, coaching from 1969 until his 1979 heart attack, after which he was assigned to the front office—a duty for which owner George Steinbrenner allegedly refused to pay him. Howard died the next year. Despite Steinbrenner's frequent managerial changes, Howard had never received consideration. "There never was any thought of it at all," Howard told Art Rust Jr. "[Yankees president] Gabe Paul told me they wanted somebody with experience, and this is something that always arises when you get into the problem of a black manager.... The whole thing you hear over and over again is the bullshit experience thing." Howard's wife, Arlene, remembered, "We always thought that since they acted like great white liberals, they might give Elston a chance.... Elston wondered why he had to be better than everyone else, why he had to be superman to manage a baseball team. They wanted you to have a PhD to manage if you were black, and about any white guy could manage. To Elston, it was like a slap in the face." Steinbrenner told her that, "managers are hired to be fired. He deserves better than that." That was a cop-out, but, given the very peculiar world of the Yankees at that time, it was also about as self-aware a thought as the Boss ever had.

Howard easily could have been the first manager of color, instead of Frank Robinson, but it didn't happen. Bill Veeck asked Howard to manage the Washington Senators when Veeck was on the verge of purchasing the team, but the deal fell through. Howard interviewed for other openings, such as with the expansion Blue Jays, but he didn't get them. Heart disease claimed him at 51. He was never in bad shape (he worked out with the players until the end), he just caught the wrong virus. It's impossible to know if he would have succeeded in his quest had he lived longer, but even if he had lived another 10 years, he still would have been squarely in the age of Al Campanis and other executive-level bigots.

> Another fella deserves credit and where would I be without him? Phew! He can give me a job in the outfield and he can catch too. Good kid, too, if they leave him alone and stop fighting the Civil War all over and they almost ruined him. He's good.
>
> **—Casey Stengel on Howard, 1955**

TINO MARTINEZ, 1B
2023 G, 1990–2005
.271/.344/.471 (112 OPS+), 29.0 WAR

An Olympian in 1988 and the 14th-overall pick in the amateur draft earlier that same year, Martinez was not a great player, but he was twice in the right place at the right time. Beginning in 1984, the Mariners had a terrific offensive first baseman in Alvin Davis. Davis wasn't a very good fielder, and, over time, he drifted towards designated hitter (at which point, his bat abruptly died). The Mariners attempted to replace him at first base with Pete O'Brien, a good fielder who was a light hitter for the position. Unfortunately, by the time they got O'Brien, he was 32 and his bat no longer rose even to its previous level—in 466 games with Seattle, O'Brien hit .237/.304/.371 (87 OPS+). In 1991, the Mariners compiled the first winning record in their history, going 83–79. O'Brien and Davis were among the reasons they were *only* that good. Martinez began playing regularly right after that. Martinez's first three full seasons in the majors were mediocre, but he was better than O'Brien and Davis, so he looked good just in contrast. After his first good season, Martinez was traded to the Yankees and reenacted the story, except that this time he was taking over for an aging-but-still-viable Don Mattingly.

Martinez was by no means a bad player, particularly because he complemented his bat with a good glove (oddly, he never won a Gold Glove; once the voters even passed him over for Rafael Palmiero in a year that the latter played only 28 games at first base), but, in a 16-year career, he had only two seasons (1995 and '97) when he was among the top first basemen in the American League in offensive production. Most of the time he was closer to the bottom. The high-offense era in which he played disguised this to a great extent. Consider 2001, when Martinez hit .280/.329/.501 with 34 home runs. He got a few down-ballot MVP votes that year, finishing 12th overall. Yet, he didn't hit lefties, didn't hit outside of Yankee Stadium (he averaged .254/.300/.412 on the road vs. .305/.357/.587 at home), and he was at a stacked position—the other first basemen on the circuit included Jason Giambi (199 OPS+), Jim Thome (170), Carlos Delgado (146), and John Olerud (136). Doug Mientkiewicz hit .306/.387/.464 and was at least as good a fielder, so there really isn't much of an argument for Martinez being a major asset. Even in 1998, when Martinez had one of his better seasons with a 124 OPS+, he was only eighth among regular first basemen.

FIRST BASEMEN BY OFFENSIVE WAR, 1992–2005

Rk	Player	oWAR	oWAR Peak	From	To	G	BA	OBP	SLG
1	Jeff Bagwell	70.2	7.7	1992	2005	1994	.297	.409	.548
2	Jim Thome	60.1	8.2	1992	2005	1711	.282	.410	.565
3	Rafael Palmeiro	52.1	5.8	1992	2005	2104	.284	.374	.533
4	Jason Giambi	50.5	8.7	1995	2005	1483	.295	.413	.539
5	Mark McGwire	47.5	9.3	1992	2001	1097	.277	.424	.663
6	John Olerud	45.7	7.5	1992	2005	1978	.299	.403	.469
7	Carlos Delgado	44.3	8.1	1993	2005	1567	.284	.393	.559
8	Todd Helton	43.8	7.2	1997	2005	1279	.337	.433	.607
9	Albert Pujols	35.6	7.9	2001	2005	790	.332	.416	.621
10	Fred McGriff	33.4	5.3	1992	2004	1729	.287	.371	.504
11	Mo Vaughn	31.7	5.4	1992	2003	1438	.294	.384	.529
12	Mark Grace	28.3	4.4	1992	2003	1652	.305	.387	.454
13	Will Clark	26.6	4.1	1992	2000	1092	.305	.393	.483
14	Andres Galarraga	24.4	5.6	1992	2004	1410	.300	.360	.537
15	Tino Martinez	23.7	4.7	1992	2005	1963	.272	.346	.475

The Yankees stuck with Martinez longer than they should have, in part because he was just good enough (that is, he was the kind of player who inspires complacency), the player who should have been pushing him, prospect Nick Johnson, couldn't stay on the field, and because they had locked Martinez into a contract that paid him only $4 million a year, a bargain even then. They also had such good offensive strength up the middle at typically less-productive positions—catcher Jorge Posada, shortstop Derek Jeter, center fielder Bernie Williams, and (from time to time) second basemen like Chuck Knoblauch—that they could tolerate a first baseman whose hitting was unexceptional. No doubt Martinez's defense helped as well, given that the preceding four were all butchers in the field.

Less explicable was what happened when the Yankees were (temporarily, as it turned out) done with him: The Cardinals signed Martinez to a three-year, $21.5-million contract (with an option on a fourth year) covering his age-34 through -36 seasons. After two nigh-identical 105 OPS+ showings (.267/.345/.434 combined), the Cardinals traded him to the Devil Rays, St. Louis paying Tampa to take him off their hands.

It's hard to say that Martinez *hurt* the Yankees, given that they went to five World Series in his initial six-year tenure and won four of them, but, as good as they were, they might have been even better had they been inclined to question his value. His sole big-league coaching job, as the Marlins' hitting coach in 2013, ended after just five months because he was too rough on players who, in his words, "Weren't working hard enough and weren't appreciating what they had." That sounds like cranky-old-ballplayer stuff, but if he was chastising them out of an appreciation for how hard he had to work to keep up with his peers, the Marlins overlooked the value of his story.

HORACE CLARKE, 2B
1272 G, 1965–74
.256/.308/.313 (83 OPS+), 15.6 WAR

It used to be fashionable to call the period between the last pennant of the Yankees dynasty in 1964 and the team's return to the postseason in 1976 the "Horace Clark Era." That was supposed to suggest a contrast: The Yankees once had greats like Babe Ruth and Joe DiMaggio, but then they had Horace. This was unfair in a number of ways. Clarke was hardly the worst Yankees regular in the history of the team (Tino Martinez as a Yankee: 16.7 WAR; Clarke: 16.0). He was just a glove-first middle infielder, who, well, sometimes had a few problems on defense. He in no way exemplified the level of talent the Yankees had, because, during his years as an everyday player (1967–73), the team regularly received huge seasons from position players such as Bobby Murcer, Thurman Munson, and the vastly underrated Roy White, as well as strong contributions from pitchers such as Mel Stottlemyre, Fritz Peterson, Al Downing, and Lindy McDaniel. The problem, then, wasn't that they had no players better than Clarke, but that they didn't have *enough* who were better, and did have several who were worse.

Yankees manager Ralph Houk exacerbated things by overexposing Clarke. In 1967, Houk parked him in the leadoff spot and left him there. Clarke would not have been a great hitter in any role, but, had he batted eighth where he belonged, no one would have complained. Instead, his skipper gave him a job that was not within his skill set and looked away. In 1968, Clarke hit .223/.249/.248 as a leadoff man, which was terrible even for that offensively arid season. It remains the worst season by a regular leadoff hitter in history, but that's on Houk, who was habitually clueless in this regard until, late in his career, he got to manage Wade Boggs.

About those problems on defense: Clarke was averse to contact with the runner when turning the double play. That is, rather than hang in on a takeout slide, he would bail out while holding the ball. Fans hated it, teammates questioned it, and management lectured him about it. In an era in which the takeout slide has been outlawed, Clarke's "cowardice" should be revisited. From 1969–71, he played 156 to 159 games a year, and that kind of durability might not have been possible had he allowed himself to be knocked into the outfield on a regular basis. It's also worth noting that his defensive numbers are quite good, and that he twice led the AL in double plays turned.

> One day early this season, Horace Clarke came out of Yankee Stadium...and there was this kid, maybe 11 or 12. "Hey Hoss, how come you can't make the double-play?" Clarke remembers the kid saying.... He remembers that he said something like, "Well, we can't all be stars. I guess I'm just a lousy ballplayer."
>
> **—Dick Young**

The day they traded Clarke to the Padres, the Yankees lost to the Twins. Covering the game in the New York *Daily News,* Young wrote, "Nobody can blame this defeat on Horace Clarke. [He] was several hundred miles away."

◆

The U.S. Virgin Islands don't produce many ballplayers, but Clarke remains the career leader in WAR for players born there:

TOP FIVE PLAYERS BORN IN THE U.S. VIRGIN ISLANDS				
Rk	Name	Pos	Years	WAR
1	Horace Clarke	2B	1965–74	15.6
2	Al McBean	RHP	1961–70	15.0
3	Jerry Browne	2B/UT	1986–95	11.9
4	Elrod Hendricks	C	1968–79	7.4
5	Midre Cummings	OF	1993–2005	0.9

> I don't care what you do for a living. I don't believe I am gifted, like Clemente, or Cedeño, or Mantle. About 10 percent of the ballplayers are gifted. For the other 90 percent of us, it is a struggle.
>
> **—Horace Clarke**

GIL MCDOUGALD, IF
1336 G, 1951–60
.276/.356/.410 (111 OPS+), 40.6 WAR

McDougald won a Rookie of the Year award and was a five-time All-Star, but there's a strong argument that old Yankee Stadium kept him from winning the kind of renown that would have put him on a higher shelf of historical memory—well, old Yankee Stadium and a tragedy. McDougald was a top-level defensive player whether manager Casey Stengel placed him at second, third, or short. In his 10 years in New York, McDougald spent seasons as the primary starter at each of the three and was an All-Star at each. In 1952, he led the AL in double plays turned by a third baseman. In 1955, he led the circuit in double plays turned by a second baseman. In 1957, he led in double plays turned by a shortstop. "If we had one of those lumberjacks on third," Casey Stengel said in March 1951, before McDougald had played a single game in the majors, "he would steal the job so fast that he'd jump two notches just like that. And if I put him on second he'd amaze you."

McDougald wasn't just a gloveman. At his peak, he hit for average and took an above-average number of walks. In 1956, he hit .311/.405/.443, but the performance flew beneath the radar because teammate Mickey Mantle won the Triple Crown. It wasn't just being in the shadow of Mantle that hurt: McDougald was a right-handed hitter, and the left-center-field fences at the original Yankee Stadium were a cab, subway, and ferry ride away from home plate. In his career, McDougald hit only .255/.333/.348 with 29 home runs in the Bronx, but .296/.379/.469 with 83 home runs on the road.

A tall, thin native of San Francisco, McDougald was signed by the Yankees in 1948 and whipped through the minors in three seasons, hitting a combined .340 and impressing no less than Rogers Hornsby, his manager at Beaumont in 1950. Having hit .336 for Hornsby, McDougald won the league MVP. Stengel then invited McDougald to his annual pre-camp rookie school; Gil played so well Casey brought him right to the majors.

It almost didn't happen. McDougald began his career with an unorthodox swing set up: he'd hold the bat at his waist, pointing the knob limply at the pitcher. Even McDougald called it "daffy-looking." When the 20-year-old tried out for the Yankees' farm team at Class-D Twin Falls with that stance, manager Charlie Metro initially rejected him. "I told him to go home. He'll never make a ballplayer the way he lets that bat droop in his hands. He looks like he's holding a lily." Yankees scout Joe Devine overruled Metro, and

McDougald made the team. Metro had failed to observe that McDougald didn't try to hit from that position; he'd raise his hands as the pitch came in.

Of course, Metro remembered it differently in his memoir *Safe by a Mile*:

> He fielded the ball way back under him and he threw it funny. And he had the worst-looking stance I'd ever seen. He held the bat parallel, way back as far as he could put it. He looked like a bird dog on point.... When he got to bat, if they threw it inside he'd hit the ball down the left-field line, and if they'd throw it outside he'd hit to right field. If they'd throw him a curve ball, he'd bust the heck out of it. About a month later, Joe Devine asked me how Gil was doing. I told him to come out and see for himself. Joe saw his batting stance and said, "He'll never hit like that." I said, "Joe, he doesn't know he can't hit."...When I got to talk with Rogers Hornsby, he told me about McDougald, and I said, "Rog, did you try to change his stance?"... He said, "Heck no. That kid could hit any way you threw him."

Divine didn't fault Metro. Scouts hadn't thought much of McDougald when they first spotted him among San Francisco sandlotters. "I guess the other scouts were afraid of the kid's physique," he said in 1951. "He was kind of awkward and carried his arms in a funny way. He didn't look like a big-league prospect to them." As Stengel put it, "He's the lousiest-looking ballplayer in the world, but he's splendid. He doesn't look like a ballplayer at the plate, in the field, or on the bases, but he produces everywhere." As McDougald continued to play well, Stengel would taunt his skeptics, asking, "How d'suppose you he wins that most valuable player prize in the Texas League last year? Do you think he went around buying votes?"

After McDougald hit a grand slam in Game 5 of the 1951 World Series, he said, "I'm not fence-happy. It has ruined some good batters. They keep trying to pull all the time then nub grounders back to the infield." That proved to be foreshadowing. After hitting .306 his rookie year, the right-handed hitting McDougald averaged only .270 over the next three seasons. Stengel pushed him to change to a more conventional stroke and be less pull-happy. "I used to spray pretty good in the minors," McDougald said in 1953. "But since coming up I have developed into a dead left-field hitter." Pitchers had also noticed he neglected the outside corner. "If the pitch was on the outside part, I would let it go up until two strikes," he told Dom Forker. "If the pitcher had control and threw it on the outside corner, you would see Gil McDougald go down on strikes. It happened many times." It took until an early-season slump in 1955 for him to accept the need to adjust. After he hit a weak .227 through the end of May, Stengel finally insisted. "If you don't change that stance—and I mean today—you won't be playing here." McDougald grumbled but adjusted and hit .302 the rest of the way.

Then came May 7, 1957. McDougald lined a ball into Cleveland pitcher Herb Score's right eye, shattering his nose, breaking his cheek, and damaging his vision. McDougald was devastated. "If he loses his sight," he said after, "I'm going to quit this game." When it seemed Score wouldn't lose his eye, McDougald backed off of his vow. "What I said last night was a spur of the moment thing. Things look better today." And yet, he wasn't unscathed. In the days around the Score incident, McDougald had a couple of other close calls with pitchers. On May 1 at Detroit, he knocked a ball off of Frank Lary's knee. Lary had to be carried off, though he suffered no long-term damage. On May 12 at Baltimore, McDougald faced Hal "Skinny" Brown. Brown was a knuckleballer, but he threw a fastball to McDougald. "I came close to decapitating him," McDougald told Forker. "His cap flew off, and the ball went right between his cap and his head, and I could see the look on his face, and I could tell he didn't want any more of pitching that day. That's when I really thought of quitting." McDougald remembered that, after the Brown incident, he decided he wasn't going to hurt anyone anymore. He would cease trying to hit the ball where it was pitched and pull everything. He was a .250 hitter from then on.

TOP AL HITTERS BY WAR, 1951-60		
Rk	Player	WAR
1	Mickey Mantle	74.2
2	Minnie Miñoso	55.6
3	Ted Williams	46.4
4	Nellie Fox	45.6
5	Yogi Berra	44.4
6	Gil McDougald	40.7
7	Al Kaline	36.2
8	Larry Doby	33.6
9	Jackie Jensen	30.7
10	Eddie Yost	29.3

Sick of it all, satisfied with his career accomplishments, and goaded by Yankees GM George Weiss, who had told him, "You need *me* to make a living," McDougald quit at the end of 1960 to go into business. He was only 32. Lucrative offers from the two 1961 expansion clubs did not tempt him to come back. It was time to be with his family. McDougald loved children. He raised four kids, adopted another, fostered more, and, when the others were all grown, adopted two biracial sons. "You don't see color or religion when you adopt," McDougald told the *Boston Herald* in 1978. "Who cares? We just wanted kids."

> The stance was as wide as a church door, with the left foot pointing in the general direction of Frank Crosetti, the third base coach. Joe DiMaggio's feet were wide too, but his was a classic pose, sternly erect with the bat held high behind his right ear. Gil's hands were waist-high and his grip so slack that the barrel of the bat sagged like a drooping banana stalk.
>
> Early in Gil's first season, the television set was on in the Williams Club on 39th Street. An old, crusty and respected member entered and took a seat just as McDougald came to bat. The old guy glowered at the screen briefly, then roared: "Have somebody fix this damn thing. The picture's all distorted."

—**Red Smith**, *New York Herald-Tribune*, January 22, 1961

> "One of these days now, I gotta figure where I'm gonna play McDougald this year.... I'll tell you somethin' about him to show you how good he is any place. I won the pennant every place he played."

—**Casey Stengel**, 1958

FRANKIE CROSETTI, SS
1683 G, 1932–48
.245/.341/.354 (83 OPS+), 24.5 WAR

In 1939, the veteran player and manager Roger Peckinpaugh said that five then-current Yankees ranked among the best players in franchise history: Joe

DiMaggio, Red Ruffing, Bill Dickey, Lefty Gomez, and Frankie Crosetti. The first four players are now Hall of Famers, so seeing Crosetti lumped in with them seems odd, but, at that moment in Yankees history, Peckinpaugh was almost correct—his fault was too much modesty. The top two shortstops in franchise history, Phil Rizzuto and Derek Jeter, had yet to come along. As of 1939, the team's top five career shortstops were Peckinpaugh (1913–21, 32.0 WAR), Crosetti (1932–39, 19.1), Kid Elberfeld (1903–09, 18.9), the much-derided Lyn Lary (1929–34, 10.5), and Mark Koenig (1925–30, 5.9).

Crosetti was the base-model shortstop of the pre-Ripken or pre-Holy Trinity (Jeter, Nomar Garciaparra, and Alex Rodriguez) period, after which baseball men were better able to conceptualize shortstops who could both field and be central to the offense. "Crow" was a strong fielder who, in a good year, could hit around the league average. He had a little bit of power. Only five AL shortstops hit 10 or more home runs in a season during the 1930s (none got to 20), and Crosetti was one of them. Joe Cronin did it five times, Crosetti four, Boob McNair twice, and Lary and Red Kress did it once each. Had he played in a more favorable park to right-handed hitters than old Yankee Stadium, Crosetti likely would have crested 20 at least once. Crow was also patient and stole a few bases, albeit not at great percentages.

That's not to say he was usually even an average hitter. Nevertheless, manager Joe McCarthy used him as the team's primary leadoff man during the team's four straight World Series–winning seasons from 1936–39. Crosetti averaged 122 runs scored per season, but did it while hitting only .255, with two seasons around .235. Some of that was the walks, some of it was the sheer ability of the hitters coming up after him, a group which included Red Rolfe, Joe DiMaggio, Lou Gehrig, and Bill Dickey typically hitting two through five in the batting order. This is the perversity of pre-OBP thinking: During these four years, the Yankees' eighth-place hitters averaged a .767 OPS, while the leadoff spot averaged .715. The Yankees were so good they scored between 966 and 1065 runs in each of these seasons, but they could have been *better*.

Just about every book about the old Yankees contains an anecdote about the team's trio of highly laconic Italianate San Franciscans driving cross-country to DiMaggio's first spring training. It was a trip marked by thousands of miles of interrupted silence. Suddenly, Crosetti turned to DiMaggio. "What?" Crosetti asked. "Shut up," Tony Lazzeri interjected. "He didn't say nothin'." After a well-pitched game in 1955, the Yankees were celebrating in the clubhouse. "For gosh sakes, do your yammering somewhere else," Crow shouted ("with a grin," according to *The New York Times*). "It's like Times Square in here. How can a fellow get dressed?"

Crosetti was far more demonstrative on the field, as illustrated by his outburst during Game 3 of the 1942 World Series against the St. Louis Cardinals. This flat description comes from *The Sporting News*: "Crosetti, playing third base for the Yanks, became embroiled in a hot dispute with Bill Summers, hefty American League arbiter, when Bill called Terry Moore safe…Crosetti jumped up, gesticulated wildly, and began shoving Summers around." It doesn't do the story justice. Crosetti and Summers had a history, with two prior ejections (and one more to come during Crow's coaching years) one of which ended with an assault. In the seventh inning of a game against the A's on August 9, 1940, Crosetti tried to score from second on an infield hit. He leaped over the catcher's glove, but Summers still called him out. According to the *Daily News* account, the arguing Crosetti, "hit the umps' [*sic*] protector in gesticulating," AL president Will Harridge suspended him three days. ("If I did that in our league," said Leo Durocher, looking on from the stands, "I'd be put out for the season.")

The World Series incident came about when Crosetti—in the game at third after starting first baseman Buddy Hassett went out with a fractured thumb (third baseman Jerry Priddy slid across the diamond to first)—was protesting a close play in which, he felt, DiMaggio's throw from center beat Moore at third. Summers, umpiring at third, disagreed. "Crosetti stormed into Summers and plowed both hands into the arbiter's ample stomach by way of emphasizing his points of argument. Summers, being a man of large and substantial proportions, pushed the trim Yankee infielder right back and sturdily held his ground against the onslaughts of all the other Yanks, including a thoroughly enraged McCarthy." Crow wasn't ejected because Commissioner Landis had reserved the power of World Series ejections for himself, but the incident was so severe that Crosetti was suspended for the first 30 games of the 1943 season and fined $250. After the game, Crow showed the press a bruise on his finger he said he received when Moore slid into him.

> Crosetti pulled Summers in on a close decision at third base, pushed him around, and generally conducted himself like a bad boy at bedtime in the orphan asylum.
>
> —*The Cincinnati Enquirer*, October 4, 1942

Crow wore three numbers for the Yankees, 5, 1, and 2, all now retired for other players. On the other hand, he is the all-time leader in World Series trophies. Crosetti coached in the majors for 25 years, 22 of them with the Yankees. During his pinstriped epoch, he participated in 23 World Series, winning 17 of them—seven as a player, 10 as a coach. Having received enough jewelry for one lifetime, he asked the Yankees to change things up for him. "The only ring I have is 1932," he remembered to the *Lassen County Times* in 1992. "Then I got a ring for my wife, then my daughter, then my son. Besides that, I got two pocket watches and three wrist watches. I didn't know what else to get after that. I'd got all the rings and watches I'd ever need.... I got a silver statue of a player swinging a bat. I got a couple of Browning over-and-under shotguns."

> "Sonny boy," he said in his Georgia drawl, "you pulled a lot of chestnuts out of the oven for me today."
>
> —**Yankees pitcher Spud Chandler,** praising Crosetti for several clutch fielding plays in the deciding fifth game of the 1943 World Series

Frank Crosetti, 37 years a New York Yankee, turned in a handwritten, six-page letter of nostalgia, announcing his resignation today, his 58th birthday. The longtime shortstop and coach's letter was a warm salute to Yankees from the days of Babe Ruth to the days of the Columbia Broadcasting System, and the salute extended to, "the butcher, the banker, the post office, the fruit store, the laundry and so many, many more people around 161st Street."

—*The New York Times,* October 5, 1968

PING BODIE, OF
1050 G, 1911–14, '17–21
.272/.335/.396 (110 OPS+), 14.8 WAR

Have you ever had a mental block about remembering something really basic, like the spelling of a particular word? I struggle to keep Ping Bodie and

Smead Jolley apart in my head. Both started out with the White Sox, but Jolley came along 19 years later. Both were Pacific Coast League stars with the San Francisco Seals. Bodie later played for the Yankees and was the primary center fielder in Babe Ruth's first year with the team. Jolley played with the Red Sox, where he was an iron-gloved corner outfielder who struggled with Duffy's Cliff, the six-foot incline that, from 1912–'33, led up to the wall that eventually come to be known as the Green Monster. Bodie was a right-handed hitter, Jolley left-handed. Bodie played in about 1,000 major league games; Jolley's defense was so bad he only got into about half that. The Red Sox briefly tried to turn the hulking Jolley into a catcher; it was a disaster. No one felt the need to do that with Bodie, but at 5-foot-8 to Jolley's 6-foot-3, he probably would have been the better candidate. Jolley twice drove in more than 100 runs, while Bodie topped out at 53. Bodie's real name was Francesco Stephano Pezzolo. Smead Jolley's was Smead Jolley. Bodie once competed against an ostrich in a pasta-eating contest. Bodie won, and the bird died; Jolley, as far as I know, never caused the death of any megafauna. Mostly, though, I like that baseball has had room for names like Ping Bodie and Smead Jolley (not to mention Fernando Valenzuela, Vladimir Guerrero, and Ichiro Suzuki). It is, or should be, the ultimate meritocracy.

WHITEY WITT, OF/SS
1139 G, 1916-17, '19-26
.287/.362/.364 (98 OPS+), 13.0 WAR

Witt had a unique career. After the Miracle Braves swept them in the 1914 World Series, Connie Mack broke up an A's team that had won four pennants in five years. He didn't try to get player-for-player value, mostly trading for cash. Almost overnight, the A's went from the best club in baseball to the equivalent of an expansion team. Witt was one of Mack's expedient replacements, going directly from his college ballfield to the big leagues. Witt was just 20 and had zero professional experience. Unsurprisingly, he was terrible. Witt could hit a bit—he had a good eye, some speed, and would eventually average .300 a couple of times in the offensively liberal 1920s—but he just wasn't prepared to be a major-league shortstop, even by the standards of 1916. He fielded .903, making 78 errors in 142 games. The A's went 36–117 that year, and Mack started thinking that maybe Witt would look better in the outfield. He did. In 1922, the Yankees bought Witt, and he was the leadoff man and starting center fielder on both the 1922 pennant-winner and the 1923 championship team.

Whitey's real name was Lawton, but he was very blonde; one paper referred to him as "The Agile Albino." The end of his run with the Yankees was abrupt. Manager Miller Huggins replaced him with Earle Combs in 1924, which was sensible, and when Combs got hurt, put Witt back in the lineup—also sensible. Combs was healthy in 1925, but Babe Ruth missed half the season. This time, Huggins didn't put Witt back in the lineup—with Huggins, there is always the possibility that he was taking revenge for earlier unspecified abuses. Witt sat for half a season and was released in early July. He was only 29, but that was basically the end of his career. Wilbert Robinson gave him a shot with the Dodgers, saying, "Whitey will be a great aid to the Dodgers, I think. He is fast, a good bunter and drag hitter, something that Brooklyn has not had in seasons…I got him reasonably and will not lose greatly should he fail to make good." He failed to make good.

In 1922, during a heated pennant-race game in St. Louis, someone skulled Witt with a bottle. The league investigated but wanted to bury the story, so they blamed the bottle for making an unprovoked attack.

ROBERTO KELLY, OF
1337 G, 1987–2000
.290/.337/.430 (106 OPS+), 20.5 WAR

Sometimes you just get lucky. Kelly was one of the few young players to evade the cordon sanitaire George Steinbrenner set up around his own minor-league prospects in the 1980s. One of eight children, the Panama-born Kelly signed with the Yankees in 1982 and then, very slowly, worked his way up through the system. His minor-league performances were unimpressive. Speed was his best skill; he didn't hit for power or average but was good for 40 or 50 stolen bases a year. He made a point of maintaining a neutral, almost bland on-field demeanor—"The less people know about Roberto Kelly, the better," he said—but he had a lot of pride in his play and in being the heir to great Yankees center fielders like Joe DiMaggio and Mickey Mantle.

Kelly was added to the 40-man roster in the winter of 1986. It's instructive to recall the four players who were promoted with him: pitchers Logan

Easley and Al Leiter and outfielders Jay Buhner and Keith Hughes. Two weeks after they added him to the roster, the Yankees traded Easley to the Pirates in their latest effort to obtain aging pitchers, in this case the 34-year-old Rick Rhoden. Hughes got four pinstriped at-bats in 1987 before the Yankees dealt him to the Phillies in the June trade that unwound the teams' previous swap of veteran outfielder Mike Easler, 36. Buhner got a *little* more of a chance, 32 games and 99 plate appearances between 1987 and '88 before the Yankees traded him to the Mariners for 33-year-old platoon DH Ken Phelps. Leiter was given 32 starts spread over three years, endured frequent injuries, had his arm pitched off by manager Dallas Green, and finally was abandoned to the Blue Jays in 1989 in return for outfielder Jesse Barfield, off-brand in being only 29, on-brand in being past his peak.

Kelly was the one kid who stuck, but it was a near thing. He was shuffled up and down from Triple-A as Rickey Henderson and manager Lou Piniella warred over the former's hamstrings. Kelly was pushed to left field for Deion Sanders and then Bernie Williams. He won the Opening Day center-field job in 1988 but slumped in May and was sent down (in favor of a platoon of the non-hitting Gary Ward and the non-fielding Claudell Washington). In 1989, Green stubbornly insisted on batting Kelly ninth, even as he blossomed and hit .330, igniting a media tempest when Piniella criticized the current manager for doing so on a Yankees broadcast. "All I wanted was a chance to play," Kelly whined. When Green was replaced by Bucky Dent, Kelly found his fielding and attentiveness criticized by a manager who had coached him for two years in the minor leagues. It was always something.

That Kelly persisted with the Yankees resulted from a series of fluke circumstances that arrived all at once: Both Henderson and Dave Winfield got hurt and were driven from the organization. Sanders was a bust. Luis Polonia, another competitor for playing time, got caught up in an underage-sex scandal and was traded. Washington and Ward's contracts ended at the same time collusion had kept the team from salting away even more free-agent outfielders. Finally, in July 1990, Steinbrenner was (temporarily) permanently banned by Commissioner Fay Vincent, and the organization suddenly learned to be patient with young players.

Through it all, Kelly tantalized with performances that suggested a far better player than he turned out to be, like the hot streak that Piniella wielded against Green, Kelly's 11-homer/24-steal second half in 1990, or the fast start that got him his first All-Star berth in 1992 (hitting .335/.373/.492 at the end of May, he averaged .242/.297/.332 over the rest of the season). Kelly did improve in some senses. In 1990, his first full season, he tried to sell out for power and struck out a then-troubling 148 times. He recognized it was a problem, chased fewer pitches (though he never became patient), and never whiffed at anything like the same rate again.

Kelly never achieved the stardom that New York writers kept predicting for him, but he was more than just the player Gene Michael traded for Paul O'Neill. If Kelly had a fault, it was that he lost his speed early; he stopped being an effective center fielder or base-stealer while still in his twenties. He remained worth rostering because he was a low-maintenance professional who had useful skills: what speed remained and a consistent ability to punish left-handed pitchers (he hit .312/.365/.470 against them). Kelly's professionalism is also exemplified by a long post-retirement career in coaching and managing, including nine years on the Giants' major-league staff.

Teammates occasionally refer to Roberto Kelly as "The Bat," but not because of his hitting prowess. No, Kelly earned the moniker for his sleeping habits. Kelly loves to sleep. Sometimes he will sleep 12 to 14 hours at a time. If he sleeps the whole day, he's particularly pleased. "To write a story about Roberto Kelly," [Randy] Velarde said, "all you need to do is type the letter 'Z' all the way across the column. Sleep is what makes him tick."

—**Jon Heyman**, *Newsday*, July 16, 1992

Kelly…had a gun pressed to his head, had an expensive car stolen and had a close friend killed during the invasion. But it also resulted in the capture of the Panamanian leader, Manuel Noriega. "I'm lucky I got out of there without getting hurt," Kelly said. "I came close. Who knows what could have happened?"…Still, when someone asked him to compare Panama to the Bronx streets surrounding Yankee Stadium, he smiled. "I'll stick with Panama," he said.

—**Michael Martinez**, *The New York Times*, March 23, 1990

DON BAYLOR, DH/OF
2292 G, 1970–88
.260/.342/.436 (118 OPS+), 28.5 WAR

Baylor was highly amusing or highly annoying depending on whether he was playing for your side or not. That was due to his famous ability to get hit by pitches—he reached base that way 267 times and led the AL in HBP eight times, maxing out at 35 in 1986. Baylor was officially 6-foot-1 and 190 pounds, but he seemed more mountainous than that, with a density that appeared to remove his fear of pain. A right-handed hitter shaped roughly like an inverted equilateral triangle with legs (topped with a huge, gap-toothed smile and a dapper mustache), he would crowd the plate, and, when the pitcher would inevitably put a pitch a little inside, he would turn his shoulders slightly into the pitch, then trot to first base.

This seemed to satisfy the rulebook stipulation that a batter try to *avoid* being hit, but if that slight, taunting twitch observed the letter of the law, it contravened the spirit, given that it moved him towards the pitch rather than away from it. Umpires mostly chose to ignore the distinction and award him first base. If the act pained him, he never let on; one had the impression that his back musculature was so thick that he didn't feel the impact. Getting hit by a pitch is supposed to be a negative for everyone, something both hitter and pitcher are meant to avoid. For Baylor, it was an elective, something he could order off the menu at will. He retired with the modern record, having surpassed pincushion second baseman Ron Hunt (243) on June 28, 1987 (Rick Rhoden of the Yankees did the honors). "I'm just glad it's over," Baylor said, as if he'd broken the home-run record. Craig Biggio subsequently surpassed him with 285, achieved in approximately 550 more games.

Think of Baylor's HBPs as walks and you can see how they changed Baylor's offensive profile. He wasn't an especially patient hitter, averaging 57 walks per 162 games played. Add in an average of 19 balls off the shoulder per annum, however, and he jumps up to 76 "walks" a season. He only paid a high price for it twice—in April 1976, when a pitch broke a bone in his left hand (he didn't miss any time but had what was, to that point, the worst offensive season of his career), and in April 1980, when he broke his right wrist. He was so strong, and his getting hit was so commonplace, that it took a while for anyone to notice the latter injury had happened. The AL MVP the year before, he fell off hard, missing 72 games.

"I've always stood close. If I backed off, I'd be giving away some of the plate. I guess I don't know how to get out of the way. That's my secret."

—**Don Baylor**, 1987

Baylor was marked not just by baseballs but by the more amorphous quality of "leadership." It's almost easier to talk about that insubstantial quality than it is his actual profile as a player, which was weird. When he was young, he was fast, peaking at 52 stolen bases with the 1976 Oakland A's, a run-mad team. For a while, it seemed as if he might become the third player, after Willie Mays and Bobby Bonds, to join the 300-homer/300-steal club (a group subsequently enlarged by another six players), but, as with many of us, his speed ebbed as he passed 30. Though he stopped running, he never ceased being a terror to middle infielders in breaking up a double play.

Baylor got his first taste of the major leagues in 1970 with a stacked Baltimore Orioles team that still had Don Buford, Paul Blair, and Frank Robinson in the outfield. As such, it took him a few years to achieve regular status. The year he made his big-league debut, he played at Triple-A Rochester and hit .327/.429/.583. The Orioles had nowhere to play him and sent him back. In 1971, he hit .313/.422/.539 while repeating the level. The O's still couldn't find a place for him.

When Baylor finally did come up, his game took some time to evolve. In his first season with more than 500 plate appearances, he hit 10 home runs. Five years later, in his MVP season with the California Angels, he hit 36. The next year, hampered by the aforementioned broken wrist and a dislocated toe, he hit just five in 90 games. That was hardly his fault, but it serves to symbolize a career pattern, in which he spent five of his 16 full seasons ranked among the league leaders in home runs and 11 in which he did not. Similarly, he had six seasons in the AL top 10 in stolen bases and 10 outside of it. He also had defensive shortcomings that increasingly limited him to designated hitter. Baylor had suffered a dislocated shoulder playing high school football and couldn't throw at all. As Orioles outfielder Merv Rettenmund once said, "Don can hit, run, and lob." Baylor's reputation as a leader grew in inverse proportion to his time in the field. Late in his career, he got passed from World Series team to World Series team, going from the 1986 Red Sox to the 1987 Twins to the 1988 A's. "The first day he got here, he became our leader," Red Sox pitcher Bob Stanley told Tracy Ringolsby in 1986. "Don gives us something this team has looked for for a long time," catcher Rich Gedman said.

Baylor also developed a reputation for clutch play that, as with all such players, was only partly deserved, but he did bear it out in a losing effort against the Brewers in the 1982 ALCS (.296 average, 10 RBIs in five games) and the Twins' World Series win over the Cardinals in 1987 (.385 in five games, including a key home run in Game 6). "I don't seem to concentrate when the runners aren't on base," he said during the 1982 ALCS, "but when they're out there, I do a lot more thinking."

Despite winning a Manager of the Year award for his stewardship of the wild-card-winning 1995 Colorado Rockies, Baylor's managerial career was not successful. As with many players known for their clubhouse leadership, the expectation had long been that Baylor would be able to translate his interpersonal skills in a way that would make him a strong dugout leader. It turns out, those aren't the same things. In 1993, sportswriter Scott Ostler had a terrific line: "Don Baylor, the new manager of the Colorado Rockies, issued a no facial-hair edict for his players. The Rockies are a very young team, though, and several of the players immediately shaved off their eyebrows." It's funny, but, between the lines, there is a suggestion that Baylor had failed to read the room.

For a former home-run hitter, Baylor the manager was overly enamored of one-run strategies that were self-defeating given the high-scoring environments of his teams. He also spent 14 years as a hitting or bench coach, roles for which he was perhaps more suited. Regardless, as an African American who got to follow his Orioles teammate and role model Frank Robinson into a managerial role, an aspect of the game in which Black players have not been proportionately represented, he deserves credit as a pioneer.

> "There's nobody—black, white or brown—who should have more opportunity or is more needed in the game after his playing days are over than Don Baylor."
>
> —Peter Ueberroth, 1987

JEFF WEAVER, RHP
355 G, 1999–2007, '09–10
104–119, 4.71 ERA (93 ERA+), 15.2 WAR

Every team has acquired a prominent player only to have that player not only disappoint but fail. It's often tempting to think that a good player on a bad team will be elevated by a good team. The 2019 trade that sent outfielder Nick Castellanos from a failed Tigers team to a competitive Cubs teams is the quintessential example: He went from hitting .273/.328/.462, which, in a very inflated offensive environment, was just okay, to .321/.356/.646. On the pitching side, the ultimate example is probably still Red Ruffing, who (to use won-lost record as a proxy for performance, inadequate though it is) went from 39–96 with a 4.61 ERA with the Red Sox to 231–124 with 3.47 ERA with the Yankees. The Red Sox were *really* bad at the time, and there have been some unsubstantiated suggestions that a frustrated Ruffing might have been trying to pitch his way out of town. There are counterexamples, as well. Weaver was one of them.

Weaver was the 14th-overall pick of the 1998 draft (CC Sabathia, who turned out to be the best pitcher of the round, went at number 20). Weaver reached the majors the next year and seemed fully formed. His only flaw, if it could be called that, was that his borderline-side-arm delivery left him vulnerable to left-handed hitters. That remained a career-long problem, with southpaw swingers hitting .296/.360/.502 against him in almost 4,200 PAs. The Tigers averaged a 67–95 record during Weaver's four years with the team. Given his collegiate and minor-league records and frequently strong performances—he led the AL with three shutouts in 2002—it was tempting to see any inconsistency as a product of his weak support. That was wrong. Though he would occasionally pitch well over the remainder of his career, any semblance of consistency vanished when he left Detroit. The Yankees were the first team to find this out when they collaborated in a tri-corner trade with the A's and Tigers to acquire Weaver in return for inexperienced lefty starter Ted Lilly and two prospects. In parts of two seasons in New York, Weaver posted a 5.35 ERA, the highest of any pitcher to have thrown at least 200 innings for the franchise.

"I thought trading Ted Lilly in essence for Weaver was terrific, and I was wrong," Yankees manager Joe Torre said in his memoir/retrospective with Tom Verducci, *The Yankee Years* (the prequel *The Mets Years* awaits publication, but it would probably be a much more compelling book). "Again, I think that's another situation where New York played a part in not being able to realize your ability." In placing Weaver on the 2003 postseason roster, leaving him to rot in the bullpen, and then bringing him into the 11th inning of Game 4 of the World Series for his first appearance in nearly a full month, *with Mariano Rivera still available,* Torre and Yankees GM Brian Cashman conspired to make one of the greatest, most obvious postseason blunders of all time. "I had no options," Torre said. "People say bring in Mariano. I had no options. It was an extra-inning game on the road."

We can talk ourselves into all sorts of self-destructive actions when we believe we have no options. "We have the wolf by the ears," Thomas Jefferson wrote of slavery, "and we can neither hold him nor safely let him go." By this, he meant that slavery was immoral and the divisions it inflicted would destroy the country, but it couldn't be ended because (as per the conventional wisdom of the time, informed by some real-world events), once freed, the former slaves would rise up and a race war would begin. And so, like Joe Torre, even those with a clear-eyed vision of the future said, "I have no options." Choosing to do nothing in the face of daunting choices was the Jeff Weaver of the early 1800s. It's not that there were no options, just no easy ones.

Weaver's career never wholly recovered from that teachable moment, but he did find himself in the postseason rotation for the World Series–winning 2006 Cardinals. He pitched well, too, which must have helped assuage the pain of 2003, not to mention the awkwardness he experienced earlier in '03, when he was bumped from the Angels' rotation in favor of his younger brother.

> It's baseball, what do you expect?
>
> —**Gail Weaver,** mother of Jeff and Jared, after the Angels designed Jeff for assignment to make room for Jared

> "Jered's human—he might be somewhat affected by it," General Manager Bill Stoneman said. "But they've been around pro baseball for a long time. If Jered's thinking about his brother now, I don't blame him, as long as baseball is on his mind Monday night."
>
> —*Los Angeles Times,* July 1, 2006.

GRANT JACKSON, LHP
692 G, 1965-82
86-75, 79 SV, 3.46 ERA (105 ERA+), 14.1 WAR

Grant Jackson was talented—anyone who spends 18 years in the majors and pitches in three World Series is, by definition, talented—but he mostly held an unglamorous role: pitching in middle relief.

> "Nothing bothers me," Jackson said, unsmiling, as if in answer to the question that wasn't asked.... It doesn't even seem to upset him when Manager Earl Weaver pulls him in mid-inning with a righthanded hitter coming up, in favor of Bob Reynolds. "I don't care," Jackson insisted. "I just work here."
>
> —*The Sporting News*, January 18, 1975

There were seasons in which Jackson was tremendously effective. He went 8–0 with nine saves and a 1.90 ERA in 80 1/3 innings for the 1973 Orioles. He helped pick up the 1976 Yankees by going 6–0 with a 1.69 ERA in 58 2/3 innings after coming over from Baltimore at the old June 15 trade deadline.

As well as Jackson pitched, that 1976 trade turned out to be one of the worst in Yankees history. The full exchange was Jackson, starting pitchers and imminent free agents Doyle Alexander and Ken Holtzman, a minor-league non-prospect pitcher named Jimmy Freeman, and veteran reserve catcher Elrod Hendricks to the Yankees in return for veteran starting pitcher Rudy May, former first-round pick (and future 20-game winner) Scott McGregor, fringe pitcher Dave Pagan, lefty reliever Tippy Martinez, and reserve catcher Rick Dempsey. The Yankees were 5 1/2 games ahead in the AL East at the time and, although they would pull away at the exact moment of the trade, the additions and subtractions didn't make the difference. Jackson helped in a small way, but Martinez and Pagan had pitched decently as well. Alexander was only slightly more effective than May had been, and Holtzman was a disaster; no one had bothered to ask manager Billy Martin if he had a problem with Jewish players (he did, especially when they pitched poorly) before the Yankees acquired Holtzman and signed him to an expensive extension. None of the players the Yankees acquired would be with them long, whereas McGregor, Martinez, and Dempsey were valuable players well into the '80s and were key contributors to the Orioles' 1983 championship. It was a typical

Steinbrenner-era youth-for-age deal. "We don't think we mortgaged our future," Yankees team president Gabe Paul said, but, even though New York would win the 1977 and 1978 World Series, they had; none of the players acquired from the Orioles in the deal contributed to those championships.

Jackson did not dominate left-handed hitters to the extent of the greatest lefty relievers. Willie Hernandez, whose career (1977–89) overlapped with Jackson's, held southpaws to .211/.264/.295 rates, impressive given that only the best left-handed hitters were allowed to hit against him. Lefties hit .251/.303/.341 against Jackson, though he did have two seasons in which he kept them under .200. Hernandez had three. In 1978, when Jackson was with Pittsburgh, same-side hitters averaged .391 (34-for-87) against him. Why? What did he do wrong? Nothing—small samples are weird, and the Pirates were a bad defensive team. Of the 34 hits, 30 were singles; the other four were doubles. Sometimes balls in play just break against you.

> Jackson is unknown, unheard, and unappreciated. It is almost as if he wants it that way.... He is not brilliant enough to draw heaps of praise, yet he seldom does anything to merit criticism. Grant Jackson seems to work at remaining obscure.... "Just being able to throw strikes in any given situation without being nervous is the key to relief pitching," Jackson said. "I don't get upset easy. I try to keep everything easy. I don't feel any pressure going in there."
>
> —*The Sporting News*

Chapter Four

ON THE FRINGES

Their stories outweigh their statistics, and may we never confuse one with the other.

TIM BLACKWELL, C
426 G, 1974–83
.228/.328/.305 (74 OPS+), 1.1 WAR

Try naming the Cubs' starting catchers between Randy Hundley and Jody Davis. It's not easy. Blackwell, generally a light hitter, was very briefly one of them. Barry Foote's 1980 back injury forced the Cubs to give the switch-hitting Blackwell 366 plate appearances, more than twice what he'd receive in any other season. Blackwell hit .312/.400/.450 in the second half, giving him respectable offensive numbers, overall. He also threw out 41 percent of attempted basestealers, an above-average rate. It was a one-off. He was the Cubs' Opening Day catcher in 1981, and, with Foote (who started the season 0-for-22) traded to the Yankees that April, the way was clear for Blackwell to establish himself as a regular at 28. He couldn't hold onto the job. Blackwell hit .216/.326/.342 through the strike (his OBP was a positive, but he was also batting eighth in the NL, so he was pitched around quite a bit), while the 24-year-old Davis, a Rule 5 pick from the Cardinals, waited on the bench. The Cardinals hadn't protected Davis because a non-baseball medical issue had put his career in doubt. The Cubs gambled and got a two-time All-Star and Gold Glove–winning catcher. Davis got a chance to play in June, and that was that for Blackwell's career as a starter.

Blackwell had his moments. He had an amazing Sam Elliott-in-a-period-film mustache, which he deployed as Carlton Fisk's backup during the Red Sox' pennant-winning 1975 season. Departing the Cubs as a free agent, Blackwell signed with the Expos to stand behind Gary Carter, perhaps more of an insult than a compliment given that Carter rarely came out of the lineup. More incredible was that the Elias Sports Bureau had classed this bench player as a "Type A" free agent; Expos general manager John McHale gave the Cubs his team's 1982 first-round pick (the 17th overall) to sign this anodyne reserve. The player the Cubs selected with the pick didn't work out, but that's not the point. Trading the possibility of a star for guaranteed mediocrity is never a winning strategy. Roy Halladay was a 17th-overall pick, and he's in the Hall of Fame, and if you feel like that's cherry-picking, you also have Cole Hamels (a four-time All-Star and the 2008 World Series MVP), Gary Matthews (the 1973 NL Rookie of the Year and later an All-Star), and Tim Anderson (an All-Star and batting champion), among others, to choose from.

TONY MUSER, 1B
663 G, 1969, '71–78
.259/.309/.323 (82 OPS+), –1.3 WAR
As manager: 748 G, 1997–2002, 317-431 (.424), no postseasons

According to the Peter Principle, we tend to rise to the level of our own incompetence. Muser seems to have done that twice. Primarily a glove man, there was nothing in his minor-league record that suggested he would be a useful major-league first baseman. He was a career .284/.347/.381 hitter at Triple-A, but he made it up anyway and was generally an impediment to his teams. During the Orioles' first base interregnum between Boog Powell and Eddie Murray, Muser was used as a part-time starter and defensive substitute in place of Lee May. Muser got into 336 games over three years, only 91 of them starts. He still accumulated roughly one full season of plate appearances (581), and what a season: He averaged .241/.293/.281 (70 OPS+) with just one home run. The most you can say about that performance is that he was a decent pinch-hitter (.277, almost all singles). Earl Weaver was a great manager, and he had a staff that pitched to contact, so perhaps he felt that

Muser's bat was the price he had to pay for his glove, but using a first baseman who hits like that is equivalent to shooting yourself in the foot and then eating the severed scraps of your toes without barbeque sauce.

After wrapping up his playing career with a stint in Japan (he hit .196 for Seibu), Muser went right into managing. He started with Stockton of the California League (in the Brewers' organization) and worked his way up. Beginning in 1985, he became a fixture on Milwaukee's major-league coaching staff and also had a long stint with the Cubs. With both teams, he bounced from third-base coach to hitting coach and even to bullpen coach and then back again. From this, it would be safe to conclude that teams found him a good guy to have around. Later in his career, he had a four-year stint as Bruce Bochy's bench coach in San Diego. In between, though, came six seasons (in whole or in part) as manager of the Royals.

Notwithstanding that this was a period in which the Royals as an organization were not serious about competing, Muser didn't distinguish himself. The Royals' top prospect of the mid-'90s was Mike Sweeney, a terrific hitter who had been miscast as a catcher. This was a problem Muser inherited, but he was in no hurry to solve it—by the time Sweeney reached his age-25 season in 1999, he had been up for all or parts of four seasons (the previous season and a half under Muser) and was no closer to becoming a regular than he was at the beginning. Sweeney's position that spring was number-three catcher and irregular DH. It was only when incumbent first baseman Jeff King abruptly retired in late May that Sweeney started getting regular chances in the field. "I'm committed, at this point, to making him our first baseman," Muser said that August. "Things can change, of course, but he's made such an improvement that we have to think about him." At that moment, Sweeney was hitting .336/.398/.551.

A couple of years later, Muser had to clarify to his team and the press that he wasn't taking a shot at Sweeney's religiosity when he said, following a loss, "Chewing on cookies and drinking milk and praying is not going to get it done.... I'd like to see 'em go out and pound tequila rather than cookies and milk." Sweeney was hitting .280/.352/.561 at the time.

"If I hurt anyone's feelings," Muser said, "I apologize for that. That was not my intent. I am a God-fearing man. My example of milk and cookies meant this wasn't Little League baseball. It's tough.... One is nasty, and one is easy to eat and get down. So, we have to suck it up and get through this together. That was my intent." Was he referring to Sweeney? "I've said many times that if there was one man on the face of this planet to marry my 18-year-old daughter it would be Michael Sweeney." Well, marriage is one thing and a glove-first first baseman having a prejudice against a bat-first first baseman (for his fielding, not his religion) is another. Even after Sweeney's breakthrough season, the relatively light-hitting Dave McCarty kept sneaking into the lineup. As for Sweeney's matrimonial prospects, it was Graig Nettles' niece he took to the altar. Muser was let go 23 games into the 2002 season.

> He's going to be a good player. You learn the strike zone by swinging the bat.
>
> —**Muser on Red Sox rookie Shea Hillenbrand,** who walked 13 times in 139 games in 2001 and averaged 24 per 162 games for his career

◆

> "I know people are happy now," one Royals official says. "They're thrilled because it looks like Tony is gone. And they will never know just how much Tony Muser gave to the Kansas City Royals. He gave his heart and soul to this team."
>
> —*Kansas City Star*, April 30, 2002

◆

> Mike Sweeney says Tony Muser turned around Sweeney's life. That's not a bad legacy.
>
> —Joe Posnanski, ibid.

PETE COSCARART, 2B
864 G, 1938–46
.243/.314/.329 (78 OPS+), 5.0 WAR

Coscarart, "the Basque ballplayer from Escondido," was the second baseman who had to be replaced for the Brooklyn Dodgers to reach their golden age. Rebuilding under team president Larry MacPhail and manager Leo

Durocher after about 15 years of being broken and bankrupt, they had gone 84–69 in 1939 and 88–65 in 1940, finishing third and second, respectively. They were nearly there, but something was missing. When Durocher said in his memoirs that he thought the one player the Dodgers needed in order to win a championship was Billy Herman, he wasn't *exactly* saying that all that stood between Brooklyn and a World Series dogpile was Pete Coscarart, but it was close.

It turned out Herman was available cheap; MacPhail was able to pick up the future Hall of Famer in return for outfielder Charlie Gilbert, utility infielder Johnny Hudson, and $65,000. MacPhail repeated the trick seven months later when he packaged Coscarart and some other spare parts the Dodgers didn't need—catcher Babe Phelps, outfielder Jimmy Wasdell, and pitcher Luke Hamlin—and acquired hard-hitting infielder Arky Vaughan from Pittsburgh. Pirates manager Frankie Frisch felt Vaughan was "10 years overdue" for being moved from shortstop to third base (as the Dodgers would indeed do), and he thought Coscarart would be a defensive upgrade.

That Frisch would swap a player who had, to that point, hit .324/.415/.472 (141 OPS+) for one who had hit .240/.318/.335 (78 OPS+) shows how fuzzy thinking about defense was until fairly recently. It once was commonplace to hear expressions like, "Ozzie Smith saves 100 runs a year with his glove." Systems for evaluating defense vary, so we should speak broadly about runs saved, but 20 runs saved over the average shortstop is a more typical league-leading total, perhaps reaching 30 in a peak year. Baseball-Reference has just one player in history—Andrelton Simmons in 2017—worth 40 defensive runs above average (41, to be exact). Restricting things to shortstops, Simmons had three seasons of 30 or more runs saved, and nine other payers had one such season each. Only 26 shortstops have saved as many as 25 runs in a season above average, including Mark Belanger four times, Simmons his three, and five other players twice each. Should we talk about second basemen, since Coscarart was one? In the modern era (since 1900), only four second basemen have saved 30 runs in a season, including Frisch himself with 37 in 1927. Only 13 second basemen have been worth as many as 25 fielding runs above average. That's it out of all the seasons by all the middle infielders since the start of the twentieth century. A bad bat will cost a team more runs than all but the greatest gloves will save.

This should have been obvious based on simple observation. In any given season, there are only so many balls put in play. Of those, only a portion of them are hit towards the shortstop. Some are hit right at short, or close enough for all but the most unqualified shortstops to field them. Only a very limited number fall into the tough-play category. Let us further stipulate that a ball that gets past the shortstop is almost certainly a single, and that only about a third of all singles score. None of this requires a Bill James to figure out, and, in fact, James *didn't* figure it out—it took a lot longer. Somehow it wasn't intuitive, even if, retroactively, it seems obvious.

Now let's return to Pete Coscarart, new Pirates shortstop of 1942. At .228/.288/.287 (67 OPS+) in everyday play, Baseball-Reference has him as 20 offensive runs below the average hitter. They also have him at –8 fielding runs, but let's say they're wrong and he was eight runs *above* average—in what sense were the Pirates ahead? "The surprise of the [traded] quartet is the heretofore unwanted Pete Coscarart," veteran sportswriter Harry Grayson wrote that May 19. Coscarart "is playing shortstop as though he were raised there. His batting average is scarcely high, but he is meeting the ball well and swatting it for distance. The Buccaneers never have made so many double killings…They are comparing Coscarart with Tommy Thevenow of whom Pittsburghers like to speak." The '41 Pirates went 81–73; the '42 team went 66–81. Thevenow was a disastrous player, too, a career .247/.285/.294 (51 OPS+) hitter. He was a good fielder, but he made more outs at the plate than he saved on defense.

A pro-union player before it was fashionable, Coscarart worked at a gas station in the offseason. He eventually became a real-estate agent in his California hometown. Like all prewar players, he was left out of the Major League Baseball pension plan. In 1997, he joined a group of similarly excluded players to sue for lost benefits. Initially victorious, the players saw the verdict reversed on appeal. Coscarart and his co-plaintiffs were ordered to pay MLB's attorneys' fees. According to a 2000 article by Steve Love of the *Akron Beacon Journal*, Coscarart, then 87, received a bill for more than $340,000. If he'd had *that*, he wouldn't have needed to get into a $10,000-per-annun pension plan; that was Major League Baseball being vindictive.

> "What is so exceptional about Coscarart?" asked one of the Brooklyn execs. "We've had him for four springs now. He's not outstanding in speed, power, fielding, making plays or smartness. And he's a wretched hitter. He does have youth on his side—but those four springs don't give any hope of his improving."
>
> —*Daily News*, March 26, 1941

With the Dodgers' pursuit of Herman an open secret during spring training 1941, Coscarart hit about .150; Durocher called him, "the only disappointment of the club this spring." Squeezed between Herman and second-year shortstop Pee Wee Reese, Pete sat on the bench all year and batted only 71 times, hitting .129. Forced into World Series play when Herman suffered a muscle strain prior to Game 3, he went 0-for-7 as the Dodgers lost to the Yankees in five. That will get your ticket out of town punched every time, Arky Vaughan or not.

**Early to Bed, Early to Rise and He Eats Wheaties…
Pete Coscarart's Wise!**

While Pete takes his morning shower, his pretty wife, June, is busy in the kitchen getting breakfast. Like many another champion's wife, Mrs. Coscarart helps make it easy for her husband to keep fit the year around. She'll tell you that her family eats a lot of Wheaties; they both like 'em especially with fresh fruit.

—1940 newspaper ad

JOHN VUKOVICH, 3B/IF
277 G, 1970-71, '73-77, '79-81
.161/.203/.222 (20 OPS+), -3.5 WAR

Baseball statistics are unique in sports in their ability to tell stories. Occasionally we can even use them to infer character. With "Vuke," they tell us that he must have been a heck of a guy, because he was (a) by one measure the worst hitter of the last 75 years, and yet was (b) a baseball lifer who spent 23 straight years on major-league coaching staffs and was the longest-serving coach in Phillies history. Beginning with the 1982 Cubs, he worked under Lee Elia, Charlie Fox, Jim Frey, Gene Michael, and Frank Lucchesi. Moving to the Phillies, he served as a lieutenant for Elia again, then Nick Leyva, Jim Fregosi, Terry Francona, and Larry Bowa.

That's a sad list filled with meaningless baseball. Vukovich's 1984 Cubs won the NL East, and his 1993 Phillies won the NL pennant. Of his 21 other teams, only one even came close to the postseason, and the coaching staff did not distinguish itself. With some teams, the managers are so few and so notable you could name them all for decades without having to jog your memory too much. Think of the major Yankees skippers from the Ruppert years up to the point George Steinbrenner became compulsive: Miller Huggins, Joe McCarthy, Bucky Harris, Casey Stengel, Ralph Houk, Yogi Berra, Johnny Keane, Ralph Houk again, Bill Virdon, Billy Martin I. We've just covered 1918 through 1975. The Dodgers are even easier, because, from 1954 through 1996 there were just two managers: Walt Alston and Tommy Lasorda. Vukovich's teams are the opposite. The Cubs and the Phillies have gone half-centuries without having managers who achieved anything that forces you to keep them in your active memory. Joe Maddon and Charlie Manuel were islands in seas of mediocrity. Most Cubs and Phillies managers aren't even memorable for being notably bad. The few that did make their marks—such as Gene Michael (as a Yankees executive), Terry Francona (as Red Sox manager), or Fregosi and Bowa (as players)—did it in entirely different contexts. Vukovich never got to manage in his own right beyond two stints as an interim skipper picking up after Frey (1986) and Elia (1988). When you can't get a job in *that* crowd, it must make for a lot of late nights.

On June 26, 1988, the Phillies, 32–39 and on the way to losing 95 games, beat the Cardinals in 10 innings, this despite a blown save by reigning NL Cy Young Award winner Steve Bedrosian. The winning rally included Bob Dernier squeezing home pinch-runner Darren Daulton, the catcher of perpetually swollen knees. Fun, right? But look at Vukovich's night. First, Phillies first baseman Von Hayes lined out in the ninth inning and bounced his helmet off of his manager in frustration. He hadn't *meant* to bounce it off of Elia, that's just the way it ricocheted, but Phillies players were making something of a habit of pelting Elia with equipment. The manager, never the coolest of cucumbers, took umbrage. "If I get hit again, I'll break your skull," Elia shouted at Hayes per *The Philadelphia Inquirer*'s family-safe version. Hayes objected to *that*, and the two nearly came to blows before bench coach Vukovich pulled them apart.

The mood must have remained tense, because, shortly thereafter, Vukovich emerged from the dugout to go over some lineup changes with plate umpire Lee Weyer and got into an argument over whether or not Weyer was "smirking" at the Phillies dugout. "I told him he doesn't have to look into our dugout," Vukovich said eloquently. Weyer, quite reasonably, ejected him. Just another night in 1980s Philadelphia. The Phillies needed a coach who acted as the voice of sanity in an insane world, but Vukovich wasn't made that way.

Rather than hire him for the full-time managerial role for which he was otherwise qualified, baseball men would whisper about his temper. Nevertheless, Cubs GM Dallas Green, a temperamental man himself, was set to give Vuke the Cubs job in 1987. Green was fired the morning of the press conference announcing the move, and Vuke's best chance went with him.

Vukovich was the 10th-overall pick of the now-defunct January phase of the amateur draft. In retrospect, there weren't any high-quality players available, so no harm done. He wasn't an automatic out in the minors, but the majors were a different story. If you rank postwar position players by OPS+ and lower the cutoff to 600 PAs, or roughly one full season, you get a career list that looks like this, counting down to the worst hitter by those qualifications:

Rk	Player	Pos	OPS+	PA	AVG/OBP/SLG
10	Mick Kelleher	IF	43	1202	.213/.266/.253
9	Jerry Zimmerman	C	42	1119	.204/.269/.239
8	Mario Mendoza	SS	41	1456	.215/.245/.262
7	Luis Gomez	SS	40	1391	.210/.261/.239
6	Brandon Wood	3B/SS	40	751	.186/.225/.289
5	Donnie Sadler	IF/OF	39	861	.202/.262/.284
4	Kevin Cash	C	37	714	.183/.248/.278
3	Michael Martinez	IF/OF	37	621	.194/.243/.261
2	Angel Salazar	SS	36	932	.212/.230/.270
1	John Vukovich	3B	20	607	.161/.203/.222

Maybe the Mendoza Line should have been the Vukovich Line. To be fair to Vuke, it's tough to get established when you play as infrequently as he did after 1973. Vukovich won rings as a member of the 1975 Reds and 1980 Phillies, which just goes to show that sometimes perseverance is rewarded before talent. "I know I can hit," the then-23-year-old Vukovich said during an 0-for-30 stretch in July 1971. "It started to get to me a little bit. It's a funny game. You see guys hit 'em [down on the bat handle] and they bloop 'em in. You wonder why it can't happen that way for you. You look up and say, 'What did I do?'" He never did work that out, although he hit six home runs in the majors off of six different pitchers, among them Nolan Ryan, Jerry Koosman, Mickey Lolich, and Sparky Lyle. That's not a bad collection for a guy who couldn't buy a single the majority of the time. Brain cancer drove him off the field and into the front office in 2005; it laid him low in 2007 at the age of 59.

> I've offended enough people along the way that don't want me to get it. But I look back and I wouldn't change a damn thing I did the last 22 years—except hit the breaking ball better.
>
> —**John Vukovich**, on the possibility of being named manager of the Cubs

> "He was probably my second dad. He was family to me.... He had a very, very rough exterior, but he had a very, very soft center."
>
> —**Ruben Amaro Jr.**, on the occasion of Vukovich's passing

BILLY HUNTER, SS
630 G, 1953–58
.219/.264/.294 (53 OPS+), –1.9 WAR

As longtime shortstop Phil Rizzuto began to slip in the 1950s, the Yankees took their time finding a long-term replacement. Hunter, whom they acquired in a 17-player trade with the Baltimore Orioles (depending on your source, we might still waiting for one PTBNL to be revealed), got a shot at the job, but only for a moment—the Yankees had too many good infielders to play a pure gloveman, and this gloveman twice led the AL in errors. "He's a showboat," said an anonymous Yankees coach in March 1955, "who makes the easy ones look hard and vice-versa." Rey Ordoñez was a better hitter than Hunter. Mark Belanger was a *much* better hitter. Due to an out of character hot streak in May of his rookie year, Hunter made the AL All-Star team along with fellow St. Louis Brown Satchel Paige. Hunter had already stopped hitting; as of the All-Star Game itself, he was averaging .245/.283/.281. It would be an exaggeration to say he never made another hit all year, but it's close: over the rest of the season, he hit .189/.218/.234 in 68 games.

Casey Stengel once said, "I don't like them fellas who drive in two runs and let in three," but he also didn't care much for players who save two runs but strand three. "Hunter can go to his left and to his right. He has a strong arm. That leaves hitting and if Billy can boost his batting average he'll have to be considered [as a starter]." That was Stengel's spring training assessment. Hunter couldn't boost his average, of course. Stengel's way of coping was to pinch-hit for him early and often. In 1955, Hunter started 91 games. He finished only 50 of them. On two occasions, Stengel pinch-hit for him as early as the third inning. In one game, the Yankees were trailing 6–4 and Hunter came up with two men on. In the other, they were ahead 5–0 and Hunter came up with the bases loaded. Stengel went to first baseman Eddie Robinson both times. In the former game, Robinson failed to plate the runners, and the Yankees went on to lose, but in the latter, Robinson hit a two-run single to turn the game into a blowout. Overall, the tactic didn't really work. Despite Stengel using three future Hall of Famers to hit for Hunter (Rizzuto, Mickey Mantle, and Country Slaughter), as well as excellent players such as Robinson (12 times), Moose Skowron, Joe Collins, Bob Cerv, Elston Howard, and Hank Bauer, Hunter pinch-hitters averaged .147 with a double, three walks, and 9 RBIs in 39 plate appearances.

After all of that, the Yankees sent Hunter down to the Denver Bears of the American Association, and it's tempting to think that, if the pinch-hitters had come through just a few more times, he might have stayed on the roster for the entire season. The Yankees, in first place since late May, had slumped in July, and the White Sox passed them at the end of the month. All of the infielders were slumping, including Hunter (he went 0-for-17 with a walk in the nine games before the demotion). With Jerry Coleman returning from a broken collarbone, Billy Martin returning from the Army, young Bobby Richardson playing well at Denver, and Rizzuto still on the roster, the middle infield was where they had the depth to make a change. Stengel, who had earlier praised Hunter for having "spark and fight," said of the demotion, "It wasn't something I wanted to do. This boy didn't play bad ball around here. We were in first place with him playing shortstop, weren't we?" About two weeks later, Hunter broke his leg sliding into second base, ending his season.

Hunter spent 14 years coaching for the Orioles—he was the third-base coach for almost all of the good years in team history (1964–77). He turned down opportunities to manage the A's, Twins, and the Reds but accepted the invitation to be the fourth Rangers manager of 1977 after Eddie Stanky abruptly resigned just one game into his reign.

Hunter was the Rangers' fourth manager in a week when he took over and their sixth manager in the six years since the team had moved from Washington to Texas. Owner Brad Corbett offered the job to Harmon Killebrew and Don Drysdale and waited for them to reject it before hiring Hunter on the recommendation of general manager Eddie Robinson—the same Robinson who had repeatedly pinch-hit for Hunter almost a quarter of a century earlier. "I think Billy is the type of guy who will jerk [the players] up if they need it," Robinson said. The team, loaded with veterans on long-term contracts, took off under Hunter. Just 34–35 and in fourth place when Hunter was hired, the Rangers went 60–33 (.645) the rest of the way and finished second. "We were a team that was waiting to have some kind of direction or guidance," catcher Jim Sundberg said. "It was kind of like a rebellious child who needed some leadership. He gave it to us."

Hunter returned in 1978 and, despite the team's frenetic roster overhaul during the offseason, had another strong year by the standards of the 1970s Rangers, going 87–75. Corbett offered him various long-term contracts, but Hunter preferred to go year-to-year—his wife didn't want to relocate from Maryland to Texas, so he wanted the flexibility to get out if he needed to. This was used against him when it turned out that not every player wanted to be jerked up. Hunter was an old-school baseball man with a disciplinarian mindset who "seldom showed more personality than a resin bag"—Frank Robinson had nicknamed him "Little Hitler" during their Orioles days. When Hunter banned the Rangers from drinking in the team hotel and on team flights, it aggravated the club's thirtysomething contingent. In May 1978, erratic/free-spirited (depending on your point of view) pitcher Dock Ellis vocally challenged the manager on a team bus ride. Hunter responded eloquently, telling Ellis to, "sit down and shut up." Ellis's response was that Hunter "may be Hitler, but he's not going to make a lampshade out of me."

Corbett told Hunter that Ellis would be traded, but Ellis outlasted Hunter in Arlington. There is a bittersweet coda: According to Ellis, he confronted Hunter at a Rangers old-timers event years later:

> I scared all the old-timers. I said, "All right all you sons of bitches, shut up! I've got something to say. Go out there and bring in Billy Hunter's ass!" They brought him in there. I said, "Man, let me tell you something. During the time you were my manager, I was a sick son of a bitch. I was an alcoholic dope fiend. In the process of recovery, I need to make amends to you!"...It blew his mind!

That came too late to save Hunter's job. Corbett said, "We had a bitter team," and needed, "a manager who can communicate," and fired him on the season's penultimate day. When there were no consequences for Ellis, Sundberg said, "maybe because Hunter's hands were tied, he let Dock get away with it and he lost the team."

Then and there, Hunter foreswore all future major-league employment. He subsequently spent nearly 20 years as the baseball coach and athletic director for Towson University. He turned down all chances to reconsider his vow and return to the majors. "I felt I had accomplished what I set out to accomplish," he said in 2013.

Hunter was developed by the Branch Rickey–era Dodgers but was traded to the Browns before ever reaching Brooklyn. "Everyone in Triple-A for the Dodgers knew more about fundamentals than the Browns," he later told John Eisenberg. That was almost certainly not hyperbole, and it's easy to imagine Hunter, who also played on two Yankees pennant winners and coached an Orioles team that did everything right, developing the belief that he knew more about how to play the game than most. He may even have been right, but acquiring the knowledge is one test, communicating it to others is a harder crucible.

> Sometimes I wonder myself whether I am doing the right thing by sending them home. Sometimes I wonder if I shouldn't stop them. One thing, for sure, the fans in the stands are very helpful.
>
> —**Billy Hunter,** Orioles third-base coach, 1972

> Was he sorry he ever accepted the Rangers job? "Yes," was the reply.
>
> —*The Dallas Morning News,* October 2, 1978

ROLLIE ZEIDER, IF
941 G, 1910–18
.240/.315/.286 (80 OPS+), 6.0 WAR

Rollie "Bunions" Zeider spent all but 50 games of his career with the three Chicago teams. Three? Yep: He started with the White Sox, spent two years with the Federal League's Whales, then wrapped up with three years with the Cubs. The 50-game exception came during the 1913 season, when he was traded to the Yankees. He was part of the much-derided return for Hal Chase, the greatest star in New York American League history to that point. On June 1, 1913, after Chase and Yankees manager Frank Chance had their final falling out, the latter dealt the black-hearted first baseman to the White Sox in return for Zeider and Babe Borton, another game-throwing first baseman. (Chase's cheating was present tense; Borton's lay in his Pacific Coast League future.) The public, not privy to Chase's corruption, was less than thrilled with the deal. Not only was the return uneven, Zeider was hurt and required minor foot surgery. New York sportswriter Mark Roth said, "The Yankees traded Chase to the White Sox for a bunion and an onion." What this joke omitted was that the word was out on Chase—Chance said that the other teams, "did not seem anxious to get Chase under any conditions or at any price." The bunion/onion combo was the best he could do.

Chance, who said he was going to replace Chase with his 36-year-old, chronically-concussed self (this didn't happen), claimed, "Zeider is a better ballplayer than he has shown. He simply needs regular work." That didn't happen either, not because Chance was lying, but because Zeider almost immediately underwent surgery on the infamous bunion and missed all but three of the games the Yankees played between early June and mid-August. His next chance at regular play would come in the Federal League with what were functionally expansion teams. Chance later requested an investigation of the deal on the grounds that Sox manager Jimmy Callahan had lied to him about the players being in condition. American League President Ban Johnson dismissed the complaint as unfounded.

Zeider had established himself as a player with the San Francisco Seals of the Pacific Coast League—he stole 93 bases (in 201 games) in 1908, the second most in league history, and was voted the most popular player on the circuit in '09—and reached the majors at 26. Once his major-league career was over, he returned to the PCL, playing for Vernon, Los Angeles, and Portland.

◆

> Rollie Zeider, the Chicago Cubs' old second sacker, was quite a jokesmith.... He was trying to make rookies on the team think

he was not afraid of Manager Frank Chance.... Chance was deaf in one ear, so Rollie would seat himself beside the manager on the bench, taking care to get on Chance's deaf side.... Every time Chance hurled some caustic bit of advice at any player, Zeider would call Chance some name, adding a remark like: "Oh, shut up! What do you know about this game?"

He got away with it until one time when Chance happened to turn his head slightly in Rollo's direction. Being a lipreader, Chance could almost tell what he had said.... "Say, young fellow," remarked Chance, "if you are calling me what I think you are, you won't be on this team very long." Zeider subsided.

—*The Laclede County Republican*, August 17, 1923

If that prank on Chance sounds cruel, worry not. Zeider got his. According to *The Garret Clipper*, during his first stint in the PCL, some of the Seals spent a bit of voluntary time at the Portland county jail, "many of the officials being ardent baseball followers." During the tour, "They came to a cell where a wild-eyed man stood at the gate, clutching the steel bars and growling.

"'This is the toughest prisoner we've ever had here,' the official told Rollie. 'It took five of our best men to get him in there, and he laid three of them out. He'll try to kill every chance he gets, and we have him in our strongest cell.'

"As he spoke, the 'prisoner' suddenly dashed against the door and it sprang open. Yelling and snorting, the man made for Zeider. His mates, who were standing back chuckling, claimed Rollie broke his own excellent sprinting record as he tore down the corridor with the man in hot pursuit.

"A cell door stood open and Zeider leaped in, closing it with a click." It had been a practical joke—the man in the cell was a guard.

◆

Zeider was never much of a hitter; speed and versatility were the benefits he provided his teams. Even during his two seasons in the Federal League, where the quality of play was lower than in the established majors, he only scraped a league-average offensive performance in the first. After retiring at 40, he went back home to Indiana and opened up a tavern.

EDDIE "MONGOOSE" LUKON, OF
213 G, 1941, '45-47
.230/.307/.408 (98 OPS+), 2.3 WAR

One of the smallest tragedies of World War II, but a tragedy nonetheless, was the loss of careers to military service. It must have been particularly painful for those who saw their baseball hopes dashed because they answered their country's call, given how briefly one is young enough to play at an elite level. For us spectators, even more than half a century after the fact, it's frustrating because it's impossible to know what we lost. Mongoose Lukon made the majors with Cincinnati as a 20-year-old just months before Pearl Harbor. Between the Reds' decision to send him back to the minors for 1942 and the war, he wouldn't appear in Reds drag again until September 1945. What he might have been had his career not been interrupted is impossible to say, but, in the limited playing time he received in 1946 and '47, he showed power and a modest ability to reach base. The point isn't that he would have been a star; most young players turn out to be much less than that. The point is that he didn't get to find out.

In the war, Lukon was a fighter pilot and a veteran of the Battle of the Bulge. In the majors, Lukon had a 5-for-5 day at Brooklyn on June 25, 1946, hitting two doubles and a home run. In 1941, *The Cincinnati Enquirer* mentioned that Lukon's father helped him by filming his swing. Not to take anything away from Tony Gwynn, but that's more than 40 years before he was noted for utilizing technology the same way.

EDDIE BROWN, OF
790 G, 1920-21, '24-28
.303/.334/.400 (98 OPS+), 7.7 WAR

Some baseball nicknames are complimentary ("Hammerin' Hank"), some descriptive ("High-Pockets Kelly"), some sort-of complimentary but in questionable taste (Mike "Superjew" Epstein), and a few are just vicious. Brown had one of the latter. He was known as "Glass Arm Eddie" because he couldn't throw. He had reasonable assist totals during his brief career, but that doesn't prove that the appellation was unfair; sometimes an outfielder will pile up high assist totals because baserunners feel safe testing his arm. He'll get a few of them, but an above-average number are still safely traveling from first to third on a single.

Brown was tall for the time (6-foot-3) and rangy, but those throwing problems were real and came close to keeping him out of the majors; they certainly damaged his efforts to stay. He spent five years in the low minors without impressing anyone, missed a year serving in the Great War, and didn't get his first cup of coffee until he was 28. John McGraw gave him a trial as a pinch-hitter in 1921. Brown hit .297 in the role, but all the Giants could see was that throwing arm. "Brown was not a success with the Giants for one reason," wrote Tommy Holmes. "He certainly could paste the old apple and his fielding, while not particularly graceful, was done in a capable manner. But Ed's throwing arm was atrocious. Cursed with a weak pegging arm, all McGraw's horses and all McGraw's men could not make a big leaguer out of the rangy Westerner in this respect."

The Dodgers acquired Brown when they were looking for the short side of an outfield platoon. Once he got to play, he proved to be a durable singles hitter who piled up the hits but didn't do much else to generate offense. He led the NL in games played in both 1925 and '27. In between, he led the league with 201 hits, averaging .328/.355/.415 (115 OPS+). He hit only two home runs and drew only 23 walks, and it says something that the Dodgers had traded him to the Braves after only two seasons. From the time he got to play, at 32, until he was 35, he had four full seasons of hitting .300, then slumped to .268 and was packed off to Toledo; when you don't become a regular until you're 29, you don't have very long until father time comes calling. Brown was probably hurt by being a .313 hitter in a league that averaged .284. Singles hitters were as cheap then as power hitters are now; think of Brown as the banjo-hitting version of Renato Núñez.

Throwing isn't everything. Brown's obituary asserts that, "Throughout his career he was noted as one of the league's outstanding defensive players." This is consistent with what was said during his career. On the occasion of Brown's trade from the Dodgers to the Braves, Brooklyn manager Wilbert "Uncle Robbie" Robinson called Brown, "the greatest catcher of long flies [I] ever saw." Reporter Thomas Rice added, "Brown has not been as spectacular as some outfielders because he runs so smoothly with his long legs that he makes star catches look easy." Yet, Rice conceded, Braves shortstop/manager Dave Bancroft, "will relay many throws from Brown."

Brown hit only 16 home runs in his career, three of them in a doubleheader against the Phillies at the tiny Baker Bowl in 1924. After his playing days were over, he worked as a carpenter at the Mare Island Naval Ammunition Depot in California. Brown was once traded for a shortstop nicknamed "Binky"; maybe "Glass Arm Eddie" wasn't so bad.

> I'm 31. There's no use lying about it, I suppose.
>
> —**Eddie Brown,** upon joining the Dodgers five weeks before his 33rd birthday

SUMPTER CLARKE, OF
36 G, 1920, '23–24
.227/.267/.300 (45 OPS+), –1.0 WAR

This comment is unusually indebted to the player's SABR biography, written by Chris Rainey. Clarke was such a fringy player it's hard to know what to say about him. It turns out there are a few things worth talking about:

1) His first name is unusual. It was his father's name. How the old man came by it, I don't know, but these were Southerners—Sumpter II was born in Savannah—so perhaps Sumpter I's folks were celebrating the kickoff of the Civil War and misspelled the name of the fort that was attacked. Sumpter is also archaic English for "pack animal," so maybe Sumpter II's grandpa had a negative feeling towards his son, but this seems unlikely. Sumpter *pere* spent some time as a traveling salesman, so it's also possible he was from Hoboken, got lucky in Georgia, and the name was a coincidence. This is what we call a "subject for further research/not time-effective." Life is full of SFFR/NTEs, and knowing and accepting them for what they are and refusing their siren song is an important skill for students of history if they are ever to get anything done.

2) Throughout his career, Sumpter was referred to as an eccentric character. He was called "high-tensioned," and a post-career article "lumped [him] with Casey Stengel and Jimmy Piersall as 'colorful' outfielders." Whereas we can give examples of Stengel and Piersall being colorful in their ways, whatever Clarke did to earn that description seems to have been lost to history due to mostly occurring in obscure minor-league games. The closest we come is the story of his taking a poke at his manager after being criticized for not hustling on a grounder. That's not colorful, it's just violent. He also caused his team, the Birmingham Barons, to be sued after he winged a patron by impulsively throwing a ball into the stands following a bad at-bat. He was standing in

left field, and the spectator was in the first-base boxes, so it must have been a heck of a throw, but the act itself was not unique to Sumpter.

3) Sump (he was actually called this) had a younger brother, Rufus, who also briefly made it to the majors, pitching for the Tigers in 1923 and '24. There doesn't appear to have been anything eccentric or colorful about him, which would seem to be an argument for nature over nurture.

4) Tris Speaker put Sump on Cleveland's Opening Day roster in 1924. Clarke was to platoon in right field with Homer Summa. If only the Sumpter/Summa platoon had been more successful so that we had more reason to invoke its nomenclatural eccentricity (Sumpter could hit a homer, but Homer couldn't hit a sumpter without getting the ASPCA after him). Alas, neither of them could hit particularly well. Sump fooled 'em with a hot start, going 7-for-20 (.350) in April, but there was no encore: He went 0-for-May (in 19 at-bats), his only positive accomplishment that month was a successfully executed sac bunt.

Going 0-fer a month is rare but not unheard of. Using Clarke's 20 plate appearances as a cutoff, we learn that:

- 17 players have gone 0-for-April, led (if that's the correct word) by Richie Scheinblum, who went 0-for-30 for the 1969 Clevelanders. If you start off the season in a slump, you don't get to stay in too long, but if you survive until May, you get more rope.

- 45 players have gone 0-for-May, first among the last being Danny Valencia, who went 0-for-25 with the 2012 Twins. Valencia was traded later that season.

- 42 players have gone 0-for-June. Pitcher Red Donahue of the 1901 Phillies went 0-for-26. The position player who had the most arid June was Joe McEwing of the 2002 Mets.

- 47 players have gone 0-for-July, with Craig Counsell going 0-for-31 for the 2011 Brewers. Counsell was 40 and in the last season of his career.

- 72 players have gone 0-for-August, with a three-way tie for first/last place between 1901 Senators pitcher Bill Carrick, 1995 Tigers outfielder Danny Bautista, and 2007 Royals catcher Jason LaRue, all at 0-for-24.

- 61 players have gone 0-for-September, topped by 1916 Giants hurler Rube Benton, who went 0-for-26. The trailing position player was outfielder Thurman Tucker (1950 Clevelands) at 0-for-24. Cleveland was four games behind the league-leading Yankees at of the end of August 1950. The team played well the rest of the way but couldn't quite catch up. Tucker was part of that—Cleveland went 2–5 in his appearances, including an inexplicable home sweep at the hands of a St. Louis Browns team that lost 98 games. Three of the four losses in that series were by one run.

Clarke was only held hitless for 23 consecutive at-bats. The Orioles' Chris Davis left him in the dust when he set a record by going 0-for-54 from mid-September 2018 to mid-April 2019. "Chris Davis" is a boring name. "Sumpter Clarke" has Davis beat all hollow in the Nomenclature Olympics.

JIMMY STEWART, PH
1963–67, '69–73
.237/.306/.305 (71 OPS+), –1.2 WAR

Stewart had more appearances as a pinch-hitter (373) than he did in left field (179), second base (122), or shortstop (107). Despite his persistence in the role, he wasn't particularly good at it, hitting .220/.289/.289. He hit .247/.314/.318 as a starter, which isn't great either, but it's closer to playable if you're a good glove.

Of Stewart's two pinch-hit home runs, one comes (retrospectively) as quite a shock. On rainy August 23, 1970, the Mets were up 5–4 on the Reds heading to the top of the seventh inning at Shea Stadium. It was the second game of a doubleheader, Tom Seaver was on the mound for New York, and some of the Reds' regulars were resting. Bernie Carbo and Tommy Helms hit back-to-back singles with one out, bringing up Cincinnati's reserve catcher, Pat Corrales. Reds manager Sparky Anderson did the logical thing and pinch-hit with Johnny Bench, but Seaver struck him out. Next up was reserve infielder Woody Woodward, a very light bat (the month before, he had hit the first home run of a career that had already run about 750 games). Anderson sent up Stewart, who wasn't that much better, but he was a switch-hitter, so at least he'd have the platoon advantage. Seaver got ahead 0–2, but his next pitch caught too much of the plate, and Stewart parked it in the right-field seats, giving the Reds a 7–5 lead. They'd go on to win by that score.

"I was afraid it wasn't going to go," Stewart said. "I hit it a little bit on the end of the bat and I usually have to get all of it to hit one out." *Usually?* The guy had eight career home runs. The credit, as well as the blame, might well be assigned to Seaver, who was experiencing a year-end slump. 17–8 with a 2.39 ERA through August 1, he went 2–7 with a 3.89 ERA the rest of the way. After Stewart's shot, manager Gil Hodges switched from a four- to a five-man rotation so that Tom Terrific could get more rest.

Stewart had an exciting month. On August 9, Bench was thumbed out of the game for throwing away the ball while protesting a play at the plate. Corrales had already been in and out of the game, so Stewart appeared at catcher for the only time in his career. Billy Grabarkewitz of the Dodgers tested him with a straight steal of home. Grabs made it, though Stewart argued he'd tagged him. It happened that 1970 was Stewart's one big year as a pinch-hitter; he went 13-for-40 (.325) with that home run against the Mets. With his help, the Reds won 102 games and went to the World Series, although he went 0-for-4 in October.

After the 1971 season, Stewart earned his share of baseball immortality by being part of the low price the Reds paid the Astros for Joe Morgan and assorted other quality players. Stewart joined Tommy Helms and Lee May in heading south. This was his second Hall of Fame–adjacent chapter: As a prospect, he had been among the players the Cubs auditioned at short in the years immediately after Ernie Banks shifted over to first base. His first real opportunity, though, came as the result of a tragedy, the February 1964 death of young Cubs second baseman Ken Hubbs in a solo-flight plane crash.

◆

As Jimmy Stewart the ballplayer was trying to break in, Jimmy Stewart the actor was in theaters with *Take Her, She's Mine*, a middling comedy with an uncomfortable theme: dad feeling threatened by his college-aged daughter's blossoming sexuality. Stewart, heading into late middle age, had just closed out a terrific second act. The Indiana, Pennsylvania and Princeton University product had broken into leading roles in the mid-1930s playing the callow youth deepened by experience. Yet, even in his twenties and early thirties, he was never "light"; his characters in *Mr. Smith Goes to Washington*, *The Shop*

Around the Corner, and *The Philadelphia Story* betray hints of darkness (Jefferson Smith is one bad day away from being a plain fascist) despite the generally fluffy goings-on. Stewart spent World War II flying (and subsequently commanding) bombing missions over occupied Europe. It was a role which brought him into contact with a great deal of death. When he returned to acting, he was no longer the same man he had been and felt no connection to the kind of characters he had played.

His first film back, Frank Capra's *It's a Wonderful Life*, drew a map to the intense performances of Stewart's middle period. His collaborations with directors such as Anthony Mann and Alfred Hitchcock are far more nuanced and challenging than any of his prewar work. In 1950, he began a series of eight pictures with Mann. Five of them, the so-called "psychological westerns"—*Winchester '73, Bend of the River, The Naked Spur, The Far Country*, and *The Man From Laramie*—depict heroes just barely holding up under the strain of trying to be even vaguely decent in a fallen world. (After he and Stewart parted ways, Mann made one more variation on this theme, *Man of the West*, in which Gary Cooper plays a reformed outlaw who just wants to get a school built but is slowly forced back towards violence by the depravity of his former associates. It's not unlike Clint Eastwood's *The Unforgiven*.) Add in Stewart's less-than-appealing characters in Alfred Hitchcock's *Rear Window* (why the heck is Grace Kelly so keen on marrying *that* guy?) and *Vertigo*, and you have a catalog of archetypical American heroes far more resonant than Mr. Smith ever was. In Scott Eyman's *Hank & Jim*, a dual biography of Stewart and Henry Fonda, the latter's son, Peter, says, "They both saw life as a series of jobs and they were determined to do them to the best of their ability." That sums up Stewart's characters in these films. They have a job to do. That's both their highest calling and the most they can offer. It wouldn't be a bad attitude for a pinch-hitter.

KENT GREENFIELD, RHP
152 G, 1924-29
41-48, 4.54 ERA (85 ERA+), -0.1 WAR

John McGraw's Giants won four consecutive pennants from 1921–24. They beat the Yankees in the 1921 and '22 World Series, lost to them in '23, and bowed to the Senators in '24. After that, McGraw was on a personal downslope, and the team went along with him. Although he'd be with the Giants until the early part of the 1932 season, his health, judgment, and luck started to slip. He also experienced some off-the-field reversals which must have been a distraction. Greenfield was a minor part of a major error on McGraw's part, his decision to let go of Hack Wilson.

Greenfield and Wilson were teammates on the 1923 Portsmouth Truckers of the Virginia League. The Truckers' owner invited McGraw to scout the 23-year-old Wilson, who was on his way to hitting .388 with power. McGraw was not impressed. "He ain't got no neck," he said. Greenfield was the Trucker he wanted. In the end, McGraw agreed to take both for $11,000 and a couple of players. Wilson got an extended trial with the Giants in 1924 and played quite well despite ankle injuries and McGraw's general reluctance to use him. When Wilson started out slowly in 1925, McGraw benched him, farmed him out, and left him unprotected in that fall's Rule 5 draft. Thus did Wilson go on to a Hall of Fame career with the Cubs.

Greenfield stayed on and proved to be aggressively mediocre. McGraw farmed him out, too, not out of disdain, but because Greenfield was only 20. He got a one-start audition in the fungible final game of the 1924 season, then spent all of 1925 as the Giants' fifth starter, going 12–8 with a 3.88 ERA. "Tall, supple, strong, the youngster broke his fast ball over the plate like a lance point," *The Sporting News* said after. "He had control and he had coolness under fire. The more important the foe, the better he pitched.... Greenfield is the quiet, conservative type.... He is forward enough in a crisis. He is the natural product of the Bluegrass Hills. From time immemorial they have had definite and rigid customs in that country. It is bad form for a Southern Kentucky boy to get flustered or excited. When a kid from that section has class, he usually has a whole lot of class."

That same piece points out that Greenfield went undefeated against the Pirates, that season's eventual World Series winners. That's true; he was 4–0 with a 2.65 ERA in seven games against Pie Traynor, Kiki Cuyler, et al. That also means he went 8–8 with a 4.18 ERA against everyone else, leading to an ERA that was just a tick above league average. Greenfield was passable again in 1926, although he led the NL in home runs allowed and, this time, he went 1–5 with a 4.29 ERA against the Pirates and was also hit hard by the Cardinals, who won the pennant. So much for the idea of being "forward enough in a crisis." McGraw dealt Greenfield to the Braves in June 1927, getting pitcher Larry Benton in return. Benton would have a 7-WAR season for the Giants in 1928, while Greenfield was two years from being out of the league. "Raised in...Kentucky feud country, he had been taught to say little and do much," noted one writer. "He had been schooled to coolness, gameness, and resourcefulness." Unfortunately, no one can school you to talent.

> "Greenfield has about everything a good pitcher should have. He has a change of pace, plenty of speed, curves, and judgment. He knows what he is doing all the time and is a student of the batters facing him. He has the physique to back him up and if he doesn't become one of the greatest of pitchers I am a bum prophet, that's all."
>
> —John McGraw

♦

> Neither McQuillan nor Greenfield has been very successful this season. The former has been successful at times, but Greenfield has been a complete loss. McGraw gave him every opportunity to make good by putting him in to finish up close games, often in the face of criticism. Kent just couldn't stem the tide, however, and invariably was rapped for a run or two more, which in most cases cost the Giants the game.
>
> —*The New York Times*, June 13, 1927.

Greenfield was 2–2 with a 9.45 ERA in 12 games for the Giants before the trade in 1927. The team's record in his appearances was 3–9.

PIRATES HUMBLED BY A GIANT ROOKIE

Greenfield Baffles Buccaneer Batsmen and McGrawmen Win With Ease by 10 to 1

COOL IN TIGHT PLACES

> ...Kent Greenfield, one of the Giants' freshman pitchers, made a baseball play hide-and-seek with the Pirates bats up at the Polo Grounds yesterday.... Greenfield was tapped often enough, but when the Pirates decorated the corners and threatened to transform

runners into runs the youngster tightened up like a vise and turned the enemy back. Greenfield comes from the bluegrass country in Kentucky. A colorful pitcher.

—**Harry Cross,** *The New York Times,* May 24, 1925

Chapter Five

THE TOO-SHORT PEAK

These players were good—sometimes very good—but then things took a turn.

BILL SCHROEDER, C
376 G, 1983-90
.240/.281/.426 (91 OPS+), 2.7 WAR

A career .280/.357/.509 hitter in the minor leagues, Schroeder appeared to have enough on the bat to play regularly in the majors, but several factors worked against him. His primary problem was injuries. He was also a very aggressive hitter for the time and didn't get on base much. Schroeder struggled to get on base even when he had the platoon advantage. A right-handed hitter, he hit 33 home runs in 514 career at-bats against southpaws, which made him *look* like a strong platoon player, but he hit only .255 against lefties and almost never walked, so his OBP against them was only .288. The big exception was 1987, when his power, a conscious effort to make more contact ("I found the homers still will come," he said), a rabbit ball, and a fluke .383 batting average on balls in play helped him hit .332/.379/.548 against all opponents in 75 games. Even then, he couldn't break out of a platoon with the young, lefty-hitting B.J. Surhoff. "Kids in the playgrounds are always yelling, 'Come on, Joey, a walk is just as good as a hit,'" observed *The Scouting Report: 1985*. "Bill Schroeder better not hear them say that. He might be the only major leaguer in history to have more homers than walks in parts of two seasons." To that point in his career, home runs were leading walks 17 to 11; they'd finish his career up 61–58.

So much of life is contingent, and Schroeder, who was behind future Hall of Famer Ted Simmons and then perennial Gold Glover Jim Sundberg when he first came up with the Brewers, had the bad timing to suffer an elbow injury almost as soon as he was named the team's starter in 1985. The problem ultimately required surgery and cost him about two-thirds of both the '85 and '86 seasons. Injuries also prevented Schroeder from following up his big '87 season. Playing infrequently, he hit .125 through May, was sent down briefly, got hurt when a Dan Plesac warmup pitch hit him in the knee, and ended up on crutches.

After 1987, he played just 100 more major-league games spread over three seasons, some coming with the Angels after the Brewers traded him for infielder Gus Polidor in December 1988. The move had been at his request; both team and player had grown frustrated with each other. He backed up Lance Parrish in Anaheim but didn't contribute. In total, over those 100 games, he hit .189/.218/.352 with 15 home runs, 10 walks, and 90 strikeouts in 334 PAs. "It's like the chicken-and-the-egg theory," he said in 1988. "Do you have to hit more to play? Or do you have to play more to hit? It's a catch-22." Of course, if you can't stay healthy enough to play, it's a moot point.

The Brewers have yet to develop or acquire a slugging catcher who has remained with the team for any length of time. The team leader in games caught is Charlie Moore (1973–87), to whom they showed unusual loyalty despite middling production. No Brewers catcher has had a full-season slugging percentage above .468, and only three, Schroeder among them, have had a partial season above .500 (Dave Nilsson and Jonathan Lucroy are the other two). The list of high points is brief: Lucroy is the team's career home-run leader among catchers with 79; Schroeder is third with 51. Lucroy had a 6-WAR season in 2014 (an outlier for both him and the team), and the Surhoff/Schroeder combination was excellent in 1987. Simmons had his moments but was at the point in his career when he spent half his time as the DH. Darrell Porter was inconsistent. Yasmani Grandal was excellent in his sole season in beery togs in 2019. These exceptions aside, they're still waiting for their Yogi, their Piazza, their Gary Carter.

WALLY JOYNER, 1B
2033 G, 1986–2001
.289/.362/.440 (117 OPS+), 35.8 WAR

Very few players have had as much go right in their rookie year as Joyner did in his. He started hot, hotter than he'd be for the rest of his career. It was a wonderful bait and switch: For the first four months of 1986, he hit .315/.362/.525 with 21 home runs. It was the fastest way to make fans forget his 3,000-hit predecessor, Rod Carew. "I'm not a home run hitter, I'm a hitter," Joyner warned early on, but who are you going to believe, the player or your own eyes? He bore a superficial resemblance to Matthew Broderick, one of the most popular movie stars of the time due to *Ferris Bueller's Day Off*, which came out that June. The Angels got hot along with Joyner and won a division title. He hit .235/.318/.310 with one homer the rest of the way (a bruised shoulder forced him to alter his hitting style). It didn't matter. "Wally World" had been proclaimed. Irrational exuberance has its own rules.

Joyner hit 34 home runs in 1987, the year everyone hit them. He played another 14 seasons and never again hit more than 21, averaging about 14 per 162 games. He was still quite good, but he was rarely spectacular. He never made an All-Star team after his rookie year, never won a Gold Glove despite being a very good first baseman, and has virtually no black ink on his baseball card. He hit .289/.363/.430 after 1987, with three full seasons over .300, four if you count 1994, and he hit some doubles.

The strangest thing about Joyner, from our perspective, is he struck out only 50 or 60 times a season. Put aside that first season, and he was the model of a number-two hitter, not the slugger he first appeared to be. "I could drag bunt, I could shorten my stroke, I could find the holes in the field. But Wally Joyner is the No. 3 hitter," Joyner said in 1988. "For the team to be successful, Wally Joyner has to drive in 100 runs. Wally Joyner has to worry that pitcher." Wally Joyner, to maintain his own convention, never drove in 100 runs after 1987. "He reminds me of a young Keith Hernandez or Rusty Staub," Angels GM Mike Port said during spring training 1986. The comp to Hernandez turned out to be just about right, though Joyner was not quite as talented.

In 1983, the Yankees burned their top three draft picks on free agents. They lost their first-round pick to the White Sox for signing outfielder Steve Kemp, their second-round pick to the Reds for signing lefty Bob Shirley, and their third-round pick to the Angels for signing Don Baylor. Joyner was the player the Angels selected with that pick. There's no telling what the Yankees would have done with the pick had they retained it, but with Don Mattingly about to establish himself in the major leagues, Joyner should probably thank whatever gods he prays to that he didn't end up being the best first baseman in the history of the Columbus Clippers.

> It's almost a case of false representation. He should at least have a warning label. A pitcher looks down the barrel and sees this bright-eyed baby face staring back at him, he doesn't know whether to give it a fastball or a lollipop.
>
> It isn't fair. You look at Wade Boggs, or even Darryl Strawberry, up there and you know you've got trouble. You look at Wally Joyner and you feel as if you might get nailed as a child molester.
>
> —Jim Murray, 1988

> After Wally Joyner shaved his head, some of the players started touching their bald heads together. "Before the game, we just all had a special handshake or something. We'd touch heads or rub heads," [Greg] Vaughn said, adding, "Wally is one of the funniest human beings you'll ever meet in your life."
>
> —Dan Good, on the 1998 Padres

DELINO DESHIELDS, 2B
1615 G, 1990–2002
.268/.352/.377 (98 OPS+), 24.4 WAR

What the heck was *that* career? DeShields was taken by the Expos with the 12th-overall pick of the 1987 amateur draft. A high school shortstop out of Delaware, he turned down a Villanova basketball scholarship to sign. Rated the game's 12th-best prospect heading into the 1990 season by *Baseball America*, DeShields had little in the way of home-run power, and, with a lot of swing-and-miss in his game, it wasn't a sure thing he would hit for any kind of average. Arguing in his favor was terrific speed and a willingness to take a walk. In 1990, the Expos made him their Opening Day second baseman despite his having played only 47 games at Triple-A. He had never played second before, but they pushed him over so they could keep playing Spike Owen at shortstop. DeShields went 4-for-6 with a stolen base in his first game and didn't look back.

More accurately, he didn't look back for about a third of a season. DeShields was hitting .304/.398/.424 on June 15 when he was hit on the hand by Joe Magrane. A broken finger kept him idled for about a month. He hit .276/.356/.367 the rest of the way. Which was the real DeShields? He gave a troubling answer in 1991, when he hit .238/.347/.332 and led the NL with 151 strikeouts. With the laudable exception of drawing 95 walks, he did nothing well. He made 27 errors. He opened the season with 12 consecutive successful steal attempts, then was caught 23 times in 67 attempts the rest of the way.

It might have seemed safe to dismiss DeShields based on one and a half seasons of mediocre performance, but that would have been underestimating a thoughtful, determined player. He cut down the strikeouts (giving back some of the walks, as well) but recovered his batting average. From 1992–93, he hit .294/.374/.386 and stole 89 bases against only 25 times caught stealing, which made him attractive enough to the Dodgers that they traded Pedro Martinez to get him.

As then–general manager Fred Claire tells it in his memoirs, the Dodgers felt pressured to acquire a second baseman because their incumbent, Jody Reed, had set too aggressive a price in free agency. They bid on the Giants' Robby Thompson, but all they succeeded in doing was pressuring San Francisco into signing Thompson to a more expensive contract. "If Jody accepts our offer, we keep Pedro Martinez." Claire wrote. "If we sign Robby Thompson, we keep Pedro, and Will Clark probably stays with the Giants." (Also a free agent, Clark left the Giants for the Rangers that winter.)

The Expos didn't know they had made one of the greatest trades in baseball history. GM Dan Duquette crowed that dumping the arbitration-eligible DeShields for the salary-controlled Martinez was, "a powerful economic move." Manager Felipe Alou was measured in his response. "This is a kid with a great arm.... Delino is on his way to being a superstar. If Martinez pitches well, this could be a good trade for both teams." Said Montreal *Gazette* columnist Michael Farber, "This is the Expos' one big deal to balance the books, one of those trades that gives Montreal baseball fans a sick feeling in their stomach." As for the Dodgers, manager Tommy Lasorda said that DeShields, "will be more valuable to us than the relief pitcher," echoing a similar statement by Claire.

The trade was made infinitely worse when DeShields stopped hitting. In 1996, he averaged .224/.288/.298 in 154 games, crashing to .184/.273/.222 in the second half. The Cardinals, desperate for a quality second baseman since the decline of Tommie Herr, signed him as a free agent and he made the Dodgers look bad one more time, hitting .293/.363/.440 over two years in St. Louis. Then an off year with the Orioles, then a good year, then the end. There must have been undisclosed injuries (in addition to several we know of, such as chicken pox early in 1993, a torn thumb ligament late that same year, and the broken thumb and quadriceps injuries that ruined his 1999) or off-the-field distractions, because few players have been so lacking in linearity.

◆

> Society's changed a lot. We grow up differently—faster, for one thing. Plus, you know, a lot of us black kids come from single-parent families and we're raised by our mothers. It's a fact, socially. A lot of us came from situations where we had to make key decisions and an early age.
>
> I was like that. The way I see it, I made some major-league decisions well before I was in the major leagues.
>
> **—Delino DeShields,** April 29, 1990

DeShields, nicknamed "Bop," was noted for cuffing his pants high in the old-fashioned style. It was his homage to his Negro Leagues forebears. "That is just my way of saying, 'Thank you for making all of this possible.'" He gave his son and major-league namesake, center fielder Delino DeShields, the middle name Diaab. "Diaab means 'one who perseveres,'" he said in 1993. "Originally, I chose that name for myself. Africans lost a lot coming over here in slavery. I felt the name fit, and I said if I ever had a little boy I'd name him that. I came through a lot to get where I am. I want my baby to have those same characteristics."

BOB HORNER, 3B
1020 G, 1978-86
.277/.340/.499 (127 OPS+), 21.8 WAR

"Bob Horner can break any home run record he wants to," Henry Aaron said in 1978, "if he just stays healthy and plays enough games." It turned out that conditional was everything. A star at Arizona State, Horner batted .386 with an NCAA career-record 56 home runs. After considering drafting Michigan State's Kirk Gibson, the Braves made Horner the first-overall pick in the 1978 draft, also eschewing players such as Lloyd Moseby, Hubie Brooks, Mike Morgan, and, well down in the second round, Cal Ripken Jr. They brought Horner directly to the majors. He arrived with plenty of arrogance—"Man, am I gonna make that Indian dance," he said, referring to the teepee-dwelling, woefully offensive human mascot the Braves kept behind the outfield wall in those days—but he also followed through, hitting a home run in his first game (off of Bert Blyleven) and smacking 22 more in 89 games, mostly by taking advantage of his "Launching Pad" home park.

Horner won the Rookie of the Year award, but the pattern for his career was set—half seasons and home-field hitting. He had a short swing that led to good contact rates for a power hitter. Constant injuries, some of which seemed to stem from a lack of conditioning (Braves manager Joe Torre tried to motivate him by making him team captain; Cardinals manager Whitey Herzog just called him "Buddha"), kept him off the field for far more than his 306 official days on the disabled list. Caught up in collusion after 1986, he went to Japan and hit 31 home runs in 93 games but also spent time on the shelf there. Herzog, asked about him that winter, said "I don't like Horner. Of his lifetime homers, about 70 percent were hit in Atlanta. He never could hit in St. Louis. He can't hit and he can't field." The Cardinals showed what they thought of Herzog's opinion, signing the portly infielder to replace departed free agent Jack Clark in January 1988. This seemed like a sign that Herzog's influence was waning, something that proved to be true over the next couple of seasons. Horner's return to the majors was what Herzog expected (.257/.348/.354). After Horner's chronically injured left shoulder prevented him from making the Orioles in 1989, he quit for good. He averaged 36 home runs per 162 games for the Braves, but he never played more than 141 games in a season.

> Horner is only 26.... so maybe it is rather early to be drawing any conclusions about his career. It is beginning to look, however, as if he never is going to have That Year.
>
> —**Bill James**, *The Bill James Baseball Abstract 1984*

> I'll never forget Opening Day in 1988.... I had a rule that everybody took infield before the game, but I didn't see Horner out at first base, so I went in the clubhouse.... He looks up at me, blinks like an old frog on a lily pad and says, "I'm tired." A hundred and sixty-two games left to play, and the man is gassed!
>
> —**Whitey Herzog**, *You're Missin' a Great Game*

NOMAR GARCIAPARRA, SS
1434 G, 1996–2009
.313/.361/.521 (124 OPS+), 44.3 WAR

Hindsight only helps us with the amateur draft to a very limited extent. Garciaparra was the 12th-overall pick of the 1994 draft. Six pitchers went in front of him. Many were clearly talented, but whether because the Mets, in their brilliance, thought it was important for Paul Wilson to lead the minor leagues in complete games, or Jaret Wright just wasn't meant to play baseball for more than a few weeks at a time, they all got hurt. The best of the position players were Ben Grieve, a born DH, and Todd Walker, ditto. If the Mets had just transplanted Wilson directly from Florida State University to the majors they couldn't have done him any more harm than they eventually did, but that wasn't knowable that day in June 1994. Thus, as far as the first round was concerned, the Red Sox got Garciaparra, and everyone else got very little at all.

Garciaparra had a half-dozen great seasons for the Sox, but it was getting rid of him that had the most decisive impact on franchise history. The 2004 season saw the confluence of four events: Garciaparra's age-30 season, his precipitous physical decline, his looming free agency, and the team's latest chance to snap a championship drought that dated back to 1918. As of that year's July 31 trading deadline, Garciaparra had missed 64 of 102 games, leaving the Red Sox reliant on the defensively excellent but offensively anemic Pokey Reese at shortstop. With averages of .219/.271/.291 in 2003 and '04, Reese might have been the worst-hitting regular in baseball at that moment. Boston general manager Theo Epstein had to choose between the increasingly notional idea of having an all-time great at shortstop in the lineup and accepting the idea that Garciaparra was, in every way that mattered, already gone.

This was a brilliant redefinition of the problem, one which disregarded Garciaparra's performances to date and took a cold, clear-eyed look at what he was likely to do for the Red Sox in the future. Once Epstein had accepted that having a diminished Nomar who was frequently unavailable was a lot like not having Nomar at all, it had to have become blindingly obvious that there was a vast qualitative space between Reese and Garciaparra, and that Red Sox didn't have to bridge it entirely to improve the team. Garciaparra was traded to the Cubs as part of a four-team swap that brought Orlando Cabrera to Fenway. Cabrera had neither the bat of Garciaparra nor the glove of Reese, but he had enough of both—as well as a crucial durability—to represent a clear upgrade. The Red Sox went on to win their first World Series since the days of Babe Ruth; Garciaparra went on to have more injuries.

Garciaparra has a congenital condition that causes the body to manufacture extra scar tissue, so perhaps that helps explain why he was so frangible. This also might have led to the early erosion on his skills. In 468 post-Red Sox games, he hit .288/.368/.441. He was playing a lot of first and third base by that time. Given the requirements of those positions and the inflationary offensive environment of the time, his production was actually disappointing. "Paul Molitor had three seasons with more than…100 days spent on the DL, on the way to logging a career total of 556 DL days," noted *Baseball Prospectus 2006*. "Nomar's got two 100-plus seasons so far (2001 and 2005) and his career total is now 367. Molitor may not have had the benefits of advances in sports medicine, but that cuts both ways; Garciaparra can be rebuilt again and again, but like a GM car, after a few too many recalls and repairs you have to wonder if it isn't time for a new set of wheels."

Garciaparra has three children with soccer great Mia Hamm, all of whom are still too young to be professional athletes. It's going to be fascinating to see where this experiment in genetics leads (though, if it leads to an MD, a degree in chemical engineering, and an MFA, that would be great, too).

BEN GRIEVE, OF
976 G, 1997–2005
.269/.367/.442 (113 OPS+), 8.4 WAR

The second-overall pick of the 1994 draft (the Mets took Paul Wilson first and pitched his arm off), Grieve made it to the majors at 22. In his first full season, he hit .288/.386/.458 with 41 doubles, 18 home runs, and 85 walks for Oakland, a performance sufficient to win him AL Rookie of the Year honors. (By WAR, he was third among rookie position players, trailing Miguel Cairo of the expansion Devil Rays and Mike Caruso of the White Sox; Cuban pitchers Rolando Arrojo and Orlando Hernandez, of the Rays and Yankees, respectively, had bigger seasons than all of the above.) Grieve was never better than he was that first year and was out of the majors at 29. In this, his career mirrored that of his father Tom Grieve, who was drafted sixth overall by the expansion Washington Senators in 1966, had a few good seasons but dropped off quickly and was through as a regular after his age-28 season. Ben still grew up around the game; his father became Texas Rangers' GM in 1984, and Ben served as the team's bat boy. "We joke about it—Kathy's no longer 'the wife of Tom Grieve,'" Tom said in 1994. "She's now 'the mother of Ben Grieve.' It's not too long before I'm 'the father of Ben Grieve.'"

> When local baseball talent is measured by the experts, Martin center fielder Ben Grieve is considered by many to be miles ahead of the competition.
>
> "Oh yes, he was the best player out there," said an area major-league scout who requested anonymity. "To me he was just heads and tails above everybody else."
>
> A basketball commitment, an alcohol-related disciplinary suspension and brief bout with mononucleosis limited Grieve's season to 15 games [but] "Grieve's the best in this area since Todd Van Poppel, by far," said another scout.
>
> —*Fort Worth Star-Telegram,* June 5, 1994

If Ben had kept hitting as he did with the A's (.280/.370/.475 in three-plus seasons), he might have lasted longer, but he trended relentlessly downwards. Even in 2000, when he hit 27 homers and drove in 104 runs, he undermined that production by hitting into 32 double plays (the third-highest total of all time) and playing poor defense. He was very slow and probably should have been a full-time designated hitter from the outset, but, with similarly limited players such as Matt Stairs, Kevin Mitchell, and John Jaha on the A's, there was always a veteran player of terrapin qualities with an equally strong argument for the spot. In that sense, he drew a bad hand. "His lack of speed causes problems in right field, where the ball often plays him," *The Scouting Notebook* opined in 1999. "When he gets to the ball he fields it cleanly, but hits do fall around him." In 2001, *Baseball Prospectus* wrote, "When a ball is hit to Ben Grieve in left field, the home crowd shows all the nervous silence of a golf gallery, complete with relieved clapping if the ball is actually caught."

It's also possible that even an organization as progressive as the A's were becoming was still subject to the prejudice against "limiting" young players to designated hitter, which had obtained since the position was established approximately 25 years earlier. That prejudice still exists. Despite teams like the Astros and Guardians taking young players with defensive limitations such as Yordan Alvarez or Franmil Reyes (respectively) and giving them extensive time at DH, the all-time leader in games played as DH at the age of 25 or younger remains the squarely built Billy "Country Breakfast" Butler, who had 338 games at the position with the Royals from 2007 to '08. It's unlikely any active player will catch him, though several deserve to (or, in the case of Nick Castellanos, should have).

Sent to the Devil Rays as part of a three-team trade (the A's also gave up shortstop Angel Berroa and catcher A.J. Hinch and netted lefty Cory Lidle, center fielder Johnny Damon, and second baseman Mark Ellis), Grieve continued to decline offensively, which didn't leave much argument for continued playing time. At 27, when he might have been expected to be nearing his peak, he lost more than half the season to thoracic outlet syndrome and thereafter was unable to reestablish himself as a regular. He had a better career than Bob Hamelin, which sounds like damning him with faint praise, but it's not meant that way—there's no correlation between winning a Rookie of the Year award and future success, and for every Cal Ripken Jr. or Derek Jeter, there's a Pat Listach or Ben Grieve. In a life in which nothing is promised, we should savor what we get, even if it's less than we desired.

I played eight years. I look at is as a positive aspect. As a kid growing up, my dream was to play in the big leagues. Maybe I should have had a dream of being in the Hall of Fame.... I had some solid years where I drove in some runs and hit some home runs, so I'm happy. When I was done, I was done. I don't feel a need to be around it anymore, which I think is a good thing for me.

—Ben Grieve, July 2007

WORST CAREERS BY WAR, ROY WINNERS					
Rk	ROY	Lg	Name	Team	Career WAR
1	2003	AL	Angel Berroa	KCR	1.0
2	2009	NL	Chris Coghlan	FLA	1.1
3	1976	NL	Butch Metzger	SDP	1.2
3	1962	NL	Ken Hubbs	CHC	1.2
5	1980	AL	Joe Charboneau	CLE	1.5
6	1994	AL	Bob Hamelin	KCR	2.5
7	1979	AL	Alfredo Griffin	TOR	3.0
8	1950	AL	Walt Dropo	BOS	3.3
9	2000	AL	Kazuhiro Sasaki	SEA	3.7
9	1989	NL	Jerome Walton	CHC	3.7
9	1952	AL	Harry Byrd	PHA	3.7
10	1992	AL	Pat Listach	MIL	4.3
10	1961	AL	Don Schwall	BOS	4.3
21	1998	AL	Ben Grieve	OAK	8.4

DAN GLADDEN, OF
1196 G, 1983–93
.270/.324/.382 (95 OPS+), 15.5 WAR

Pity the poor tweener, the outfielder who isn't quite a center fielder defensively but isn't a left or right fielder with the bat. A few of them break through to become fourth outfielders, and the rest fall through the cracks. That was very nearly Dan Gladden's story. Signed by the Giants as an undrafted free agent in 1979, he was a consistent .300 hitter in the minor leagues. He didn't have a great deal of power, but he was by no means a singles-only hitter, and he stole 50 bases a year. Any number of less-talented players built along that model had significant major-league careers in the 1980s and weren't left sitting at Triple-A for three and a half years before they got their chance, like Gladden was.

Part of the delay was a case of bad timing. The Giants were poorly run during the 1970s and early '80s, mixing in 90-loss seasons with the occasional third-place finish. They also had one foot out the door under the old, dissipated Stoneham-family ownership and, subsequently, under Bob Lurie; the latter saved them from going to Toronto but still wanted to move the team out of Candlestick Park. The Giants would make no postseason appearances between 1971 and '87, as management had its attention everywhere but on the roster. For example, between the end of Willie McCovey's first tour, in 1973, and the arrival of Will Clark, in 1986, the Giants routinely tolerated miserable seasons from their first basemen. In 1980, Mike Ivie, Rich Murray, and an aging McCovey hit a combined .239/.295/.352; in 1985, David Green, Dan Driessen, and pals combined to hit .233/.289/.332 with nine home runs.

What the Giants *did* have, though, particularly as Gladden was climbing the ladder, were good outfielders, such as Chili Davis, Jeff Leonard, and Jack Clark. Gladden couldn't even get a bench spot, because he was blocked by Max Venable, a choice that's hard to decipher all these years later. Despite a September 1983 cup of coffee, it took a season-ending knee injury to Clark and a simultaneous hamstring injury suffered by Dusty Baker in June of 1984 for Gladden to get back to the majors. In a case of fortuitous timing, he had just changed his stroke. "I always believed if you were going to play outfield in the big leagues," he said, "you had to drive in runs and hit home runs. But [the Giants] suggested I try a heavier bat, choke up on it, and go for line drives. I didn't like it." Maybe not, but he hit .397 prior to his call-up.

Gladden had a little more than half a season to prove himself. What he did remains one of the best rookie campaigns in Giants history. He hit .351/.410/.447 (145 OPS+) in 86 games, stealing 31 bases, and scoring 71 runs. There's no guarantee he would have done the same thing with more playing time, but it's fun to extrapolate that to a full season and imagine he might have had 226 hits, 58 steals, and 133 runs scored. It would have been a peak Ichiro Suzuki season, except a little better.

Gladden wasn't that good, of course; few players are. Today we might have looked at his .384 batting average on balls in play and guessed he was going to crash. He did, but his glove played up in left, and, in the years in which he was able to keep his batting average in a decent place, he made up for his other shortcomings. He played a key role on two Twins championship teams and hit .314/.397/.490 in 58 postseason plate appearances for the 1987 champs, including a grand slam in Game 1 of the World Series that was very gratifying for fans of underdog players.

> Will Gladden start tomorrow night in the opener of a three-game series with the Houston Astros?
>
> "He may," [manager Frank] Robinson said. "Joe Niekro's going and I don't know if he's ever faced a knuckleball pitcher before."
>
> "Tell Frank yes," Gladden said. "Tell him I faced a knuckleball pitcher in every series we played down in Phoenix."
>
> —*San Francisco Examiner*, September 9, 1983

> I didn't know anything about the Twins other than I used to collect Rod Carew, Tony Oliva, and Harmon Killebrew baseball cards. I had to look in the encyclopedia to see where Minnesota was.
>
> —Dan Gladden, 1988

TRACY JONES, OF
493 G, 1986-91
.273/.329/.388 (97 OPS+), 2.4 WAR

In the 1980s, the Reds developed several compelling outfielders in a relatively short period of time, Eric Davis, Kal Daniels, Paul O'Neill, and Jones among them. Somehow, they ended up winning the World Series in 1990 with Billy Hatcher in left field. (He hit .750 in the Series, so we can't really hold it against them.) Jones probably had the least inherent talent of the group, but, for a while, he made up for it with hustle. "What kind of guy pops a hamstring as he rounds first base, hops almost all the way to second, falls down with 12 feet to go and crawls the rest of the way just to get a double?" asked Greg Hoard of *The Cincinnati Enquirer* about the rookie Jones in 1986.

"Me and [pitcher Tom] Browning call him Norman Bates, the guy in *Psycho*, 'cause he's crazy out there," commented closer John Franco.

> Several weeks ago in spring training, Reds' hitting guru Billy DeMars pointed to the 25-year-old Jones and said to Reds player-manager Pete Rose: That's you 23 years ago.
>
> —*The Cincinnati Enquirer,* April 8, 1986

It didn't last. By 1990, *The Scouting Report* was denigrating Jones as someone who, "has gotten the reputation for having an attitude problem. He's considered moody, stubborn, and difficult to manage." By then, he'd gone from the Reds to the Expos to the Giants to the Tigers. Before the season was over, he would be with the Mariners. It seems like a contradiction in terms, but he was simultaneously dispensable and in demand. This gaslighting by baseball had Jones, in his words, confused and depressed. "I always thought I was a pretty good ballplayer but I had to wonder. My feelings were really hurt."

The disparity between the effort Jones was making and the perception baseball had of him seems to have paralleled the disparity between his early results (he had hit .299/.351/.417 with 56 steals in 71 attempts over his first three seasons) and what he was able to contribute thereafter (.246/.305/.357 with 6 steals in 10 attempts). Even as his skills and his ability to stay on the field eroded, he was an enticing possibility as a platoon bat. From '86 through '89, he had hit .333/.394/.468 against left-handed pitchers in 501 plate appearances; that was the third-highest batting average against southpaws over that span, trailing Pat Tabler, Kirby Puckett, and tied with Barry Larkin. Alas, by 1990, even that had gone.

What had come in between were a seemingly endless series of knee injuries. Tall, lanky, also successful in amateur football and basketball, and confident—"I tell Pete [Rose] I'm a Pete Rose with talent. He doesn't like that"—Jones lacked power and patience but compensated with speed and those Rose-like qualities, but even a Charley Hustle can only achieve so much when his legs limit him to a lower gear. He was still there in spirit, but he couldn't be there in body.

> I'm very high strung. It's tough to put a guy in the infield who's so high strung…I only have to 30 steps to first base. I enjoy running a mile [to the outfield] to run off some of the energy that I have.
>
> —**Tracy Jones,** on a potential move to first base, *The Cincinnati Enquirer*, April 20, 1987

"He does things I never thought of doing," Rose said. "He'll slide into a bag and he'll act like he's hurt. You go out there and ask him how he's feeling and he'll say he's just decoying. So now when he gets hurt, he can be dead and I'm going to stay in the dugout."

—*The Cincinnati Enquirer*, July 2, 1987

SAM HORN, DH
389 G, 1987-93, '95
.240/.328/.468 (119 OPS+), 2.3 WAR

Horn, a lumbering 6-foot-5 with some pounds on him, was called "The Fenway Fridge," a reference to the massive Chicago Bears defensive tackle William "The Refrigerator" Perry. It was a little unfair. Perry was officially 6-foot-2 and 335 pounds; Horn was officially 6-foot-5 and 215. No doubt Horn was heavier than that, but not Perry heavy.

The Red Sox made Horn the 16th-overall pick of the 1982 amateur draft. Even with the benefit of hindsight, you can't say they missed much—the big man of the first round, Dwight Gooden, was long gone at that point, and only four players tabbed after him in that round made the bigs. They were first baseman Franklin Stubbs, pitchers Rich Monteleone and Todd Worrell, and shortstop Dale Sveum. Worrell had his moments as a closer for the Cardinals and Dodgers, but they were fewer than you think. The second round held Barry Bonds, David Wells, and Barry Larkin, but you can't fault the Red Sox for missing them given that every team had misclassified them. The first overall pick was shortstop Shawon Dunston. The old joke was that, of course Dunston went ahead of Gooden—he had a better arm. Dunston threw so hard, it might have been true.

A first baseman is under tremendous pressure to hit, a pure DH like Horn—he made just nine starts in the field across eight major-league seasons—even more so. Horn never found offensive consistency in the majors or the minors, and it took more than five years for the Sox to give Horn a shot. To get that shot in 1987, he had to hit .321/.389/.649 with 30 home runs in 94 games for Triple-A Pawtucket. Horn homered in his first two major league games, the first Boston player ever to do that, and had five home runs through his first eight games, but no one maintains a 1.000 slugging percentage forever. Horn's inevitable slump was exacerbated by a combination of a lack of opportunity (resulting from inviolate Red Sox oldsters Jim Rice and Dwight Evans occupying the only position Horn could play) and remaining a stubborn pull hitter, even when fed a steady diet of offspeed pitches on the outside corner. Playing in an extra-inning game on July 17, 1991, he went 1-for-7 with six strikeouts; that was Horn.

The Sox gave Horn only 135 plate appearances across 57 games between 1988 and '89, and when he hit only .148/.267/.217, they flat released him. Signed by a rebuilding Orioles team, he hit well, and even lost weight, but gradually lost playing time he would never recover. The chief beneficiary was veteran first baseman Glenn Davis, whose expensive acquisition had to be justified. Exiled to Triple-A by Cleveland in 1993, Horn hit .269/.361/.600 with 38 home runs, then popped four more round-trippers while going 15-for-33 as a late-September call-up. They weren't interested.

Horn had his limitations, but he hit .239/.328/.469 (122 OPS+) for Baltimore, and the Orioles have often done a lot worse than that at DH.

ORIOLES AS DESIGNATED HITTER BY OPS (MIN. 500 PA)								
Rk	Player	OPS	G	PA	HR	BA	OBP	SLG
1	Harold Baines	.885	602	2355	107	.301	.379	.505
2	Luke Scott	.853	212	872	45	.266	.348	.505
3	Eddie Murray	.838	262	1106	47	.286	.354	.485
4	Aubrey Huff	.832	194	821	33	.280	.341	.491
5	Sam Horn	.804	210	748	38	.244	.330	.473
6	Renato Núñez	.804	132	554	27	.257	.327	.477
7	Terry Crowley	.744	196	651	17	.259	.358	.386
8	Ken Singleton	.742	477	1972	46	.257	.357	.385
9	Vladimir Guerrero	.740	137	582	13	.292	.320	.421
10	Glenn Davis	.721	122	509	16	.254	.321	.400

The still-active Trey Mancini would rank fourth at this writing.

Horn's post-major-league career had a long tail. He played on through the minors, the Mexican League, and the independent Big South and Atlantic Leagues. Except for 11 pinch-hitting appearances with the Rangers in September 1995, he never got another big-league chance. There were always teams suffering at DH—it's a deceptively hard position to fill—but Horn was never in the right place at the right time.

> Glenn Davis had come over as a free agent and was originally supposed to be the first baseman. But after injuries cropped up early, Davis moved to DH, leaving Horn without a spot…"I looked forward to that '92 season because everyone was banking on, 'Sam Horn is going to hit the warehouse,'" Horn said. "Trust me, it was hard to hit the warehouse from where I was sitting."
>
> —Ian Browne, MLB.com

SLOPPY THURSTON, RHP
288 G, 1923-27, '30-33
89-86, 4.24 ERA (94 ERA+), 15.8 WAR

Everyone has a special anniversary. Everyone has a birthday. These are days that are important to us, and they should be, but expecting anyone else to care to the same extent would be toxically solipsistic. We should take the same approach to 20-win seasons by major-league pitchers. Winning 20 games is not always the mark of a special season or a special pitcher, it's just something that happened to someone in the same way your anniversary happened to you. Hollis "Sloppy" Thurston had his "special" year in 1924, when he went 20–14 with a 3.80 ERA. He pitched 291 innings, allowed 330 hits, walked 60, and struck out 37. He led the AL in both earned runs and home runs allowed (and, more positively, complete games, with 28). He ranked 17th in the league in ERA and ERA+, the later with a 108 mark (Walter Johnson led both categories with 2.72 and 149, respectively).

It was a—pardon the expression—sloppy season. We need a baseball category covering "superficial success/aesthetic failure," but let's give the then-25-year-old a little credit: The White Sox, still in the backwash of the Black Sox scandal, were a bad team. Despite fielding five future Hall of Famers, they went 66–87–1, due primarily to the shortcomings of their pitching staff. That Sox team, which scored about five runs per game, better than league average, scored about six for Thurston, and he pitched just well enough to win 20, but even that was a close thing—he was 16–4 with a 3.23 ERA through mid-July but was pounded thereafter, not just in the 1924 season, but largely for the rest of his career.

As the low strikeout totals suggest, Thurston was a junkballer who pitched off a screwball or "fadeaway," letting batters put the ball in play. Among those who did was Babe Ruth. George Herman owned Sloppy, hitting .396/.475/.774 with five homers in 62 plate appearances. In Ruth's record-setting 1927 season, he went 8-for-15 against Thurston with three of his 60 home runs. History thanks you, Sloppy. Asked which of his pitches Ruth had hit, Thurston replied, "Everything I threw up there."

Thurston seems to have been a little oppositional. Slightly delayed by a hitch in the navy during World War I, the Los Angeles native started his professional career with the Salt Lake City Bees of the PCL in 1920. In his third season, he was briefly suspended for insubordination by manager Duffy Lewis. "According to the available information, Hollis thought he should not be required to do certain things," reported *The Salt Lake Tribune*, "the certain things asked of him being that he should pitch to the batters." He claimed he had a sore arm. Then he blamed the weather. "I can cut loose all right," Thurston said, "but I won't cut loose in this wind." Nevertheless, the next year the Browns purchased him for $15,000. "Perhaps the most talented young right-hander in the Coast league," said the *Deseret News*, "the only big fault Thurston has is his occasional failures to take his work seriously."

Thurston lasted two games in the big leagues before he was suspended again. This time, his crime was refusing manager Lee Fohl's order to throw batting practice; once again, he insisted he had a sore arm. The Browns put him on waivers with the intention of passing him back to Salt Lake City, but the White Sox put in a claim and got a year and a half of decent pitching out of it, including the aforementioned 20-win season.

After 1924, Thurston struggled for three years, wound up back in the PCL (this time with the Seals), and, after two years, was claimed by the desperate-for-anyone Brooklyn Dodgers. He pitched well at first. After starting the 1930 campaign in the bullpen, he moved to the rotation and pitched consecutive shutouts against the Cardinals and Braves. He hung on as a swing man for three years after that, not so much because he was effective as that the Dodgers weren't trying. The lowlight of this period came on August 13, 1932, in the first game of a Polo Grounds doubleheader against the Giants. Sloppy pitched a complete game, allowing nine runs. He walked none, struck out none, and allowed *six* home runs, thus tying a modern record that has been equaled eight more times (most recently by Matt Swarmer of the Cubs in June 2022) but never surpassed. Again, give Thurston this much credit: All six homers were hit by future Hall of Famers: Bill Terry hit three, Mel Ott two, and Freddie Lindstrom one. Sloppy was a man of refined taste and discretion.

Speaking of which, James K. Skipper's *Baseball Nicknames* gives three different explanations for Thurston's nickname: (1) His father had a restaurant called, "Sloppy's Place" in Tombstone, Arizona; (2) he was a slob; (3) he was *not* a slob. For what it's worth, he looks pretty well put together in his photographs.

An outfielder as an amateur, Sloppy was a good hitter for a pitcher, averaging .270/.399/.383 with five home runs in nearly 700 career plate appearances. After retirement, he became a scout and was noted for signing Ralph Kiner for $250.

> Hollis Thurston's ding-dong delivery made the game last half an hour longer than it should have under other conditions.... If there is a slower pitcher in the league than Thurston, I don't want to see him.
>
> —**John J. Peri,** *Stockton Daily Evening Record,* 1934

BILL CAUDILL, RHP
445 G, 1979-87
35-52, 106 SV, 3.68 ERA (110 ERA+), 11.0 WAR

Caudill, who closed games for the Mariners, A's, and Blue Jays, points up the vacuity of the saves rule. In 1982, he had a 2.35 ERA and saved 26 games. In 1983, he had a 4.71 ERA and saved 26 games. His save percentage was actually higher in the latter season because he was deployed in softer situations and blew only three saves—even the worst major league pitcher can usually get three outs before giving up three runs.

SAVES VS. WAR: WORST SEASONS, 25 OR MORE SAVES									
Rk	Player	Year	Team	W	L	SV	ERA	ERA+	WAR
1	Brad Lidge	2009	PHI	0	8	31	7.21	59	-2.6
2	Mike Stanton	1993	ATL	4	6	27	4.67	86	-1.7
3	Shawn Chacón	2004	COL	1	9	35	7.11	70	-1.5
4	Mike Williams	2003	PHI/PIT	1	7	28	6.14	69	-1.3
t5	Alfredo Aceves	2012	BOS	2	10	25	5.36	79	-1.2
t5	John Axford	2012	MIL	5	8	35	4.67	88	-1.2
7	Matt Capps	2009	PIT	4	8	27	5.80	72	-1.1
8	Brad Lidge	2006	HOU	1	5	32	5.28	85	-1.0
t9	Ron Davis	1984	MIN	7	11	29	4.55	93	-0.9
t9	Randy Myers	1992	SDP	3	6	38	4.29	84	-0.9
t9	Doug Jones	1993	HOU	4	10	26	4.54	85	-0.9
t9	Rod Beck	1995	SFG	5	6	33	4.45	91	-0.9

Caudill's 1982 and 1983 seasons were worth 4.4 and 0.3 WAR, respectively.

The weakness of the saves statistic aside, Caudill was often quite valuable during his brief career. He was a one-pitch pitcher who never quite mastered the fine art of control, but that one pitch—in his case a hard fastball—was often so good that no one could complain about the walks. He had two seasons worth more than 4.0 WAR. The first came with the Cubs in 1980, when he set up for Bruce Sutter; in 127 2/3 innings (including two starts), Caudill compiled a 2.19 ERA. Two years later, he had the aforementioned 1982 season for the Mariners, a season in which he pitched 95 2/3 innings.

Perhaps due to those high innings totals, not uncommon for a reliever in Caudill's day, there was an on/off rhythm to his career—1981 and 1983 were as bad as 1980 and 1982 were good. Caudill, who was Scott Boras's first client, was known as a goofball, but it was perhaps more because of his inconsistency and wildness that he was so frequently traded. He was drafted by the Cardinals and showed promise, but they dealt him to the Reds while he was still a teenager for young utility man Joel Youngblood. The Reds kept Caudill for one minor-league season, during which he walked 103 in 158 innings while whiffing 118, and then sent him and veteran lefty Woody Fryman on to the Cubs in return for former 20-game-loser Bill Bonham. Dallas Green traded Caudill away from the Cubs in the spring of 1982, using him to complete an earlier deal in which Chicago had received former first-round pick Pat Tabler from the Yankees (making unmotivated trades of top prospects is what the Yankees were all about in those days). "There's no question in my mind he had a good arm," Cubs manager Lee Elia said, "[but] I did my homework and found out he couldn't put his body down at night. History had shown here that he couldn't adapt to day games." Possibly Elia intended his audience to make an inference about Caudill's tendency to, in his words, go out to "celebrate" if the team won and to "forget" if they lost.

The Yankees didn't keep Caudill, almost immediately passing him on to the Mariners (along with fellow righty Gene Nelson and outfielder Bobby Brown) for lefty Shane Rawley. It was Mariners manager Rene Lachemann who made Caudill, then with his fifth organization, a closer for the first time.

Rk	Player	Year	WAR	G	W	L	SV	IP	H	BB	SO	ERA
	BEST RELIEF SEASONS IN MARINERS HISTORY BY WAR											
1	Bill Caudill	1982	4.4	70	12	9	26	95.2	65	35	111	2.35
2	J.J. Putz	2007	4.0	68	6	1	40	71.2	37	13	82	1.38
3	Bill Swift	1991	3.7	71	1	2	17	90.1	74	26	48	1.99
4	Edwin Díaz	2018	3.3	73	0	4	57	73.1	41	17	124	1.96
5	S. Hasegawa	2003	3.2	63	2	4	16	73	62	18	32	1.48
6	Ed Vande Berg	1982	3.2	78	9	4	5	76	54	32	60	2.37
7	Enrique Romo	1977	3.2	58	8	10	16	114.1	93	39	105	2.83
8	Jeff Nelson	1995	2.9	62	7	3	2	78.2	58	27	96	2.17
9	J.J. Putz	2006	2.8	72	4	1	36	78.1	59	13	104	2.30
10	Arthur Rhodes	2002	2.7	66	10	4	2	69.2	45	13	81	2.33

Caudill endeared himself to the team and the fans with his eccentric style. He was called "Cuffs" and "The Inspector." "In addition to his repertoire of pitches," wrote E. M. Swift in *Sports Illustrated*, "Caudill possesses a genuine customs inspector's badge, a pair of handcuffs, two pink panthers, a calabash pipe, a Sherlock Holmes hat, two magnifying glasses, a Beldar the Conehead mask and, some Mariners suspect, several dozen packages of Jell-O." "The Inspector" appellation came about after the Mariners went 2–7 on a road trip. Caudill donned his deerstalker cap, picked up his magnifying glass, and inspected the team's bats for missing hits. Thereafter, the organist would play

Henry Mancini's *Pink Panther* theme when he entered games—he wasn't just any inspector, but Peter Sellers' Inspector Clouseau.

Whereas Herbert Lom never got to trade his frustrating inspector, teams just kept moving Caudill. After two years, the Mariners dealt him to the A's, for whom he pitched well, but he was arbitration-eligible, so they traded him, too, to the Blue Jays. Boras got the Jays' signature on a lucrative five-year contract, but they got very little value in return—although his ERA was deceptively good, Caudill's velocity and strikeout rate were dropping. After he blew his fifth save of the season in August 1985, manager Bobby Cox gave the closer's role to Tom Henke and never looked back. He didn't call on Caudill even once in the ensuing seven-game ALCS. The next year, shoulder problems set in, and it was all over quickly.

Chapter Six

TEAM OF GREATS II

Nine of the ten players in this chapter are in the Hall of Fame (the exception, Ellis Kinder, deserves to be in a Hall of Something, maybe not fame but endurance in the face of both great obligation and great dissipation). Two of them still haven't received notification and never will, having been made to wait past the point that they departed this veil of tears. Perhaps this chapter would be better titled, "Seven Great Players Who Got to Feel Really, Really Chuffed after Getting a Career-Achievement Award, Two Sad, Snubbed Wallflowers...and Ellis Kinder, Who at Least Enjoyed Himself."

RICK FERRELL, C
1884 G, 1929–45, '47
.281/.378/.363 (95 OPS+), 30.8 WAR

    It's frustrating when we play dumb. Rick Ferrell was elected to the Hall of Fame by the Veterans Committee in 1984, and, ever since then, he's been one of the main arguments for how deleterious the actions of that particular body have been. The VC, in all its incarnations, *has* been miserable, profligate in the gifts it bestows on baseball's lower-magnitude stars. The problem with getting too exercised about that is that, as Bill James has pointed out, the Hall of Fame is a self-defining institution. "Fame" has no true definition, so, if a group of voters say that Ferrell has "fame," he does. Another way of stating that is that it's the Hall's game and, therefore, the Hall's rules, and if you expect consistency from them, or virtually anyone else this side of your mom, you're naïve (and some of us have erratic moms, too). Over the years, most baseball observers have come to define "fame" via minimal statistical thresholds, and Ferrell fails on that score. That is, however, a very narrow and narrow-minded criteria. Ferrell was very good and pretty damned "famous," not to mention the kind of baseball lifer—a player, scout, and general manager—who deserves a prominent place in a museum dedicated to honoring great careers in the game, *not* just great numbers.

If any of the foregoing incenses you, please consider that (a) none of this is of the slightest import, (b) do you suppose they were still arguing about what scrolls to put in the Library of Alexandria when it burned? and (c) [insert Emerson quote about foolish consistency being the hobgoblin of small minds, which is no less true for its ubiquity]. Aside from various immutable laws of science, every fact, custom, folkway, belief, and structure of human existence can be boiled down to—as felt philosopher Kermit the Frog put it— "somebody thought of that, and someone believed it." The Hall of Fame is a mutable concept, the money in your wallet is just paper, and even your need to put on pants before leaving the house is a societal construct that might disappear tomorrow. To put it another way, Edna St. Vincent Millay was once considered a great poet, then a hack, and now she's touted as a late-arriving master of the sonnet. The wheel turns, opinions are revisited and revised, and this is not so much an argument for Ferrell to be in the Hall as for the irrelevance of the Hall itself.

The BBWAA was incensed by Ferrell's enshrinement, because he had been considered on the regular ballot and barely registered, picking up a solitary vote in each of three elections. All that means is that the VC was operating on different principles than the BBWAA voters, who have themselves proved myopic in their own considerations. That doesn't make the VC standards, such as they were, better or worse, just different. In Ferrell's case, he was the AL's all-time leader in games caught (since surpassed), a noted defender, and an eight-time All-Star. His brother Wes, the pitching great, is quoted in Rick's SABR biography as praising his glove: "Brother or no brother, he was a real classy catcher. You never saw him lunge for the ball. He never took a strike away from you. He'd get more strikes for a pitcher than anybody I ever saw because he made catching look easy." Wes was praising Rick's framing, or presentation, which means Rick had it where it counts for us when we look at modern backstops.

As a hitter, Ferrell was no star, but he got on base at a higher clip than most, no doubt due, in part, to spending a lot of time batting in front of the pitcher. Mickey Cochrane, Bill Dickey, Gabby Hartnett, and Ernie Lombardi were the top offensive catchers during Ferrell's career. Ferrell was also less of a hitter than Spud Davis, Babe Phelps, and Frankie Hayes, but they weren't the defenders he was, and he was more durable. During Ferrell's career, the average major-league catcher had a .703 OPS. His was .741. Combine that with good defense, and you have a high-quality player and career baseballist whose enshrinement is no more an embarrassment to the Hall of Fame than the pretense that there's no justification for Ferrell's enshrinement when we know darned well what it was.

BILL TERRY, 1B
1721 G, 1923–36
.341/.393/.506 (136 OPS+), 56.5 WAR
As manager: 1496 G, 1932–41, 823-661 (.555),
3 pennants, 1 championship

Terry was one of the most self-possessed men to have a prominent career in baseball. He knew what he was worth and didn't suffer fools gladly. This was helpful to him in some ways and a handicap in others. An unsentimental man confident in his ability to walk away from the game and earn his daily bread by other means if he must—he had done it while in the minors and would do it again—he was impervious to low-ball offers and the threat of demotion implicit in the abusive tactics of his manager, John McGraw. After 1929, Terry largely ignored him, and McGraw, realizing Terry could not be intimidated, left him alone. Conversely, once Terry succeeded McGraw as manager in 1932, these same qualities made him a bit distant, a bit too inflexible in his personality, static in his tactics, and unwilling to romance the press. He was smart enough to know that public relations is a big part of the manager's job, but it wasn't something he was interested in. Maybe he couldn't have been any different—one 1933 profile made a point of insisting, "In the words of the world-renowned Popeye, 'he yam what he yam and that's all he yam'"—but he might have had a better time of it (and a faster trip to Cooperstown) if he had given the writers just a little of what they needed instead of insisting they were "$3-a-week ribbon clerks."

> Bill Terry was approached by people from all walks of life last night.... They asked him queer questions, silly questions, impossible questions, and a few even found it possible to ask sensible questions. Bill Terry accepted them all with a smile. He tried to be polite to everyone. But he talked little, if any, baseball.
>
> —*The Knoxville Journal,* December 21, 1933

William Harold Terry was born in Atlanta and came up on the sandlots, impressing both as a hitter and left-handed pitcher. He got his first minor-league berth in 1915, when he was only 16 years old. He married young, though, and soon had a child to support, so, after the 1917 season, he took a fulltime job. For four years, his only contact with the game was playing and managing for his Standard Oil company team. Former big-league shortstop Kid Elberfeld, then managing in the minors, was impressed with Terry and arranged for him to meet with McGraw in the spring of 1922. When McGraw offered Terry a chance to join the Giants organization, Terry coolly asked what McGraw was proposing to pay. He wasn't going to sign unless it improved his financial position.

McGraw was undoubtedly flabbergasted. Peter Williams' biography of Terry, *When the Giants Were Giants*, helps explain both why Terry quit the minors and his insistence on watching the bottom line thereafter. Terry married Elvina Sneed in November 1916, not long after his 18th birthday. The following spring, he reported to the Shreveport Gassers of the Texas League. Elvina followed Bill to spring training and arrived in Shreveport in the interregnum between when players reported and when they got paid. Terry, broke, was put in the embarrassing position of having to ask his young wife to return her engagement ring. He needed to pawn it for cash to buy food. It wasn't the first time he had been in that position; his parents' marriage had broken up when he was a child, and he was forced to drop out of school at 13 and go to work to support himself. As strong as he appeared to be on the outside, the shame and fear of moments like these must have haunted him.

> One spring when I did not sign my contract until after the season started...John McGraw did not conceal the fact that my attitude and actions were not making a hit with him.

The first day I reported, the Giants had the bases loaded with two outs in the ninth. McGraw sent me up as a pinch-hitter. I struck out.

As we walked off the field, McGraw, very sore, turned to me and exclaimed, "Terry, you can ask for more money in the winter and do less for me in the summer than any player I ever had."

—**Bill Terry** (This does not seem to have happened the way Terry recalled it, at least not in the regular season.)

◆

Terry will be of little use to us for weeks. Terry is older than the average. He needs the spring training more than anyone else.... I know there is very little sentiment in professional baseball, but just the same I think Terry is ungrateful after all I have personally done for him with the business office.

—**John McGraw,** March 4, 1932

Terry's career was short but exemplary. McGraw wasn't one to let a promising player stew in the minors, so once Terry had put in about a year and a half at Toledo, McGraw got him to the majors at 24. That's not terribly late, as rookie seasons go, but McGraw had George Kelly in front of Terry. He waffled in picking one of them, sometimes moving Kelly to second base to make room for Terry, sometimes changing his mind and pushing Terry back to the bench. In mid-May 1924, Kelly sat for five days as the result of some rough dental work. Finally given a handful of starts after 13 consecutive pinch-hitting appearances to begin the season, Terry went 8-for-20 (.400) with three home runs. Despite moments like these, McGraw's period of indecision persisted for three years. Even then, the great manager, beginning to slip, let the Reds decide for him. He offered Terry to Cincinnati for pitcher Dolf Luque, but, when the Reds demurred, he gave them Kelly for outfielder Edd Roush, instead.

By the time Terry's career as a regular began in earnest, he was 28. He proved to be an excellent player, an all-fields line-drive hitter who was also agile around the first-base bag. "When I joined the Giants, I was a pull-hitter," Terry said, "but McGraw wanted me to learn to hit to the opposite field. Later on, he wondered why I didn't pull the ball." His career high in home runs was 28, but, in the rabbit-ball year of 1930, he became the last National Leaguer to date to post a .400 batting average. It was a good season, but, placed in context, it's only cosmetically better than Terry's 1932, when he hit .350.

It's hard to think of a modern comparable for Terry; Baseball-Reference's similarity scores suggest there are no true comps and lists Don Mattingly as the nearest reasonable facsimile. Although the two men were built very differently, there is an interesting commonality. Terry was tall by the standards of his time, and Mattingly was not, but both seem to have contorted themselves while hitting. Pictures of Terry at bat show him compressing his head into his shoulders, while Mattingly crouched to generate power. Terry's motives might have been the same as Mattingly's, or perhaps his crouch was just an idiosyncrasy.

Knee problems started to trouble Terry in his mid-thirties, and he last played in 1936. Unlike many former player-managers whose main asset as skipper was their own presence on the field, Terry won a pennant while sticking to the dugout. It was as if sitting on the bench freed up his mind. He normally set his lineup and stuck with the starters until they dropped, with the result that his teams would fall off in the second half. This happened most dramatically in 1934, when the Giants blew a seven-game September lead to the Cardinals. They also performed a vanishing act in 1935, 1938, and 1940. In 1937, though, he gambled in August, changing out his first baseman and gambling that veteran outfielder Mel Ott could play third base so the team could upgrade both there and right field simultaneously. The Giants went from seven games back to winning the pennant by three games.

Terry replacing McGraw in 1932 was a surprise to most observers given the strained relationship between the two men (according to Terry, they patched things up before McGraw passed in 1934). Whatever his flaws, the team improved as soon as Terry took over and won the World Series the next year. "Bill managed like he played," Carl Hubbell, his pitching "meal ticket," said. "It was a business to him, not fun, and he was successful." Terry held the position through 1941, leaving the team in a bad way. His pennant-winning core had aged out and, with World War II on the horizon, there would be no way to rebuild in the short term. He left the majors after one year as the Giants' general manager, saying, "Baseball is too cheap for me." He spent four years as president of the South Atlantic League, but his main focus was amassing a fortune, which he achieved through investments and an auto dealership (this possibly understates things; as Arthur Daley reported it in 1957, Terry was, "One of the country's biggest Buick distributors.... He owns a handsome, modern block-long showroom and service depot [in Jacksonville, Florida], a foreign car agency across the street, a used car center downtown, a financing firm and heavens knows what else. Mr. Terry is loaded.") On a couple of occasions he tried to buy a team, but it never worked out.

When Terry was finally voted into the Hall of Fame, in 1954, he was typically brusque: "I have nothing at all to say. I have found that when somebody in my position says something it's usually the wrong thing." At the actual induction, he surprised himself by choking up. That didn't stop him from remembering who the bad guys were. "I didn't know I'd ever feel like this.... I didn't know what kept me out [of the Hall], newspapermen or just that you didn't want me up here, but I finally made it and I thank God for it."

> It is impossible to reconcile his two natures. All he had to do was put a little effort into being nice and he could have won over all the persons who became his implacable foes. The newspaper men disliked him and, it might be added, the feeling was entirely mutual. There were one or two non-members of the Hate Terry Club and they served as liaison offices for the others who never spoke to the Brain.
>
> —**Arthur Daley,** *The New York Times,* January 11, 1944

◆

> Bill hasn't the glamour, the color, the fire of a McGraw. He doesn't love baseball. It's not the national game to him; it's strictly a business. Every time he rounds first base he is figuring out that hit in dollars and cents.... He doesn't want the glory or the applause of the crowd. The only two things he reads are his bank book and his official record.... He never reads a book, hates the movies, is a poor bridge player, scowls when he loses at poker and is a very strict parent. He disciplines his kids like a German oberlieutenant [*sic*].
>
> —**Sidney Skolsky,** New York *Daily News,* June 15, 1932

◆

Flushed with success over the pennant and World Series success of his 1933 team, Terry, in response to a question concerning Brooklyn answered with another question. His purported answer ran "Brooklyn? Are they still in the league?" Brooklyn answered that question all right.... Brooklyn beat the Giants in both games of a tremendous final week-end series at the Polo Grounds. The twin setbacks enabled the Cardinals to grab the flag on the last day of the season.

Last spring the fellow who was responsible for the whole thing, Roscoe McGowan, dean of baseball writers now covering the Brooklyn Dodgers [ran into] Terry, a mellower Terry, now rich and therefore friendly.... He spied McGown and he grinned and joshed, "There's the fellow that put the words in my mouth that ruined me in baseball. Chased me out of New York, that's what he did." (Terry didn't leave until eight or nine years later.)

—Harold Rosenthal, *New York Herald Tribune*, May 18, 1952

NELLIE FOX, 2B
2367 G, 1947–65
.288/.348/.363 (94 OPS+), 49.5 WAR

Once, while slumping, Mickey Mantle cried out, "Look, I am doing the best I can. Not everybody can be a Nellie Fox!" Mantle meant that he couldn't will himself to big-league success. Fox, 5-foot-10 and 140 pounds—150 if you count the huge chaw of tobacco he was always working—was not equipped by nature to be a great player. Obviously, he had *some* gifts to play as well as he did for as long as he did, but it was always the impression of those who saw him play that he had outperformed his physical tools. He didn't try to do too much; using a bottle-style bat, he hit singles and bunted men over, played excellent defense, put the bat on the ball (those last two are where the gifts come in), and hit .300 or better six times during the 1950s by going with the pitch.

Those running the Philadelphia A's for the increasingly spaced-out Connie Mack did not make an indefensibly bad decision when they traded Fox to the White Sox for the thirsty reserve catcher Joe Tipton after the 1949. Rather, they made the reasonable evaluation that Fox—whom Mack had signed in 1944, when Fox was an even-more-undersized 16-year-old first baseman, and then only because he wasn't draft-eligible—would not be the one player out of dozens who looked like him to become great.

> He's a rip-snorting 23-year-old, so light that he refused to be interested in a weighing machine. With much prodding he finally got aboard one such thing at last spring's training camp. The needle worked its way so high that the onlookers quickly appreciated they had been hoaxed. A search revealed he had his pockets filled with stones and bits of scrap iron. So nobody knows his exact poundage.
>
> —Irving Vaughan, *The Sporting News*, July 4, 1951

Even when Fox was at the height of his powers, his manager, Al Lopez, sounded like he needed to be convinced of his bona fides, telling *Sports Illustrated*, "Nellie Fox isn't real fast, and he doesn't have a great arm. He doesn't have good hands. No, wait a minute. He never bobbles a ball. I'd say he does have a good glove hand. He works hard, and he knows the hitters as well as anyone in the league. The big thing with Fox is he anticipates where the ball is going." Lopez said that in 1959, the year Fox won the AL MVP award. Fox himself put it this way: "I'm no ballet dancer, but I know we still get our share of double plays."

◆

Jacob Nelson Fox was killed by cancer at the age of 47. To that point, the BBWAA had voted on him five times. Only a fifth of them saw Fox as a Hall of Famer. After he was dead, he seemed to improve as a player, as 45 percent of the writers gained an appreciation for him, perhaps via some messenger from the afterlife, like an angel or a talking crow. By 1985, when Fox was about to drop off the ballot, 74.7 percent of them had awakened to the abilities of a player who, by then, had not played for 20 years. The Hall refused to round up.

One wonders why a group that could look at a self-made player who was a 15-time All-Star, multiple Gold Glove winner, an MVP, hit .300 a half-dozen times, led the AL in hits four times, made 2,663 career hits, scored 100 runs four times, was the hardest man in the league to strike out for 10 straight seasons, rarely missed a game, and was looked upon as the heady captain of his infield and *not* see a player deserving of a career-achievement award should not have been immediately disqualified from voting for anything, anywhere, at any time. Then again, Hall of Fame voters are just a subset of Americans, and we know who Americans have chosen in elections. Put in that light, it's less amazing that the voters missed on Fox than it is that they haven't yet enshrined an eggplant.

> I just loved him. He was such a loyal little guy.
>
> —**Ted Williams**, on the occasion of Fox's passing in 1974

> He's got a new system on those double plays. He doesn't touch the bag. Got it down so pat, though, that he even fools the umpires. By not having to stop and touch second, he gets the ball away faster and he also avoids being jostled by the runner.
>
> —**Casey Stengel**, 1951

> He gets into high gear in two steps, that's why he's so good. He can cover 25 yards for ya. He goes to his left after he's already gone to his right.
>
> —**Casey Stengel**, 1959

RON SANTO, 3B
2243 G, 1960–74
.277/.362/.464 (125 OPS+), 70.5 WAR

Shame on Hall of Fame voters and the Veterans Committee for making Santo wait until 2012 for enshrinement. He had died two years earlier at 70 years of age. He never knew that he had achieved the pinnacle of his profession, something he desperately wanted to live to see. That the Hall argument was eventually resolved in his favor is meaningless compared to the joy that a plaque would have brought him. We can utter some mealy mouthed sentiment about how the important thing is that the museum has a more complete, historically accurate collection of plaques, but we'd be vastly overstating the importance and impact of what is, in the final analysis, a jumped-up piece of wall art. The next time you take the kiddies to the local museum of natural history, ask yourself how the taxidermied ex-tiger feels about the honor of being under glass. Then ask yourself which would have had more impact on them: a dead tiger or a live one.

There is a counterargument in defense of the "complete" position: You might visit any large art museum—say the Metropolitan Museum of Art in New York or the Louvre in Paris—and, after taking in all the galleries, pull a docent aside and ask where all the *other* art is. They'll explain that there's too much of it to collect in any one place, that what you're seeing is just the tip of their own collections, most of which is in storage, that some of what you might consider art's greatest hits is held by other institutions, and that what matters is that the visitor is presented with a representative sampling. In that case, the belated inclusion of Santo makes sense—he and Brooks Robinson were the best third basemen of the 1960s, with Santo leading on offense and Robinson on defense. Simultaneously, it also diminishes the inclusion or exclusion of any one player, the odd Jackie Robinson or Babe Ruth aside.

During Santo's peak, which lasted from 1963 through '69, he hit .292/.380/.502 at a time when pitchers disproportionately dominated the game—that line translates to a 144 OPS+—and won five consecutive Gold Gloves. He was way ahead of the third-base class. For example, in that same period, Brooks Robinson hit .280/.327/.432 (117 OPS+). Alex Bregman, who hit .289/.391/.533 (147 OPS+) from 2017 through '19, has had similarly-shaped production, but is less of a defensive standout. Since 2019, injuries have eroded Bregman's production, whereas Santo maintained his while playing nearly every game and managing a case of diabetes. He once spoke of his dawning realization, while waiting out a long Billy Williams at-bat in the on-deck circle, that his blood sugar was dropping. Williams walked to load the bases. Feeling faint, Santo decided to swing at the first pitch so he could sooner get back to the dugout and his supply of candy bars and orange juice. Four runs scored on that swing. (Santo didn't specify the game, but it was likely April 26, 1970; the grand slam came off of Larry Dierker of the Astros.)

Perhaps the BBWAA missed on Santo because he hit only .277 and had neither 3,000 hits nor 500 home runs. He had been involved in a few clubhouse controversies and the collapse of the 1969 Cubs, and perhaps that hurt him. Maybe they were unable to place his statistics in the context of the low-scoring era in which he played. He was probably also hurt by an accident of timing: By the time he reached eligibility, in 1980, there had been a flood of great third basemen, including all-time greats Mike Schmidt and George Brett, as well as several who were nearly that good, including Sal Bando, Graig Nettles, Buddy Bell, Darrell Evans, and Ron Cey. Add in Brooks Robinson and Ken Boyer winning MVP awards during his career (Santo finished in the top 10 four times but never higher than fourth) and, in retrospect, he must have seemed tertiary. He wasn't.

Give the BBWAA that pile of excuses. It carries them through 1998 (the year Brett was elected). Santo still had 12 years to live, though, so whoever failed to correct their oversight in the years after will have to live with themselves. A Van Gogh in the museum does nothing for Vincent, either.

PEE WEE REESE, SS
2166 G, 1940–42, '46–58
.269/.366/.377 (99 OPS+), 68.4 WAR

Two of the best stories about Reese are mythical. It has long been said that the Red Sox purchased the Louisville Colonels solely to acquire Reese, who was property of the team in 1938 and '39. That may or may not be true, but what isn't is that the July 18, 1939, trade of Reese to the Brooklyn Dodgers was done at the instigation of Joe Cronin, Boston's manager and starting shortstop, in order to protect his own position. The true explanation is even worse: He wasn't trying to protect his position; he was only 32 in 1939, was still playing extremely well, and would continue to play well for another two years. He simply thought Reese wasn't a prospect. That was it. He wasn't venal, he just blew it. We might even exonerate Cronin completely: In some tellings of the tale, it was Tom Yawkey's partners in purchasing the Colonels (Donie Bush and Frank McKinney) who prompted the sale so that they could realize the highest possible price on a top prospect rather than be shortchanged by a related-party transaction.

Sadly, the famous May 1947 embrace of Jackie Robinson by Reese in Cincinnati, supposedly in response to racist hecklers, probably didn't happen, either, at least not then. Reese, a Kentuckian, was actually a little ambivalent about having a player of color on the team, but he got past it. That's important. That matters. That Reese didn't make a public spectacle of his support in 1947 diminishes the fairy-tale aspect of the story a bit, but that was always a lie, anyway. The result of the Robinson "experiment" was not the magical erasure of hundreds of years of received prejudices; Robinson helped move American conceptions of race by inches, not miles. It's possible that Reese's embrace—more metaphorical than physical—did take place the next year, in Boston ("letting the Boston players know that I was a friend of his," said Robinson), and that's plenty good enough, even if it's not neat. "A really nice man is a rare man, and the crowd always spots him," Robinson told John Lardner in 1949. "They sure guessed right about Pee Wee." Given our legacy of white intransigence, we shouldn't take "nice" for granted.

> A familiar scene around Ebbets Field is an exchange between the fans in the boxes near the field and Reese, at his shortstop post. Often, some rabid Dodgers follower would yell in a raucous voice, "Hey, Peewee, have you had your milk today?"—and Reese always waves and nods his head, with a big smile on his face, to the delight of the crowd.
>
> —*Famous American Athletes of Today*, 1947

Reese was an unusual player, and trying to find a recent analogue for him is difficult, especially given the three key seasons (ages 24–26) he missed due to World War II. Reese started out as a light-hitting gloveman but developed a little pop along the way. He also had excellent plate judgment, ran the bases well, and hit for good averages, though he only topped .286 once. That was in 1954, when he hit .309/.405/.455. If you could mix Willie Randolph and Alan Trammell you'd about have him, or Randolph and Chuck Knoblauch—which is to say, he had all of Randolph's skills plus Knoblauch's slightly greater power. (Hitter-friendly Ebbets Field didn't have a notable effect on his power numbers—from 1940 through 1957, he had an isolated power of .107 at home and .107 on the road.)

> Pee Wee Reese should go on to become one of the best shortstops in the history of the league.
>
> —**veteran catcher Spud Davis**, 1941

> When I finally decided to go and play ball in 1938, the man who got me the job at the telephone company said to me, "Pee Wee, I think you're making a big mistake by quitting your job and going away to play baseball." I said, "Mr. Lane, I'm young. I may as well give it shot." And thank Heavens I did.
>
> —Pee Wee Reese

> He played shortstop for three generations of Brooklyn teams, and came to sport droll cockiness. Yet near the end, sitting on a friend's front porch and watching a brown telephone truck scuttle by, he said with total seriousness, "I still can't figure why the guy driving that thing isn't me."
>
> —Roger Kahn, *The Boys of Summer*

HENRY AARON, OF
3298 G, 1954-76
.305/.374/.555 (155 OPS+), 143.0 WAR

How do you bottle this? What combination of nature and nurture goes into making a ballplayer *this* good? Science has revealed a great deal about how human beings are put together, but it hasn't yet explained that.

◆

It was Hammerin' Hank's misfortune to play in smaller markets at the same time that Willie Mays and Mickey Mantle were headlining the big room. It's hard to say that a player who won an MVP award and made 25 All-Star teams was underappreciated, but Mays won the Rookie of the Year award and *two* MVPs, and Mantle won three. More food for thought: Using a league-leading WAR total as a rough proxy for "Should have won the MVP award," Mays led his league nine times, Mantle six times, and Aaron just twice. Aaron ranked second in WAR among NL position players five times; in three of those seasons,

Mays was the leader. In the other, 1959, Ernie Banks led. In 1969, Aaron was tied with Willie McCovey. Banks and McCovey won the MVP in those years. It was a crowded era and a great one; after Branch Rickey and Jackie Robinson uncorked the bottle, the 1950s saw the full flowering of African American athletes in baseball. Look at the names mentioned here—Aaron, Mays, Banks, McCovey—they all have something in common. They were Robinson's heirs; they took his point about Black players being more than able to compete with whites and, to whatever extent there were still doubters, proved it.

Note that they proved it objectively. It is a different task than "silencing the bigots" or any other trite construction we might employ. Bigots are definitionally incapable of learning.

The American League, dominated by the racist owners of the Tigers, Red Sox, and Yankees, was much slower to embrace integration. You can see this in the awards voting: The league didn't see its first non-white MVP until Elston Howard won in 1963, 16 years after Robinson's arrival. Conversely, from 1949 through '62, the NL had only three white players win the award—Jim Konstanty, Hank Sauer, and Dick Groat. In addition to Aaron, Mays, and Banks, the NL MVP winners during that span included Robinson himself, Roy Campanella (three times), Don Newcombe, Frank Robinson, and Maury Wills.

It would be as naïve to say that Aaron completed the integration story of baseball by wresting the all-time home-run title away from Babe Ruth as it was to say that the election of Barack Obama marked the end of racism in America. In fact, it was the opposite; both proved, in the ire their accomplishments aroused, how much further there was to go. Of the many pieces of hate mail that Aaron received during his drive to the record, the most moving (though not in the way the author intended) asked him to refrain from hitting home runs *for the sake of the children*:

> I just can't bring myself to rooting for you, Mr. Aaron. I pray that you let the record books stand.
>
> When a little kid thinks of baseball he thinks of home runs. And when a little kid turns the page in a record book and looks for home runs, and sees at the top of the list: Babe Ruth 714, he

asks, "Who's Babe Ruth, dad?"... Therefore, how could you, Mr. Aaron, ruin, destroy, and shatter to pieces the one record which separates Babe Ruth from any other man to play the great game of baseball? How could you do it, Mr. Aaron? Are you ready to destroy that child's dreams?

The author of the letter protested he had not written, "one of the thousands of hate letters you are receiving every day," and that, if Mickey Mantle were about to break the record, "there is no doubt in my mind that this letter would be going right to him." Neither Aaron nor Mantle had the slightest power to reach back in time and diminish Ruth in any way. Indeed, the arduous nature of their individual pursuits (whether of the career or single-season home-run record or simply a career in baseball) tends to exalt Ruth: Chasing him was like climbing Mt. Everest. Yet, in the mind of Aaron's correspondent, Aaron was in the process of displacing Ruth, and, at that point the child's aspirations would become inaccessible. Despite the writer's inclusion of Mantle, it seems certain that the reason was Aaron's complexion.

In explaining his feelings about racism, Branch Rickey would refer back to his days as a college baseball coach in the early 1910s. He had one African American player, first baseman Charles "Tommy" Thomas. A hotel had denied Thomas a room. Rickey threatened to pull his team from the establishment, and a compromise was reached: Thomas would room with Rickey. Thomas, Rickey remembered, was badly shaken:

> Tommy stood in the corner, tense and brooding and in silence. I asked him to sit in a chair and relax. Instead, he sat on the end of the cot, his huge shoulders hunched and his large hands clasped between his knees.... Tears welled in the large, staring eyes. They spilled down his black face and splashed to the floor. Then his shoulders heaved convulsively, and he rubbed one great hand over the other with all the power of his body, muttering, "Black skin... black skin. If I could only make 'em white." He kept rubbing and rubbing as though he would remove the blackness by sheer friction.

The color of Thomas's skin should have been irrelevant, but, of course, it wasn't. He, and all Americans of color, were trapped in a Kafkaesque scenario. They stood accused not of something they had done, but of the fact of their genetic heritage. They were second-class citizens, and the only way to become a first-class citizen was to change the unchangeable and become someone else. The notion that Blacks were inferior was so deeply embedded in American society that many Blacks passively absorbed it (this is one of the subjects of Ibram X. Kendi's history of American racism, *Stamped from the Beginning*). Thus, Thomas was not moved to prideful defiance but rather surrender, wanting, in that moment, to remove what he had learned to view as a stain. The letter Aaron received is just another expression of the idea that to be Black was to be inferior, even if the writer never explicitly says so. Babe Ruth is an aspirational figure; Aaron, who grew up poor in the segregated South, should have been just as valuable a role model, but for *some reason* he couldn't be.

As Bill James pointed out in the first edition of his *Historical Abstract*, Aaron was held back quite a bit by Milwaukee County Stadium, but his late-career move to Atlanta Fulton County Stadium paid him back in full. The exchange of ballparks helped balance his career record and allowed him to pass Ruth, but his ballparks cost posterity just the same. Had Aaron played in a better offensive environment, he likely would have had a couple of 50-home-run seasons instead of topping out at 47. To cite just one example, in 1962 he hit .340/.408/.693 with 27 home runs on the road versus .304/.371/.538 with 18 home runs at home. This is, of course, a minor cavil. Aaron's accomplishments are as much a joy to consider as any Tom, Dick, or Trout's, and that includes Willie Mays and Babe Ruth.

AL SIMMONS, OF
2215 G, 1924-41, '43-44
.334/.380/.535 (133 OPS+), 68.2 WAR

The best Al Simmons story is the one he's not in. On August 23, 1931, his teammate, Lefty Grove, was on the mound against the Browns and bidding for the American League record for consecutive wins; he was tied with Walter Johnson and Joe Wood at 16. The A's were very good. The Browns were very bad. Simmons, who normally would have been in left field, was back in his hometown of Milwaukee nursing a badly injured ankle. With the game scoreless, two outs in the bottom of the second inning, and a runner on first, light-hitting second baseman Ski Melillo hit a liner to left. Simmons' understudy, Jimmy Moore, misjudged it, and the runner scored. Philadelphia's hitters could do nothing with opposing starter Dick Coffman, and that's how Grove's streak ended, with a 1–0 loss to a miserable team. Grove was *furious*, but he didn't blame Moore for misplaying the ball, he blamed Simmons for not being there. "His ankle wasn't so bad," Grove grumbled.

To Grove's ire, we can add our own for Simmons' interference with another historic event. On July 4, 1932, Lou Gehrig hit four home runs at Philadelphia. He would have hit a fifth, something no one has ever done, but Simmons made a leaping catch at the center-field wall to steal back his final drive.

> Lefty Grove called Simmons "a good fly-chaser, but a little lazy." When Roger Cramer became Philadelphia's center fielder, Connie Mack told right fielder Bing Miller, "Edmund, let Roger roam in your territory a little today."
>
> Overhearing the remark, Simmons asked, "Can he roam little in mine too, Mr. Mack?"
>
> **—Harold Kaese,** *The Boston Globe*

All of the foregoing emphasizes Simmons' glove, but he was also a monster hitter. Simmons, a.k.a. Bucketfoot Al, a.k.a. Aloysius Syzmanski bears some resemblance to Vladimir Guerrero, another right-handed hitter with an unorthodox style. Simmons peaked with consecutive batting titles in his age-28 and -29 seasons (1930 and '31) and then had a long, slow decline in which he was merely very good instead of an MVP-level player. Although not the world's warmest personality, he had great loyalty to Connie Mack and, from 1945 through '49, served as the bench coach and de facto in-game manager, lovingly protecting the increasingly senescent Mack. The old man's two elder sons removed Simmons from the role, one of their many crimes against their father.

> In his excitement these days, Mister Mack sometimes makes plainly discernible mistakes in simple strategy.... When he signals for an obviously wrong move these days Al Simmons turns his back a bit sadly on the old man, as if he did not detect the signal, and calls

for the right move. But this never fools Mister Mack. When Al comes back to the bench at the end of the inning, Mister Mack usually speaks up. "You used better judgment than I did, Al," he will say quietly, and then go about his timeless task of wagging his scorecard at his fielders.

—Bob Considine, *Life,* August 9, 1948

Simmons' protecting baseball paterfamilias Mack might not have been mere loyalty but a reflection of values instilled in him by the example of his mother, widowed and responsible for six children from the time he was eight years old. "There were long periods of doubt while I was being sent from one small league to a smaller one," he said in 1931, "when it seemed as though I would have to go back to work in a factory, or maybe driving a truck. And the one big driving force that kept me at it was the memory of how Mother had slaved to keep her family together and the heroism of her sacrifice.... 'Al,' I'd say, 'you weak-kneed quitter! You're on velvet compared with the little lady at home, and here you are crying over a stomach ache.'"

◆

In mid-July [1939] the shortstop [Eddie Miller] collided with Simmons on a play in short left field. Simmons came away unscathed, but Miller had a hairline fracture of the left ankle and missed most of the rest of the season.

Al Lopez remembered, "Everybody went running out there to see how Miller was. He was the bright young ballplayer, the one they had the investment in. Hardly anybody paid any attention to Simmons."

For Simmons, the accident served as a reminder of how far he had fallen as a thirty-seven-year-old player on the Boston Bees. Afterwards, he approached Al Lopez. "You know something Al? Ten years ago, when I was playing for Mr. Mack, if that collision had happened, they would have sent a goddamned kid shortstop nine hundred miles from Philadelphia for running into me."

—*Forging Genius: The Making of Casey Stengel.*

MEL OTT, OF/3B
2730 G, 1926-47
.304/.414/.533 (155 OPS+), 106.8 WAR

You might think of Ott as Jose Altuve playing the outfield. He was a little guy at 5-foot-9 (though he was not as short compared to the average male of his generation as Altuve is to his), and he generated power with a big leg kick and a pull-oriented, left-handed swing geared to a home park that was less than 258 feet down the right-field line. "Master Melvin" homered once every 14 at-bats at home but only once every 26 at-bats on the road. That's the difference between 39 home runs in a 550 at-bat season and 21. In no way does that take away from Ott's greatness. First, he was a career .311/.408/.510 hitter on the road. If you just double his away stats, you get those averages plus 1,808 runs scored, 3,032 hits, 623 doubles, 102 triples, 376 home runs, and 1,840 RBIs. He was *huge* regardless of park effects. Second, what he did at the Polo Grounds represents a skill. All ballparks help players in certain ways and hinder them in others. Not all players are capable of overcoming the limitations inflicted by their environment or of exploiting its potential advantages. In short, if Ott's accomplishments were purely a gift of the park, every Giants hitter might have done what he did. When Ott retired, he held numerous NL records, including for career runs, RBI, and home runs. The specific nature of the latter record was due to his ballpark, but his overall output was not—if the Polo Grounds bestowed its gifts indiscriminately, there would have been many Otts, but there was only one.

It was Ott whom Leo Durocher was speaking of when he (sort of) said, "Nice guys finish last." Ott is actually a good example of the opposite. Durocher was assaying Ott's abilities as a manager, and, yes, in that endeavor his nice-guyism was a bust (although four of his seven seasons heading the Giants took place during World War II, when rosters were patched together with whatever teams could find, and at no time did he possess the requisite pitching to compete). In every other facet of his life, though, people found Ott so likeable that they went out of their way to help him succeed, even though he was, at first glance, too small to play. That was how he got a paying job as a ballplayer while still in his teens, why he was recommended to the New York Giants, and the reason he became a major leaguer at 17. John McGraw preferred having Ott sit next to him on the bench to sending him to the minors; McGraw sure didn't do that with Hack Wilson. "This kid was a big leaguer the day he was born," said McGraw, and it would be a mistake to think he wasn't talking as much about bearing as he was talent. The Giants let Ott go—with great reluctance—during the 1948 season and replaced him as manager with Durocher, but Ott continued to get jobs in and around baseball because, though he might have been guilty of blandness, he was good to have around.

On August 7, 1940, the Giants held a night for Ott at the Polo Grounds before a game against the Dodgers. The team's second-largest crowd of the season (53,997) came out to pay him tribute. He was given a set of golf clubs by his teammates, a lifetime membership in the BBWAA by the writers, and a silver tea set and 208 pieces of silverware on behalf of the fans. Ott's thank-you speech, in full: "I shall always remember these gifts as an expression of you fans and I wish to thank you sincerely for all your loyalty and support over the years." Lou Gehrig wasn't an eloquent man, either, but, compared to Ott, he was Dorothy Parker.

One of Ott's early supporters was Louisiana businessman and aviation pioneer Harry Williams, who owned a semi-pro team. Williams had died by the time Ott received his day at the Polo Grounds—he crashed, as aviation pioneers are wont to do—but his widow, the stage and silent-film star Marguerite Clark, sent a gift on his behalf. Clark was a hugely popular actress up until her 1918 retirement. If you look at her few surviving films, you can see why—short, round-cheeked, with big brown eyes, she was doll-like and yet projected warmth. Walt Disney seems to have modeled his version of Snow White on hers. During her career, she played opposite DeWolf Hopper (now remembered, if at all, for performing "Casey at the Bat"), John Barrymore, and Richard Barthelmess. After her husband's death, she carried on as president of the Wedell-Williams Air Service Corporation and even submitted aircraft designs to the War Department. Clark died seven weeks after Mel Ott Night at the Polo Grounds. Ott, in kind, sent a wreath to her funeral. Her story, which only *just* intersects with Ott's, is much more interesting than his. All he was was good, and *nice*, too. It's far too easy to undervalue that, as Durocher did.

PEDRO MARTINEZ, RHP
476 G, 1992–2009
219–100, 2.93 ERA (154 ERA+), 83.9 WAR

Martinez ranks 128th since 1900 on the career ERA list, but account for context, with ERA+, and the true nature of his ability becomes clear: He ranks fourth. Even that adjustment doesn't give us a fair depiction, because Mariano Rivera ranks first, and his burdens, as a relief pitcher, were of a different kind than Martinez's. Clayton Kershaw and Jacob deGrom presently separate the two, but they're not done yet. Barring sudden, Koufaxian retirements, their inevitable decline phases will push them down the list.

The term "pitch tunneling," which refers to a pitcher's ability to keep his various pitches on the same plane long enough to force the hitter to make a swing decision before they diverge, had not yet been coined in Martinez's time. He should have inspired it, as his fastball-change combination succeeded via identical deliveries but varying speeds. Early in his career, he hit enough batters that they had to think about it from then on; no doubt that worked in his favor, as well.

On November 18, 1997, the Dodgers traded Martinez to the Montréal Expos for second baseman Delino DeShields, straight up. In his book *My 30 Years in Dodger Blue*, then-GM Fred Claire shares responsibility for the deal with manager Tommy Lasorda and Ralph Avila, who ran the Dodgers' operations in the Dominican Republic. "I told both men they had veto rights on the trade. Both agreed it was a good deal for the Dodgers in that we would solve our problem at second with an outstanding young player." If true, that makes the trade even more astounding: Any one person can misjudge a player's talent, but three? Remember, Martinez was coming off his age-21 season and, in 115 career innings, had a career ERA of 2.58 and had struck out 9.9 per nine innings, a more impressive figure then than now. That's a small sample, but it's one that speaks loudly. The Dodgers' "baseball men" didn't hear it. If charisma and ability to irritate opposing fans rated a grade on the 20–80 scale, their failure to value Martinez would be that much more perplexing.

Among the many highlights the Dodgers traded away was Martinez's 2000 season, in which he posted a 1.74 ERA in 217 innings at the height of the juiced era. Baseball-Reference ranks it the 12th-best pitching season of the modern era (since 1901). The only reason it doesn't rank higher is that old-time pitchers had many more innings in which to compile value. Cap the innings at 250 and, once again, it appears that no one has ever been better.

> Pedro was rated the second-best prospect in the minors (behind the Giants' Royce Clayton) in *The Sporting News* rankings. Martinez has a major league fastball and slider, but he's very slender

(154 pounds) and there's no guarantee that his arm will hold up on Lasorda-style usage. He's still a tremendous prospect at this point.

—*The Scouting Report: 1992*

ELLIS KINDER, RHP
484 G, 1946-57
102-71, 104 SV, 3.43 ERA (125 ERA+), 28.9 WAR

"Old Folks" was amazing, a top starter *and* a top reliever despite not reaching the majors until he was 31 years old, and he was generally intoxicated while serving in both roles.

Role	W	L	ERA	G	SHO	SV	IP	H	BB	SO
Starter	57	42	3.87	122	10	0	869	885	318	436
Reliever	45	29	2.80	362	0	104	610 2/3	537	220	315

Kinder was a sharecropper's son with a seventh-grade education. In 1937, when Kinder was 23, his mother died. Since his father had predeceased her, Kinder took in his three younger brothers (his older brother took in the remaining child, a sister). Ellis already was married with a child of his own, so the additional dependents left him little time for baseball. He supported his family by working for a road contractor. In 1938, he was spotted by a scout while pitching a semi-pro game in the middle of nowhere, but it wasn't until 1939 that Kinder's boss agreed to hold his job for him while he played a full season. In 1940, he went 21–9 with a league-leading 2.38 ERA in 276 innings for the Class-D Jackson Generals. Kinder, said *The Jackson Sun*, "wandered out of the mountains of Arkansas and started burning up the Kitty League with his powerful right arm and beaucoup pitching speed."

Kinder's remaining journey through the minors was slow and disrupted by the World War. In early 1941, the Yankees conditionally purchased Kinder and moved him up to Binghamton of the Eastern League, but, though he pitched well, they apparently decided the then-26-year-old was too old to progress and returned him to Jackson in June. In 1942, he was sold again, this time to Memphis of the Southern Association, but he pitched poorly. The next year, Kinder held out for the entire season and worked as a pipe fitter for the

Illinois Central Railroad. The wartime manpower shortage meant Memphis had to see it his way, so he came back in 1944, went 19–6 with a 2.80 ERA... and was drafted. He missed all of 1945, but his contract was picked up by the St. Louis Browns, an organization that, like Memphis, wasn't choosy about the age of its pitchers—not because of the war, but because they were the Browns and didn't really care who they threw out there.

Kinder spent two seasons with the Browns. His record was a superficially mediocre 11–18 with a 4.13 ERA, a performance at least partially attributable to the Browns fielding a poor defense while playing in a bandbox. He might have been headed back to the pipe-fitting line, but, at that moment, wealthy Red Sox owner Tom Yawkey bailed out the bankrupt Browns with a huge cash infusion. All he asked for in return was the Browns' best players, and he got them. On consecutive days in November, 1947, the Browns and Red Sox consummated two trades—one suspects they were broken up to disguise just how much money was being moved. The Red Sox got pitchers Kinder and Jack Kramer, shortstop Vern Stephens, and utility infielder Billy Hitchcock in return for pitchers Joe Ostrowski, Clem Dreisewerd, and Al Widmar, outfielder Pete Layden, catcher Roy Partee, utility infielders Sam Dente, Eddie Pellagrini, and Bill Sommers, and (the only part that really mattered) $375,000.

As so often happens, when a pitcher is backed by a better team he comes to life, but, given Kinder's age and the mileage he put on himself, his transformation was more unlikely than most. At 33, Kinder was just one long series of injuries. His arm hurt, batters lined balls off his body and broke bones, and, in 1952, he suffered a bad back injury. "Slipped off back of box while holding runner on bag," he said, apparently speaking in American telegram, "got sacroiliac. Broken disc in spine." Through it all, he was drinking heavily. One of the stories about Kinder that shows up in most books about the Red Sox of this period was told by sportswriter Roy Mumpton about a trip the Sox took to Chicago in July of 1948. On July 3, Mumpton and fellow writer Bob Holbrook went out on a hot summer evening:

> We came out of the train and it was only about two blocks from the train station to the hotel, and there was a drunk lying on the steps. I didn't pay any attention. Bob said to me, "I think that's our new pitcher." Kinder had joined the club two days before.... We got him in the hotel, got him up to bed, got his tie off and his shoes off, and left him.

The next day they announced, "Pitching for the Red Sox, Ellis Kinder." Bob and I looked at each other. I had never seen a guy so out of it. But he won the ballgame. He pitched the whole nine innings in that awful heat.

The story is inaccurate. First, Kinder had been with the team all season, not since "two days before." Second, on July 3, the Sox were not in Chicago but home against the A's. Kinder did pitch a complete game on July 4 against those same A's. He won but was hardly dominant, giving up 10 hits and five runs, including two homers. Finally, Mumpton remembered, "God, it was hot. It was 95," the night they found Kinder sleeping rough. Actually, the high was 82 degrees. That said, two parts of the story ring true. Kinder's love of spirits was well-established—"To the degree Ellis trained at all," a friend said, "he trained on the hard stuff"—with story after story of his being severely inebriated in public. He also had a special knack for beating the White Sox; over the course of his career, he went 20–8 with a 2.65 ERA against them.

Kinder tore the ligaments in his pitching forearm in spring training 1948, but, in '49, he had a Cy Young–level season, going 23–6 with a 3.36 ERA and a league-leading six shutouts. On the final day of the schedule, Kinder and the Yankees' Vic Raschi faced off in what was functionally a playoff game. Red Sox manager Joe McCarthy pinch-hit for Kinder in the seventh with the Sox trailing 1–0. The at-bat came to nothing, and the Yankees scored four runs off of Kinder's replacements. The Sox scored three runs in the top of the ninth, but it was moot. Kinder always believed he would have held the Bombers and accused McCarthy and his teammates of choking.

As age and injuries set in, Kinder was shifted to the bullpen. He was tremendous in the role. In 1953, he went 10–6 with a 1.85 ERA in an American League–record 69 appearances. Saves had not yet been invented, but he had compiled 27 of them, tying Joe Page's major-league record. Kinder was then 38 years old. His career ended when he was 42. Thanks to his habits, he lasted only a dozen years thereafter. "Bless his heart," his wife Hazel said. "Ellis did love a good time." He wrung out his life-force in a hurry, but he left us one of the great American stories in doing so.

"Me old?" he exclaims, and as he chuckles the crow's feet wrinkle briskly in the corners of his blue eyes. "Why, I'm just starting. I've got three or four more good years left in me and I'll tell you why.

Look at that arm," he said, and lifted his tanned and muscular arm up in the air. "She's just as loose and free as she was ten years ago. And look at that shoulder," he continued, and you could see the muscles rippling under the bronzed skin.

—*The Sporting News*, September 28, 1949

Arthur Richman, then a reporter for the *New York Daily Mirror*.... was one of his best friends and even tells of the time in Tennessee when Kinder took him to a Ku Klux Klan meeting.

"Why are we going here?" Richman wanted to know.

"Because it's Sunday morning and this is the only place I know where you can get a drink," was the answer Kinder gave, so Richman followed along, wondering if any of the Klansmen knew there was a Jewish kid from New York in the midst.

—**John Steadman**, *The Baltimore Evening Sun*

Chapter Seven

MORE YANKEES OF VARYING QUALITY

This chapter has a rubber arm.

RON HASSEY, C
1192 G, 1978–91
.266/.340/.382 (100 OPS+), 14.7 WAR

Hassey was a tough player to figure. Prized for his left-handed bat, frequently mocked for being one of the slowest runners in the majors, he didn't hit all that much—except when he did. Regarded as more of a catcher/DH than a gloveman, he spent three late-career seasons with a very successful Oakland A's team fulfilling the traditional role of grizzled old handler of pitchers, primarily by serving as Bob Welch's personal catcher. Hassey went through college as a third baseman and converted to catching late. Whatever the resultant defensive shortcomings, he is the only catcher ever to catch multiple perfect games in the major-leagues, doing so for Len Barker in 1981 and Dennis Martinez in 1991.

Another thing that makes Hassey memorable is the game of ping-pong the White Sox and Yankees played with his very corpus in the mid-1980s. The Yankees acquired Hassey from the Cubs in December 1984 and he was great for them the following season, hitting .296/.369/.509 in 298 PAs. It was far more than they reasonably could have hoped for given that he had been a career .272/.346/.373 hitter to that point. "We got him to pull the ball more," Yankees manager Lou Piniella explained. "He's ideal in this park." Roughly a year after acquiring him, they sent him back to Chicago, to the White Sox this time, as part of a package for ill-starred starting pitcher Britt Burns and a pair of minor leaguers. Maybe the Yankees reasoned that he wouldn't do it again. Maybe there was no reason at all other than this was the period of High Steinbrennerism, in which very little the Yankees did made sense. "I heard they were looking for a left-handed-hitting catcher," Hassey said during the following spring training. "They had one and they got rid of him."

The White Sox, also massively confused at this time (Hawk Harrelson was the GM), had aging future Hall of Famer Carlton Fisk playing every day behind the plate and were locked into 1983 Rookie of the Year Ron Kittle at DH. The plan seems to have been to follow the Hassey acquisition by sending Fisk to the Yankees for disgruntled DH Don Baylor. Bizarrely, Fisk was a free agent at the time, but, with collusion preventing player movement via free agency, the White Sox knew they'd eventually re-sign him. Both Baylor and Fisk had no-trade clauses (Fisk automatically by virtue of being a 10-and-5 player) and insisted they be incentivized (read: paid) to waive their rights. "Our catching needs will be taken care of," Piniella said, hinting at the shoe yet to drop. It never did, so the part of the sequence that would have made the whole thing sensible for the Yankees never happened. What the White Sox would have done with both Kittle and Baylor will remain a mystery.

Now the Yankees had no catcher except the fading, extremely unhappy Butch Wynegar and prospect Scott Bradley—the Yankees refused to play prospects at the time, so, functionally, they only had Wynegar—and the White Sox had a Hassey they didn't need. In February 1986, just two months after the Britt Burns trade, the two clubs made a seven-player swap which sent Hassey back to the Bronx. He again played way over his head in pinstripes, hitting .298/.381/.466. Teammates began calling him "Babe." Yet, at the trading deadline, the Yankees sent him back to the White Sox. "It's something I have no control over," Hassey said. "At least I'm going where I'm wanted.... I've been there before, I think."

There was almost one last act to this drama: Hassey reported to the Sox with sore knees, Harrelson protested, and Steinbrenner offered to rescind the trade. In the end, the Sox backed down, and Hassey played well for the rest of the season. As for the Yankees, they began the year dreaming of Fisk and ended it with Joel Skinner. "More than halfway through the season," Yankees closer Dave Righetti said, "and we have two catchers who don't have any idea what we throw." According to Mike Petriello, no team has ever won a World Series with a catcher acquired in-season. This is why.

> "Clyde," said Madden, "there's a rumor running rampant in the press box that you guys have a big trade with the White Sox going."
>
> "If there is," said King, "I don't know anything about it. Then again, George does his own deals with the White Sox. I'm not allowed to talk to them."
>
> —**Bill Madden to Yankees GM Clyde King**, July 30, 1986

◆

> Still, the news shocked Hassey.... He pinch hit in the ninth tonight, not knowing the deal had already been agreed upon, and singled.
>
> Then he came into the locker room a few minutes later. Rickey Henderson greeted him by saying, "You've been traded."
>
> —*The New York Times*, July 30, 1986

The Hassey family had a small-scale baseball dynasty: Ron's father Bill was an outfielder in the Yankees' system, while Ron's son Brad spent five years as an infielder in the Blue Jays chain.... In 1991, Hassey became a Yankee for a third time, albeit this time as an advance scout.

CHRIS CHAMBLISS, 1B
2175 G, 1971–86, '88
.279/.334/.415 (109 OPS+), 27.5 WAR

Carroll Christopher Chambliss was steady, not spectacular, and disproportionately celebrated for moments such as his ACLS-ending home run in 1976. He had only moderate power for a first baseman and was a contact hitter who didn't walk much, so when he hit less than .290, he wasn't really helping at the plate. That said, he was legitimately very good for the 1976 Yankees team that broke the team's 12-year postseason drought, hitting .293/.323/.441 (124 OPS+) in a low-offense year and then upping things a notch in the postseason, hitting .432 (16 for 37). He didn't draw a single walk in nine games, but if a guy is hitting .400, there's no reason to complain.

As with Chambliss's later pinch-hitting prowess, clutch hitting is less about grace under pressure than capturing a bit of luck—his other postseason performances weren't of the same quality, including his 1982 NLCS with the Braves, when he went 0-for-10 in three games. He was sometimes there, sometimes not, winning a Rookie of the Year award in a weak class, winning a Gold Glove once and getting picked for one All-Star team. There is no black ink in his career, no 100s in the RBI or runs-scored columns.

For all the credit he got for the big hit in 1976, it's worth noting that the 1974 Yankees, who finished two games behind the Orioles, might have won had they put almost anyone else at first base. They began the season with light-hitting gloveman Mike Hegan at first, but, in late April, Yankees president Gabe Paul, in the process of raiding his old team, traded four pitchers to Cleveland to get Chambliss, Dick Tidrow, and Cecil Upshaw. Whatever Chambliss would contribute to the franchise in the future, he was a disaster over the remainder of that campaign, hitting .243/.282/.343 (80 OPS+) in 110 games. Other things would go wrong with the Yankees that year, including a late, self-inflicted injury to Bobby Murcer (his thumb was stepped on and broken during an internecine brawl), but all you need to lose a close race is a first baseman who hits like Alcides Escobar. By the time Chambliss found his stroke in September, it was too late.

◆

While acting as Billy Martin's hitting coach in 1988, the 39-year-old Chambliss was activated for one game—one of that strange manager's many flights of fancy—but struck out looking in his only at-bat. Martin might have been tempted by Chambliss's strong showing as a pinch-hitter in his final full season two years earlier, when Chambliss led NL pinch-hitters with 20 safeties and batted .294. The year before, he hit .204 in the role—hitting on demand is a job that requires a lot of luck.

◆

The first six years Chris Chambliss was in the league, I thought he was a deaf-mute. When I called a strike on him, I thought he just didn't understand the situation.

—Umpire Ron Luciano

I would hate to be sitting under a falling safe opposite Chris Chambliss. Chris would probably be trying to decide whether he knew me well enough to tell me about it.

—An ex-teammate, 1983

STEVE SAX, 2B
1769 G, 1981-94
.281/.335/.358 (95 OPS+), 25.7 WAR

Sax, the 1982 NL Rookie of the Year, was not a great player, but he was often an entertaining one. He was a speedy contact hitter with a short, quick swing geared for singles. He preferred to hit his way on base and was shaky on defense—sometimes pathologically so—but he played with an outsized enthusiasm. At his best, he was a durable, hustling .300 hitter who added some extra bases with his speed and was solid enough at the keystone.

Sax hit .300 three times (1986, '89, '91). Otherwise, he was a league-average hitter or a little worse than that. In 1985, he hit .279/.352/.318 with just 13 extra-base hits in 136 games (eight doubles, four triples, one home run). He saved his season to some extent with one of his higher walk totals (54), but even that's a little deceptive—60 percent of those walks came after Tommy Lasorda dropped him from leadoff to eighth in the batting order. You can see why Sax never drove in or scored 100 runs, even though he started more than 1,100 games as his team's leadoff hitter: He just didn't do that much to get on base or to move other runners around the bases.

We should give Sax credit for Dodger Stadium, which was tough on batting average. During his Dodgers phase (1981-88), Sax hit .288 on the road but only .277 at home. Still, consider the value of what we used to call "peripherals." They're actually "centrals." During the 10 years spanning his Rookie of the Year campaign through his departure from the Yankees, Sax hit .286/.340/.363. He ranked 22nd in batting average among the 54 players who had 5,000 or more plate appearances during that span but was 46th in OPS and 28th in offensive WAR. His eagerness to excel made up for quite a bit; Sax was such a gamer he broke third-base coach Joey Amalfitano's thumb low-fiving him after hitting a walk-off home run against the Giants. "I should have known better," Amalfitano said. "I saw his eyes when he hit third base." ("No longer will I congratulate them on the field," he added. "I'll congratulate them in the clubhouse after the game.")

After the 1988 season, the Yankees allowed Willie Randolph, their second baseman for 13 seasons, to depart as a free agent. He was going on 34 and coming off the worst season of his career. They replaced him with Sax, 29, also a free agent. Randolph signed with the Dodgers. Functionally, the teams had made a challenge trade—my second baseman for yours, and devil take the hindmost. Sax stayed in New York for three years; Randolph was a regular for another three. Here's how it worked out:

Player	G	R	H	2B	3B	HR	RBI	BB	SB/CS	BA	OBP	SLG	WAR
Sax	471	243	563	88	7	18	161	142	117/37	.294	.392	.376	10.0
Randolph	388	174	397	45	6	4	120	191	18/9	.290	.377	.341	11.3

There's something a bit sad about a player whose best attribute is hustle spending what's left of his prime with a team as lost as the Yankees were in the late 1980s and early '90s. What is hustle in pursuit of nothing if not wasted energy?

"I thought I'd be treated special after we won the World Series," Sax said after leaving the Dodgers, "but I felt like I was just another number and that was the biggest reason I left. It was a turn-off." For all Sax's limitations, consider that, in all the years since then and of all the second basemen the Dodgers have had, none has stayed long enough to get even halfway to Sax's 1,100 games with the team, nor to his 15.9 WAR, while only Randolph (1989) and Orlando Hudson (2009) came close to his 1986 peak (4.8 WAR from 157 games of hitting .332/.390/.441 with 43 doubles and 40 steals).

> In time, Steve Sax will learn to give it a rest.... Third baseman Ron Cey figures the only way to calm down this crazed rookie

is to "kidnap him an hour before the game and put him in an isolation tank."

—*The San Bernardino County Sun*, April 7, 1982

◆

Steven Louis Sax, the leadoff man, is such a tangle of fast, furious, perpetual motion that some teammates who have been with him two years don't know what he looks like. He goes through life as if he were double-parked or late for a bus or wanted in Colorado.... He's Pete Rose II. Son of Charlie Hustle. A Rose by any other name.

— Jim Murray, *Los Angeles Times*, March 20, 1983

RED ROLFE, 3B
1175 G, 1931, 1934–42
.289/.360/.413 (99 OPS+), 29.1 WAR

Robert Rolfe came up as a shortstop but moved to third because (a) Frankie Crosetti was the better glove and (b) the Yankees were momentarily without a third baseman. Here's a fun and impossible trivia challenge: Name the Yankees' starting third basemen—excluding Rolfe—between the end of Jumping Joe Dugan's reign in 1928 and the advent of Clete Boyer in 1960. The Yankees were always patching or platooning. Some of those improvisations turned out to be quite good, but, for most of team history, they've bounced from one solution to another. They've had three Hall of Famers at the position, but they weren't Hall of Famers for *them*—Home Run Baker, Joe Sewell, and Wade Boggs did their best work elsewhere. In terms of career value, only a half-dozen third basemen have compiled double-figure WAR with the Yankees: Alex Rodriguez (54.0), Graig Nettles (44.4), Rolfe (28.1), Baker (20.5), Boyer (19.6), and Boggs (18.3). The peak list is dominated by the same players, joined by Scott Brosius, who hit .300/.371/.472 with excellent defense in 1998. It was for this condition of transience that Rolfe, "The Pride of Penacook," New Hampshire, was hailed as the greatest third baseman in Yankees history upon his passing in 1969. To that point, he was the only player in team history to log 1,000 games at third and the only third baseman other than Baker to shine offensively.

BEST SEASONS BY YANKEES THIRD BASEMEN THROUGH 1969													
Player	WAR	Year	AB	R	H	2B	3B	HR	RBI	BB	BA	OBP	SLG	OPS+
Red Rolfe	6.7	1939	648	139	213	46	10	14	80	81	.329	.404	.495	130
Red Rolfe	5.0	1936	568	116	181	39	15	10	70	68	.319	.392	.493	120
Frank Baker	4.9	1918	504	65	154	24	5	6	62	38	.306	.357	.409	129
Clete Boyer	4.6	1962	566	85	154	24	1	18	68	51	.272	.331	.413	101
Red Rolfe	4.6	1938	631	132	196	36	8	10	80	74	.311	.386	.441	107
Frank Baker	4.5	1917	553	57	156	24	2	6	71	48	.282	.345	.365	116
Red Rolfe	4.3	1935	639	108	192	33	9	5	67	57	.300	.361	.404	101
Wid Conroy	4.2	1904	489	58	119	18	12	1	52	43	.243	.314	.335	101
Frank Baker	4.0	1919	567	70	166	22	1	10	83	44	.293	.346	.388	106
Gil McDougald	3.9	1952	555	65	146	16	5	11	78	57	.263	.336	.369	101
Joe Sewell	3.9	1931	484	102	146	22	1	6	64	61	.302	.390	.388	109

Rolfe is an odd duck in any group of third basemen. He was (approximately) the 1930s version of Bill Mueller. At his best, he anticipated Boggs' style, hitting for good averages with doubles and walks. Unlike Boggs, he hit a lot of triples. If Boggs lined the ball the other way, it bounced off the Green Monster for a double or even a single; if Rolfe, also a lefty, did the same at old Yankee Stadium, it had room to roll all the way to Yonkers. Note, though, that batting average was cheaper in Rolfe's day than in Boggs'. Although Red had four seasons hitting .300 or better, he only finished in the top 10 in batting average once, and his OPS+ for the five-year span over which he hit .307 (1935–39) was only 108.

Rolfe spent his entire career hitting second behind Crosetti, an inferior hitter. Manager Joe McCarthy liked the idea of having the left-handed Rolfe batting with a hole on the left side, assuming Crow got on. You can't say it didn't work: Although Crow couldn't hit for average, he did walk a lot. He scored more than 100 runs from 1936 through '39, and Rolfe exceeded that mark for seven straight seasons. Only three players (Jimmie Foxx, Harlond Clift, and Mel Ott) scored more runs than Rolfe did in those years. Of course, the rest of the Yankees' lineup was so good that Alfredo Griffin might have scored 100 times batting ahead of those guys.

Rolfe's career had no second half; he ceased to be a good player at 31 and retired to coach Yale at 34. If he had retired after the 1939 season, he would have gone into the books with career averages of .305/.379/.433. In the 344 games left to him, he hit only .250/.314/.363. His early decline was blamed on the cumulative wear and distraction inflicted by chronic colitis. A product of Dartmouth, where he would later spend 13 years as athletic director, Rolfe was lauded for being detail oriented, buttoned down, and professional (he was famous for taking notes on game situations; excerpts from his journals would be published decades after his death). Some of these qualities were a detriment to him when he was hired to manage the Detroit Tigers in 1949. He was initially successful, but a manager who forgets to speak up except when he's required to be critical will soon lose his clubhouse. Rolfe did.

◆

> Blessed with an easy temperament, Rolfe was seen to flare up only once during his nine seasons with the Yankees. That brief outburst occurred at Yankee Stadium one day after the umpire called him out on strikes for the fourth time during a game in which Bob Feller was pitching for Cleveland. Rolfe whirled and shouted at the umpire. He waved his bat menacingly but his anger subsided and he returned to the dugout.
>
> **—United Press International**, July 9, 1969

This anecdote seems to have been inspired by the game of August 6, 1937, the only one in which Rolfe, who whiffed 40 to 50 times a season, struck out four times. The strikeout in question came not at Feller's hands, but via Joe Heving, who relieved Rapid Robert in the bottom of the 10th. The Yankees were trailing 6–5. Rolfe came to bat with runners on second and third and one out. Although he was 1-for-5 with three Ks to that point, his game hadn't been a total loss, as he'd slashed an RBI triple earlier on. Heving's 2–2 pitch came in low, the catcher having to pick it out of the dirt. Rolfe began to swing, then checked. Plate umpire Charles Johnston called strike three. When McCarthy came out to argue, insisting that Rolfe had barely swung, Johnston said that wasn't the issue, but rather that Rolfe had foul-tipped the ball, and the catcher had made a clean catch. McCarthy then changed tactics, asking how the catcher could have caught the ball if it had hit the dirt. "Oh," the umpire said, or words to that effect, and reversed the call. Cleveland manager Steve O'Neill then charged out of the dugout and demanded the base umpire be consulted. Johnston acceded, at which point *that* ump said that the catcher had indeed caught the foul tip. The reversal was reversed, and Rolfe had struck out for the fourth time. One suspects no one was shocked if even this unflappable (or at least very-hard-to-flap) man was exercised at this sequence of events. The postscript is that Joe DiMaggio came up next and pulled a double just fair down the left-field line to score both the tying and winning runs. Or maybe it was just foul. The umpires reversed themselves on that one, too, and Cleveland protested the game.

> I always hoped when I was a kid that I might play big-league baseball someday. But not even in the heights of my imagination did I ever think it would come true. Babe Ruth, to me, was a god. The next thing I knew, I was his teammate.

—Red Rolfe

ÁLVARO ESPINOSA, SS
942 G, 1984–86, '88–91, '93–97
.254/.279/.331 (66 OPS+), 3.9 WAR

Even more than the senior prom, Espinosa was the bane of my late teen-aged years. I hadn't yet shaken off my hereditary Yankees fandom, I knew the team desperately needed a quality shortstop, but I also had drunk at the fountain of Bill James and understood what on-base percentage was. Espinosa had a good glove, but he couldn't get on base if you gave him a ticket. His 1990 season, in which he hit .224/.258/.274 (50 OPS+), is among the worst offensive seasons in franchise history recorded by anyone who was not actually a giant chicken pretending to be a ballplayer. That Phil Rizzuto would nightly praise Espinosa's improved bunting (he sacrificed 23 times in 1989, finishing second in the AL behind Félix Fermín, an almost equally hopeless hitter whom the Yankees nearly preferred to Derek Jeter in 1996) in no way made up for his sheer inability to hit same-side pitching. It must be conceded that he was sometimes kinda-sorta okay against lefties, which is why he got a few extra years in as a platoon infield reserve on some good Cleveland teams in the early '90s.

As now, when I was a teenager, I had opinions. *Because* I was a teenager, I was free with them. Espinosa seemed to possess a good temperament, and, between his smile and his glove, he was popular, even as he was busy making outs. This drove me crazy, and I frequently said so. Close friends enjoyed taunting me with praise for him. I wonder if they would have persisted had they known the whole reason he was available to the Yankees. Espinoza had been beaten out for the Twins' shortstop job by Greg Gagne, a vastly superior player whom *the Yankees had given away to Minnesota so they could relieve the Twins of the sore-backed Roy Smalley Jr.* Smalley was one of a million failed shortstops in the years between Phil Rizzuto and Derek Jeter—a sad lineage of which Espinosa was firmly a part.

Since his retirement, Espinosa has become an American citizen and has coached defense in the minors for more than a decade. The game takes care of the good guys, even if they can't hit.

GENE WOODLING, OF
1796 G, 1943, '46-47, '49-62
.284/.386/.431 (123 OPS+), 33.3 WAR

Woodling had a quite a career, one of the most successful ever, and that's true even though he made just one All-Star team and never received a single vote for the Hall of Fame. Start with the fact that he was one of a handful of players to have a spot on all five of the Yankees' consecutive World Series winners of 1949–53. They didn't keep him around because he was the groundskeeper. He was excellent in all of those World Series, hitting .318/.442/.529 in 26 games, and was also excellent in the regular season, hitting .291/.393/.447 in those seasons and leading the AL in on-base percentage in 1953. He was patient and hit for good averages (he batted over .300 in five full seasons). He was also a strong defensive outfielder who rarely made mistakes—with the notable exception of Game 4 of the 1950 World Series, when his two-out error in the bottom of the ninth cost Whitey Ford a shutout, though not the victory.

Sometimes those who write about the Yankees in this period will say that Woodling was platooned with Hank Bauer. It's not wholly true. Yes, Woodling was platooned; Casey Stengel sat him against many left-handers. No, it mostly wasn't with Bauer, who played more regularly. "Woodling split the left-field assignment with Hank Bauer in those days," *The New York Times* said when the Mets acquired Gene in June of 1962. Woodling and Bauer overlapped for six seasons. In the last of those, Woodling missed significant time with an injury (he ran his right wrist into Fenway Park's Green Monster and had to miss the final month of the season), so set that one aside. From 1949–53, Woodling started 479 games in left compared to 114 for Bauer and 197 for assorted others, some of whom, like Bill Renna, were more like platoon partners than Bauer was. Conversely, Cliff Mapes was Bauer's original alternate, not Woodling. Others who preempted either or both, such as Jackie Jensen, were top prospects whom the Yankees were trying to squeeze into the lineup. Sometimes Stengel just liked the matchups better with a different set of players.

During this period, Bauer started 408 games in right, and the two were often in the lineup simultaneously. Woodling had 2,319 plate appearances in those five seasons, Bauer 2,314. As Woodling told Dom Forker, "Hank Bauer used to say to Casey, 'When you're five games ahead you platoon. When you're one game ahead, both Gene and I play.'" Woodling would berate Stengel for restricting his playing time, and the two would have terrific shouting matches, but the older man was never bothered. "Sure, I got mad at him," Woodling told author Larry Moffi. "I admit it. And I called him some names, but the more I called him an SOB the more I played. He knew people." Years later, one of Woodling's daughters would name her own daughter after Casey.

> During one clubhouse meeting Stengel said, "There is one guy in this room who don't talk behind my back." All the Yankees turned and looked toward Woodling.
>
> —Peter Golenbock, *Dynasty*

◆

> The year that Casey and I fussed a lot, we won the pennant and World Series, as usual. After we won the Series, I went into his office and said, "Hey, Casey?" He cut me off quickly. "Hey, don't come in here and apologize for making me look good all year."
>
> —Gene Woodling

Stengel had the last laugh about this when the 1962 Mets purchased Woodling's contract from the Washington Senators. "Woodling used to fuss with me to play him more with the Yankees," Casey said. "Well, he can play all he wants over here." Woodling was 39 and just about done.

That Woodling played at all, never mind played until he was nearly 40, took both a great deal of excellence and a great deal of luck. "Gene Woodling is a fellow who, throughout his career, has refused to take 'no' for an answer," wrote Gordon Cobbledick of the *Cleveland Plain Dealer* in 1958. "He first heard the negative monosyllable back in 1946 when Lou Boudreau, then managing the Indians, took one casual look and decided he wouldn't hit." One wonders if this was the "evaluation" by Boudreau that prompted Cleveland exec Hank Greenberg to write the following in September 1954:

> Each new player delivered in the spring to a big-league manager under this farm system method represents upwards of $100,000 of corporate spending for bonus and salary, scouting, study, optioning, supervision, transportation, teaching and even medical bills.... Regardless of the exact amount, most of it is spent before the manager sees the boy under big league pressure. Extension of the front office operation, then, comes as the manager tests the new player under big league conditions. A single look, a few innings of competition in a game already lost will not suffice. He represents a small fortune. Was it wasted or not?
>
> If a big-league manager's pride and ego thrive upon his unique ability to detect talent or lack of it when others can't, he'll never get along with the front office.... Decisions based on whim and caprice are useless.... He cannot win ball games by force of personality, his own lifetime batting average or friendship. He must get results from players handed over to him or give a valid reason for their failure.

Boudreau was actually pretty excited about Woodling at first, because, for a few minutes, Wooding seemed like the new Ty Cobb. Even that was unlikely; The Ohio native grew up more interested in competitive swimming than baseball. Cleveland scout Bill Bradley signed him anyway. At first, despite his rather small, "chunky" stature (5-foot-9 and around 200 pounds), it seemed like they had found a natural. In 1940, his first pro season, Woodling led the Ohio State League in batting at .398. In year two, he led the Michigan State League at .394. After a broken ankle curtailed his 1942 season at 39 games, he hit .314 in 1943 to lead the Eastern League. This earned him his first call-up. "I've never even seen the boy in uniform," Boudreau said late that September, "but if he looks as good as reports on him indicate I'll give him a chance at the first opportunity."

Boudreau was as good as his word, and Woodling capitalized, hitting .320 in eight games and hitting his first home run, off Hank Borowy at Yankee Stadium. And then the war came. Woodling joined the Navy and spent the duration playing ball for the boys. Just before he returned, Cleveland traded outfielder Jeff Heath to Washington for stolen-base specialist George Washington Case, a highly uneven trade unless it was required by Heath's sunny disposition. It meant that Woodling hit the bench, as left field was given to Case. Woodling had a shot at the center field job, and appeared to have won it, but a late-spring-training slump inspired Boudreau to give the job to 25-year-old Bob Lemon, who was such a good hitter that he's in the Hall of Fame as a pitcher. Great judge of horseflesh, Lou Boudreau. Woodling couldn't get going in sporadic action—he was on the roster all year but started only 28 times—and, that winter, new owner Bill Veeck dealt him to the Pirates for the 38-year-old Al Lopez to satisfy Boudreau's request for a quality reserve catcher.

The Pirates couldn't give Woodling much of a shot; Ralph Kiner was well-ensconced in left. They sent Woodling to the minors. "Net result of the transaction," wrote Vince Johnson of the *Pittsburgh Post-Gazette*, somehow identifying Woodling as 30 when he was only 24, "is that the Pirates lost a badly-needed catcher and got absolutely nothing they were able to use in return." Had Woodling been 30, this likely would have been it for him, but, at 24, there was still time. Late in 1947, the Bucs dealt him, a pile of players, and cash to the San Francisco Seals for pitching prospect Bob Chesnes. The Seals were managed by the great Lefty O'Doul. Lefty helped Woodling revamp his swing, changing him from an upright, all-fields hitter to a crouching pull hitter. Woodling hit .385/.483/.603 in 146 games—this despite missing six weeks with a broken ankle, the result of his spikes catching as he slid into the third-base bag (the PCL played a *long* season)—and won his fourth minors batting title. "Everyone says [the swing] is a copy of Stan Musial's," Woodling said. "Well, I didn't consciously copy Stan or any other hitter. I just followed Lefty's instructions." In another interview, he added, "I didn't feel comfortable. I still don't. But the way I hit out there I'm not asking any questions."

Also important for his future, Casey Stengel was in the league, managing the Oakland Oaks. Bill James notes that Woodling made a good impression in the best way possible: He hit .493 with five home runs against the Oaks. When Casey went up to the Yankees that offseason, one of his first moves was to tell GM George Weiss to get Woodling. (You will note that Woodling was acquired in late September of 1948, and Stengel wasn't officially named manager until the second week of October; the deal had already been done.) "He is not the Yankee type of power hitter," the New York *Daily News* sneered. "He hit only 22 homers in a league where the fences are short and the ball is lively. Jack Graham, former Giant and Dodger, thumped 48 and Nick Etten, ex-Yankees, clubbed 42 there this year."

The Yankees dealt Woodling away after his truncated, disappointing (.257/.354/.384) 1954 season, including him in a massive swap with the Orioles. The Yankees wouldn't have another long-term starter in left field until Roy White came along 14 years later. Meanwhile, Woodling rolled on, hitting a valuable .287/.390/.438 (126 OPS+) over another 1,007 games. His career ended in March 1963, following his intervention in Marv Throneberry's holdout. Weiss, now with the Mets, had refused to negotiate with the first baseman. Woodling, signed as a player-coach, got into a shouting match with Mets assistant GM Johnny Murphy over Weiss's stance, saying, "This guy Throneberry is down here [at spring training] on his own money. The least Weiss can do is see him." Weiss gave in, but was resentful. "The whole situation with Woodling has become an intolerable mess," Weiss said, and released him.

Woodling, who parlayed his many World Series shares into a working farm and a comfortable retirement (there turned out to be oil under the cornfield), exemplified the kind of sharecropper thinking that Marvin Miller would later have to combat when he took over the Players Association. Simply put, Woodling hadn't understood much of what had happened to him. "You know, when I was playing we knew that the [reserve clause] was illegal," he said in a 1977 interview. "But I believe that we knew it was necessary, too, so we didn't do anything about it.... In all the years I played, I can't recall a single player who was hurt by it. Things always worked out." We need not list all of the players who were demonstrably hurt by it, including Woodling himself, to perceive the rose-colored tint of his memories. To give just one example, in 1958 Cleveland GM Frank Lane gave Woodling what the latter felt was an insufficient raise after he'd hit .321. He refused to sign, and Lane responded by threatening to deduct $100 from his offer for every day of practice missed. "I'd quit the Indians before I'd let him fine me," Woodling shouted. "Who does Lane think he is, a dictator?" He threatened to go to the commissioner. He was also an outspoken advocate for player pensions during his career. He always remembered the bad press it got him, but he had forgotten his own powerlessness.

> I had good parents, taught me right from wrong, pay your bills. My old man bought nothing unless he paid for it. He told me, "If you ever get in serious trouble, I'm not coming to help you."
>
> —Gene Woodling

◆

> I led four leagues in hitting my first four years.... And then I came to the big leagues with Ceveland and Boudreau said I couldn't hit. Shit!
>
> —Gene Woodling

GERALD WILLIAMS, OF
1168 G, 1992–2005
.255/.301/.410 (82 OPS+), 6.5 WAR

For a team that punted both its first- and second-round picks (to sign free agents Gary Ward and Rick Cerone), the Yankees had a decent 1987 draft, tabbing two good defenders in Gerald "Ice" Williams and catcher Brad Ausmus in the 14th and 48th stanzas, respectively. They never did use the future Gold Glove catcher, leaving him unprotected in the November 1992 expansion draft long enough for the Rockies to snag him, but Grambling State–product Williams would prove to be a useful reserve/platoon outfielder over seven pinstriped seasons. Any time a team tried to make more of him than that, such as in 2000, when he started in center field for the Devil Rays, his weaknesses came to the fore: He was an excellent outfielder with speed and a strong arm, and he had decent power, but he lacked plate judgment, couldn't hit same-side pitching, and was a miserable baserunner. Let that

2000 season sum it all up: He hit .274/.312/.427 (87 OPS+) in 146 games, knocked 30 doubles and 21 home runs, took 34 walks, and stole 12 bases in 24 attempts. And yet, the right-handed-hitting Williams might have been an All-Star that year had he just kept up his usual production against lefties; that year he was roughly the same hitter against all comers. For his career, he hit .279/.330/.482 against southpaws. Special merit citation: He took Randy Johnson deep three times, including twice in the same game.

The Yankees traded Williams to the Brewers in August 1996 as part of a largely redundant trade that returned damaged infielder Pat Listach and lefty spot-reliever Graeme Lloyd. The Brewers tried to make a starter of Williams with even worse results than the Rays would later have. He bounced around a lot after that because every team can use a reserve like Ice Williams, but no one wants to pay the costs associated with locking one up.

On August 29, 2000, the Red Sox visited the Rays. The matchup was Pedro Martinez versus Dave Eiland, another ex-Yankee who came out of the ruins of their 1987 draft board. Williams led off the game for Tampa. With the count 1–2, Martinez came inside with a fastball and hit Williams on the wrist. Williams charged the mound and decked Martinez with a right hook, touching off a 12-minute brawl. It lasted that long not only because the benches cleared and some serious combat ensued, but because every time Williams was pulled out of the pile he tried to break away and reenter the battle.

"I escaped all right," Martinez said. "Gerald seemed to be complaining a lot and crying for people to get off him. He was scared down there; I wasn't. He was crying a lot, saying, 'Just get them off me, get them off me.' If you're going to charge the mound, you'd better be responsible for the things that happened down there."

Williams refrained from commenting, saying being hit by Martinez spoke for itself, and that, "I just want to remain professional." The Rays, as a team, did not remain professional. Williams was ejected, while manager Larry Rothschild was thumbed for arguing too vehemently that Martinez should be ejected, too. Over the remainder of the game, three Rays pitchers and two coaches were ejected for either hitting or attempting to hit Red Sox batters. It was an eight-ejection day for plate umpire Phil Cuzzi. The player who remained professional was Martinez, who stayed in the game and held the Rays hitless until catcher John Flaherty led off the bottom of the ninth with a single. Martinez's final line: 9 innings, 1 hit, 0 runs, 0 walks, 13 strikeouts. The Red Sox won 8–0. Major League Baseball, in the person of Frank Robinson, then the league's vice president of on-field operations, iced Ice for five games and $2,000, reduced to three games and $1,500 on appeal. "For me," Williams said, "the most significant thing is I have closure."

Sadly, there is only one true closure. In 2022, Williams was taken by cancer at the all-too-young age of 55. If you're fortunate enough to visit a major league clubhouse on Old-Timers Day, note the varying ways these formerly elite athletes are abused by time. Some are just lightly gone over and look ready to, if not play with their old flair, run a seniors marathon without too much trouble. Conversely, some are wider than they are high, having been both shrunken and enlarged over time. Some get to come back year after year, participating even from walkers and wheelchairs. Others are gone well before then. There's no reason to it, for ballplayers or any of us.

GEORGE SELKIRK, OF
846 G, 1934–42
.290/.400/.483 (127 OPS+), 23.4 WAR

"Twinkletoes" Selkirk is a great argument for why the reserve clause was pernicious. A corner outfielder, the Canadian first reached the highest level of the minor leagues in 1927, when he was 19, yet he didn't make it to the majors until he was 26. If you've heard of Selkirk, even a little bit, you know that he was the poor sap who followed Babe Ruth as the Yankees' right fielder, even picking up the Babe's uniform number. He did pretty well with the job, too; imagine a Paul O'Neill–style hitter with a little more patience. The only fault one can find with Selkirk's performance is that he was often injured.

The most dramatic of Selkirk's many woundings came on July 1, 1937, when Selkirk dove for a short fly ball off the bat of A's outfielder Jack Rothrock. The impact fractured his collarbone. "Under the momentum of a spirited dash for the fly and the difficult angle at which he made the catch," James Dawson of *The New York Times* wrote, "Selkirk plunged headlong to the ground as a ladies' day crowd of 11,894 looked on in dismay." He had also separated his shoulder and was later found to have fractured in his elbow, as well. The arm locked up on him, and when he tried to force it into position, he broke it in a new place. In 1935, he missed time with sinus problems. On Opening Day 1938, he broke his right wrist on a slide. In 1939, he made the questionable decision to soak his bruised thumb in iodine and suffered chemical burns.

He never played 140 games in a season and only surpassed 100 games four times in nine years. By the time World War II curtailed his career, manager Joe McCarthy had already cut back his playing time; just as Ruth had blocked him early on, Tommy Henrich and Charlie Keller blocked him late. "You had to hustle because once out of the lineup it was tough to get back in," Selkirk said in 1952. "I pulled a slight charlie-horse in the back of my leg and should have been out a few games, but it was two months before I got back in. Tommy Henrich, a kid that used to baby-sit for us, had my job."

On March 6, 1940, the *Herald Tribune* ran an article with the headline, "SELKIRK, RID OF INJURIES, CERTAIN HE WILL START AS YANKEE REGULAR." He was more right than not but also had to exit he season's penultimate game in the third because, as it turned out, his appendix was about to rupture.

But had Ruth really blocked him? Observers certainly had that impression at the time. "RUTH HAS SIGNED—PITY POOR GEORGE SELKIRK," read the headline on Henry McLemore's March 1932 syndicated column:

> George Selkirk has been standing out there in right field in St. Petersburgh! Sweating under that Florida sun, and dreaming.... George, just think how you'll feel when you step out there in the stadium, with 80,000 folks a-lookin' on. And you-a taking the place of the mighty Babe. George Selkirk probably doesn't like to think about those dreams now. The Babe is in right field.... I know what it is to have your dreams go haywire. I once dreamed an uncle of mine in Australia left me $100 and a housebroken kangaroo.

Yet, the Yankees had more than one spot to offer. They generally carried five outfielders. Maybe there was a strong argument for carrying Sammy Byrd, Myril Hoag, Dusty Cooke, or Dixie Walker instead of Selkirk (the ability to play center, one suspects), but, in a fairer world, those decisions would have been informed by minor-league free agency, at the very least. There was no pressure on the Yankees to use or move Selkirk, so they didn't. The result was that he spent his baseball youth on the fields of Jersey City and Newark. That wasn't *all* on the Yankees; Selkirk reached the International League at 19 and languished there until he was 23. When the Yankees bought his contract in November 1931, the *New York Herald Tribune* commented, "No terms were announced, but Selkirk must have cost a fair sum, since several clubs were watching his play." He was sold to the highest bidder, not to the club most likely to play him. The Yankees were willing to pay the most for him, but didn't let the price dictate their lineup. Almost stubbornly, they decided that the line didn't start or end with Ruth, but also included every other outfielder in creation.

"In my day," Selkirk said in 1968, "the Triple-A clubs were full of dedicated minor leaguers who could wear out that ball. I wonder what became of them?... It would be fun to have the minors filled with those dedicated guys who'd hit .380 or something. Every once in a while one would come up to the majors and hit fairly well, just enough to help a little." He was talking about minor league greats like Ike Boone and Buzz Arlett, but he could also have been referring to himself.

Once Selkirk did replace Ruth, the sports pages were full of irrelevant comparisons. "The press tried to put pressure on me," he said in 1983 when he was inducted into the Canadian Baseball Hall of Fame, "but there was no way I could replace the Babe.... All I wanted to do was stay in New York."

After Selkirk's playing career ended, he scouted, managed in the minors for the Yankees and Braves. He was sometimes rumored to be Casey Stengel's heir, but here he was again stuck behind another great, and the opportunity never came. He did become the general manager of the expansion Washington Senators—a very different sort of opportunity—from winter 1962 through spring training 1969. He nudged that team towards respectability. In December 1964, he executed what is still one of the best trades in the short history of the Senators (or the longer history of the Senators and Rangers), acquiring slugging outfielder Frank Howard, third baseman Ken McMullen, first baseman Dick Nen, and pitchers Pete Richert and Phil Ortega from the Dodgers in return for infielder John Kennedy, pitcher Claude Osteen, and $100,000. Selkirk also started the managerial career of Gil Hodges. Then again, he also called himself, "an old-fashioned baseball man," grumbling things like, "I don't care how many pitches a pitcher throws. I don't even want to know." He tended to criticize players in grumpy-old-man terms, like, "Too many of them are more concerned with their own base hits than winning a ball game."

◆

Only one thing has Selkirk against the Babe, and it's all in fun, which makes it worse. Selkirk is extremely ticklish and the Babe not only knows it but takes every possible advantage of it.... They say too, that last season when Selkirk came up from Newark... he'd have been even better than the .300 hitter, classy fielder and smart runner he turned out to be, if the Babe had let him alone.

"Why don't you belt the big guy once and for all?" asked a teammate. "That'd stop him."

Selkirk, a powerhouse of an athlete with a well-nigh perfect record in free-for-alls, stared. "What?" he gasped. "Hit the Babe?"

—**Associated Press,** January 25, 1934

BOB PORTERFIELD, RHP
318 G, 1948–59
87–97, 3.79 ERA (103 ERA+), 17.6 WAR

As with many pitchers, Porterfield's career comes down to a handful of quality seasons bookended by a good deal of injury and mediocrity. From 1951 through '54, Porterfield compiled a 3.20 ERA (117 ERA+) in 866 2/3 innings while pitching for mediocre Washington Senators teams. He helped elevate them to that exalted status—they went from being a D-/F team to being a solid C when Porterfield was at his best. His peak came in 1953, when he went 22–10 with a 3.35 ERA and led the AL in wins, complete games, and shutouts. He even hit three home runs. Porterfield pitched to contact and, in his Senators years, walked only three batters per nine innings, a refreshing change in an era in which a pitcher walking 100 batters a year was commonplace.

Among Porterfield's nine shutouts in 1953 was a five-hit blanking of the Yankees, which must have been satisfying given his experience with them. The immediate postwar period was a tumultuous one for the Yankees. There were a series of rapid-fire changes including: The team being sold and put in the hands of managing partner Larry MacPhail; MacPhail hounding manager Joe McCarthy off of the team; Bucky Harris becoming manager even though MacPhail wanted Leo Durocher; an almost accidental World Series win in 1947, which Harris nearly handed to the Dodgers with unforced errors; MacPhail assaulting farm director George Weiss and permanently leaving baseball; Weiss taking over as general manager.

Harris and Weiss had many areas of disagreement. Porterfield was one of them. The 1948 American League pennant race was one of the best of all time, with Cleveland, Boston, Philadelphia, and New York all bunched at the top of the standings. Porterfield was then with the Yankees' Triple-A team, the Newark Bears, and pitching exceedingly well (he'd lead the International League with a 2.17 ERA). Harris wanted him called up; Weiss didn't think he was ready. Harris got his way in August and, for a while, he was once again the "boy genius" manager who had skippered the Senators to 1924's championship: Porterfield's ERA through his first five starts was 1.38. Then it was Weiss's turn to laugh, however sourly. The league adjusted, or Porterfield got tired, or hurt, or both, or all three. Over the five weeks remaining in the season, he managed just one more quality start as opponents handed him a 7.62 ERA in 39 innings. In seven starts, Porterfield was knocked out in the fourth inning once, the third three times, and on September 12 against the Senators, Harris had to hook him after one. Harris stubbornly stuck by the kid, giving him the ball on the last day of the season's win-or-go-home game at Boston. The Yankees were up 2–0 heading for the bottom of the third, when the Red Sox blasted Porterfield for five runs. The loss meant that Cleveland and Boston ended the regular season in a tie and advanced to a playoff game, while the Yankees were out. Porterfield's flameout was a major contributor to the shortfall.

Weiss fired Harris and replaced him with Casey Stengel. Porterfield got a chance to make the team in 1949 and pitched well enough to do so, but, late in the exhibition season, he strained his pitching arm. Once recovered, he was subject to a series of new injuries which kept him off the mound. Batting-practice liners seemed to have an affinity for him—in late May, reserve first baseman Dick Kryhoski hit one off of Porterfield's pitching arm, putting him out for 10 days. No sooner had Porterfield returned than he tore a muscle in that same arm and was out another month.

This was typical of his early seasons. As Stengel said with his usual sensitivity, "There was always something wrong—sore arm, sore head, sore back, sore legs." "Sore head" may be a reference to the events of June 9, 1950. The Tigers had scored nine runs against starter Eddie Lopat and another two against reliever Don Johnson. Stengel threw Porterfield into the game in the sixth, hoping he would staunch what proved to be an eight-run inning for the Tigers (he didn't). Porterfield led off the bottom of the seventh against Tigers' reliever Paul Calvert. Calvert was perhaps not meant to do this major-league baseball thing—his career record was 9–22 with a 5.31 ERA, but we'll save that for his own entry. Calvert threw what he later called "a sinker that didn't sink" inside. ("I never had a chance to yell 'Look out.' It sort of slipped out of my hand.") Porterfield couldn't get out of the way, and the ball smacked into his left cheekbone. "He fell to the ground," *The New York Times* reported, "made a feeble effort to arise, then collapsed.... Porterfield remained unconscious for twenty minutes, flicked his eyes briefly then lapsed into a coma." The Yankees, including teammate Dr. Bobby Brown (who had just received his MD), tried and failed to revive him. Porterfield was taken to by ambulance to the hospital, were doctors were finally able to bring him around. He had suffered a broken jaw along with a severe concussion. He was gone for almost fourth months and was still feeling dizziness even after he came back.

By that time, the Yankees had supplemented their veteran rotation of Vic Raschi, Allie Reynolds, and Eddie Lopat with young Whitey Ford and didn't need this magnet for baseballs. "Porterfield is much improved and needs work," said Stengel in May 1951, "but I am not in a position to give it to him." They dealt him and two other pitchers to the Senators at the 1951 trade deadline in return for lefty swingman Bob Kuzava, who became the hero of Game 7 in the 1952 World Series. He did leave with a parting gift: The Yankees had changed his delivery so he finished in a position that would allow him to field comebackers rather than be maimed by them (he continued to be hit nonetheless; a 1954 spring-training liner to the left temple put him in the hospital). Nevertheless, the reviews in the D.C. press were not kind: "Nats Fans Disappointed Over Kuzava Trade For 3 Yanks Has-Beens," shouted *The Evening Star;* "Nats Pick Up Three Losers From Yankees" was the version in the *Post*. Who was managing the Senators at that moment? Bucky Harris. He was still trying to win the argument with Weiss.

Porterfield's birthname was Erwin Cooledge Porterfield, but somehow he became Bob. Another thing about him that's not quite accurate is his World War II service. It was common for profiles from his time in the big leagues to say that he was a decorated combat veteran with the 82nd Airborne Division. "He jumped into France on D-Day, was in on the assault on Aachen and was with the American forces tearing towards Berlin," Tom Meany wrote in 1956. Porterfield's SABR biography argues that, in truth, he was assigned to a division which never saw combat.

In a short baseball career, starting in 1948, baseballs have hit Porterfield, in earnest, on the leg, the shinbone, the neck, the side of the face, the seat of the pants and the temple. He has hurt his back, his elbow, his side, his arm and the finger on his pitching hand. He has been hit by thrown balls, pitched balls and line drives and this has happened in batting practice, exhibition games, spring training workouts and legal contests. He has been beaned four times, on three occasions seriously. Once he fell down a flight of clubhouse stairs. He also suffered mental anguish for a whole season, he maintains, when he had to work under Charlie Dressen, the fiery little Washington manager…He was nicked by a piece of flying shrapnel when he landed at Bastogne, but it was just a scratch, he says, and he was back in action in two days. Even his minor baseball injuries have kept him out longer than that.

—Tom Meany, *The Boston Red Sox*

"I didn't throw the ball when he lost seventeen."

—Chuck Dressen

PORTERFIELD OVERCOMES EARACHE, TIGERS, 4-1

—*Washington Post* **headline**, August 6, 1954

BOB SHIRLEY, LHP
434 G, 1977–87
67-94, 3.82 ERA (96 ERA+), 9.7 WAR

Shirley was a swingman with the Yankees from 1983–87. His best years were 1984 and '85, when he pitched a total of 223 1/3 innings with a 3.02 ERA. He gave up very few home runs, just 13 in those two years. Baseball misses those 100-inning flex pitchers who allowed managers to keep their bullpens from overrunning all available roster spots. That's not to say that

Shirley didn't inspire his share of frustration. Yankees broadcasters loved to comment that he had "a rubber arm," meaning he could pitch often, but he also sometimes made rubber pitches—as hard as it was to take him deep, he wasn't equally good at suppressing hits. Four of his five Yankees teams made serious runs at the AL East title before falling short. Second-line pitching was always a problem. It's unfair to pretend that, if Shirley had been as good in 1986 (when he went 0–4 with a 5.35 ERA, including 0–3 with a 6.35 ERA in six starts) as he had been the previous two seasons, the Yankees might have bridged the 5 1/2–game gap that separated them from the Red Sox, but most of the teams of the Shirley years tempt the sort of thinking, that, for want of a nail, the kingdom was lost.

Having forfeited their 1983 first-round draft pick to sign free agent outfielder Steve Kemp on December 9, 1982, the Yankees could only surrender their second-round pick for signing Shirley the next day. The Reds used the pick to select catcher Joe Oliver.

> Billy Martin…was loath to use him in almost any situation…. In one stretch of Billy IV in 1985, Shirley went 23 days without appearing in a game…. The only reason it turned out Martin used him on this occasion was because Rich Bordi, the pitcher he wanted to use, had been given permission to go over to a San Francisco hospital to be with his wife, who was giving birth…. After the game, reporters flocked to Shirley, who had kept a sign at his locker which updated his "days in captivity." "It was nothing," Shirley said. "The only reason I got in there was because of something that happened in the Bordi bedroom nine months ago."
>
> —**Bill Madden and Moss Klein**, *Damned Yankees*

Chapter Eight

GETTING ON BASE

*Ten men with patience at the plate,
and one pitcher who walked everyone.*

FRANK FERNANDEZ, C
285 G, 1967-72
.199/.350/.395 (114 OPS+), 6.8 WAR

    We like to pretend that baseball is the one sport without a clock, but it has one in the form of 27 outs. The art of winning baseball is avoiding making outs on offense, or spacing them as far apart as possible, while getting your opponent to burn theirs up. That's why on-base percentage is the *sine qua non* of offensive success: The higher a player or team's OBP, the fewer outs they make as a percentage of their times at the plate. Fernandez, a low-average hitter at a time of low averages, looks superficially awful, but, because of his patience, he was still good at slowing down the clock—he got on base more often than many players who were more adept at hitting their way aboard.

> Frank Fernandez went to bat four times yesterday for the Yankees against the Kansas City Royals all the box score shows for his times at bat is a zero. Fernandez walked four straight times, figuring in two of his team's runs… "I'd like to hit," the right-handed

batting catcher said in complaint. "But I don't seem to get many pitches to hit."

— *The New York Times*, September 1, 1969

Fernandez was a Staten Island kid whose Yankees term came in the three-year interregnum between Elston Howard and Thurman Munson. The Yankees' starting catcher during that period was former Ole Miss star quarterback Jake Gibbs. Munson made his major-league debut about 14 months after being drafted fourth-overall in June 1968, Gibbs became his backup, and Fernandez became redundant. Fernandez threw well and, given his patience and power, he would have made a more potent understudy for Munson than Gibbs, who had neither.

Whereas we can't know how Fernandez's career would have gone had he remained in the Bronx, the Yankees would spend Munson's entire career looking for a decent reserve. Munson caught 130 to 140 games a year with the result that he was increasingly unable to stand the wear of the position. Better alternatives would have given him more time at DH and the outfield corners. Instead, Fernandez was packed off to Oakland with pitcher Al Downing in return for light-hitting corner infielder Danny Cater, a deal that would be redeemed two years later when the Red Sox accepted Cater in trade for future Cy Young award winner Sparky Lyle.

"I was only about nine years old when I started to dream about catching for the Yankees one day," Fernandez said in September 1967. "It has been my goal ever since I signed my first contract, now I have reached it and I hope I have 2,140 games to go." He had his opportunities. He was the Yankees' Opening Day catcher in 1968 and homered off of Angels' starter George Brunet for the only run in a 1–0 win. He also earned laughs from his teammates—after he caught the ceremonial first pitch from 81-year-old poet Marianne Moore, he impulsively kissed her on the cheek while returning the ball; as ceremonial ball-throwers were often male politicians, no one had ever seen that before. "I just did it on the spur of the moment," Fernandez said later. Leonard Koppett of the *Times* noted, "He didn't deny that subliminal inspiration may have stemmed from the presence in a nearby seat of Jill Spavin, Miss World Airline Stewardess of 1968."

> The defensive play of the day was made by a Yankee—Frank Fernandez, a catcher doubling as a right fielder. He had just gone to right field in the seventh when [Don] Buford drove a "home run" toward the lower box seats. But Fernandez leaped high, grabbed

the ball in his glove at the peak of his leap, landed on the railing and jack-knifed into a front-row seat holding the ball. It was the most acrobatic catch on the premises since Frank Robinson's famous "phantom catch" into the same box seats two summers ago.

—*The New York Times*, July 7, 1968

Fernandez was also the A's Opening Day catcher in 1970, but, in both cases, he had trouble sticking in the lineup. Yankees manager Ralph Houk kept benching him for Gibbs—he didn't start for a week after his game-winning homer in '68—and in Oakland there was competition for playing time from Dave Duncan and Gene Tenace. Fernandez also suffered the usual catcher's injuries and was sidelined by military-service obligations. "Perhaps I didn't use Fernandez as much as I might have," Ralph Houk said in December 1968. "Off his offensive record, which has nothing to do with his batting average.... If he can take over the number-one job, more power to him." It never happened. In Oakland, manager John McNamara turned the job over to Duncan within a week of the season starting.

> How can anyone hit that good pitching after sitting around two or three weeks? You not only lose your batting eye, but you lose competitive sharpness just sitting around, never playing. I like to be part of the action and in the game, but it doesn't look too promising.
>
> —**Frank Fernandez,** February 1969

When Fernandez played at least semi-regularly, he was good. Add up his 1969–70 numbers and you get about a full season of at-bats with rates of .218/.363/.414, 27 home runs, 105 walks, and yes, a then-crazy-high 144 strikeouts, but, adjust for context, and he was about 20 percent more productive than the average hitter. Twenty years later, Sparky Anderson would have welcomed Fernandez onto any of his Tigers rosters, which were full of players like him. Fernandez also hit four home runs in just 32 at-bats in Fenway Park, but he never did get to play regularly in a park so favorable to him.

> Now that Fernandez is going to work on the Pacific Coast, he plans to live there. At the moment, Fernandez is thinking about San Mateo as a place to live in the San Francisco-Oakland Bay

Area. Fernandez explains: "I'm single and I hear San Mateo has plenty of stewardesses because that's where the airport is. I want plenty of opportunities."

—*The Sporting News*, March 21, 1970

Catcher Frank Fernandez let his Latin temper get the best of him last night in the Oakland Athletics' 6–4 loss at Baltimore, and it cost him cash money. He smashed a hard grounder off third baseman Brooks Robinson's shin in the eighth inning. The ball caromed over to shortstop Mark Belanger, who threw it into the A's dugout.... It was ruled an error on Belanger. Three batters later, Fernandez scored and threw his batting helmet halfway up the screen towards the press box and official scorer Phil Jackman of the *Baltimore Evening Sun*.

—*Oakland Tribune*, August 28, 1970

ELBIE FLETCHER, 1B
1415 G, 1934–35, '37–43, '46–47, '49
.271/.384/.390 (117 OPS+), 33.3 WAR

The Pirates have never received an MVP-level performance from a first baseman. Given that the Pirates franchise goes back to 1882, that's astounding. Yes, Pirates first baseman Willie Stargell shared the award with Keith Hernandez in 1979, but that was a career-achievement trophy given for a 2.5-WAR season. Beginning with 1931, when both leagues began giving out the award, and excluding the truncated 1981, '94, and '95 seasons, the average position-player MVP has been worth 7.7 wins above replacement. Here are the top five performances by a Pirates first baseman to date:

Player	WAR	Year	G	AB	R	H	2B	3B	HR	RBI	BB	BA	OBP	SLG
Elbie Fletcher	5.8	1941	151	521	95	150	29	13	11	74	118	.288	.421	.457
Kevin Young	5.6	1999	156	584	103	174	41	6	26	106	75	.298	.387	.522
Gus Suhr	5.4	1936	156	583	111	182	33	12	11	118	95	.312	.410	.467
Elbie Fletcher	5.0	1942	145	506	86	146	22	5	7	57	105	.289	.417	.393
Elbie Fletcher	4.9	1940	147	510	94	139	22	7	16	104	119	.273	.418	.437

Writing about Fletcher in the most recent version of his *Historical Baseball Abstract*, Bill James referred to him as a member "of a sort of 'rump legislature' of first basemen who didn't hit for much power but made an offensive contribution by hitting for a good average with 10–12 home runs and a hundred walks a year. Ferris Fain, Lu Blue, Joe Cunningham, and Fred Tenney were a few other exemplars of the type, which was never common, and which I believe is now extinct." There have been other members of the breed, ranging from Mike Hargrove to Dave Magadan and perhaps even late-career Joe Mauer.

Fletcher was ill-served by both his teams and his times. A Massachusetts native, he signed with the Boston Braves during the lowest period in franchise history and was rushed to the majors while still a teen. It took him a few years and a return to the minors to figure out how to play, but as soon as he was ready to succeed, the Braves, having benched him for veteran contact hitter Buddy Hassett, traded him to the Pirates for Broadway Bill Schuster, a middling middle-infield prospect, and cash. This sequence shows how desperately baseball needed the concepts of on-base and slugging percentage. Hassett was capable of hitting .300 but with so few walks or extra-base hits that he was less valuable than a player with less pure hitting ability who could accumulate those other things. Fletcher averaged .271 for his career, topping out at .290, but he had more power than Hassett and drew up to 119 walks a season. He also had the better glove. "Fletcher is a fine boy," said Boston manager Casey Stengel, "and he never caused any trouble while with the Bees." He simply felt Hassett was a better hitter, which, in a very narrow sense, he was.

A star player in high school, Fletcher won a contest to attend spring training with the Braves in 1934. Since he was a minor, he still had to go to school. He told interviewer Brent Kelley that each day he reported to what he called, "Miss Aiken's Open-Air School." "And so mornings I'd go with [manager] Bill McKechnie's daughter, Babe Ruth's daughter, and we'd go out to school early in the morning and then at 10 o'clock I'd be free and that's when practice would start." The 1934 date doesn't quite match up with Ruth's stay, which began almost exactly a year later. That notwithstanding, it's reasonable to wonder if Fletcher's early association with the Braves sealed his fate with them. As any parent can tell you, sometimes it's hard to view your maturing child as an adult with evolving capabilities. Perhaps in 1939 the Braves still saw "a fine boy" rather than a 23-year-old player.

Only two Pirates have drawn 100 or more walks in more than two seasons: Ralph Kiner (five times) and Fletcher (four). Fletcher led the NL in OBP for three straight seasons and finished a very respectable fourth (at .395) in the fourth. At that point, the war came. Fletcher disappeared from the majors for two years. He largely played ball for Uncle Sam, but, as with most players, the service game was not conducted at a high-enough level to keep his skills from atrophying and time was passing. When Fletcher returned in 1946, he still possessed the same patience, drawing 111 walks in 148 games, but his batting average was down 40 points. There's an argument to be made that the Pirates downgraded Fletcher based merely on bad luck on balls in play (his BABIP that year was .269 versus .292 prior to the war), but they decided they'd rather have an aging Hank Greenberg. Fletcher went back to the Braves for a year and was misjudged *again*—playing in an extreme pitcher's park, he hit only .227/.381/.378 at home but poked a robust .289/.409/.421 on the road. He was out of the majors after that. Today, teams would be lining up to sign him. That includes the Pirates, who still haven't found anyone better.

MAX BISHOP, 2B
1338 G, 1924–35
.271/.423/.366 (103 OPS+), 37.4 WAR

It's possible that pitchers are now too good for players like "Camera Eye" Bishop, Eddie Stanky, Eddie Joost, and Ed Yost to exist. These players built their games around an extremely discerning sense of the strike zone. Pitchers issue walks at a slightly higher rate now than they did then, but they are much pickier about who gets them.

Bishop had only nine seasons in which he played more than 100 games, and he walked more than 100 times in eight of them. For his career, he averaged 140 walks per 162 games (though they played only 154 in his day). Bishop walked in 20 percent of his plate appearances, Stanky, Joost, and Yost did so in 18 percent. With the exception of Barry Bonds, who benefited from the mass delusion that he simply could not be safely pitched to, no one with at least 2,500 PAs in this century has walked more than 17.2 percent of the time. Normally, the batters who walk most frequently in today's game are power hitters who are given extreme (though not Bondsian) deference by the pitchers. The aforementioned hitters had career slugging percentages under .400—no one was scared of throwing one down the pipe. The closest modern analogue might have been Nick Johnson, who was extremely selective without being a threat to hit 35 or 40 home runs. Note, too, that Joey Votto, who averaged a 16-percent walk rate through 2018, walked only 12.5 percent of the time in 2019; when his power disappeared, so did pitchers' fears.

Bishop wasn't always obsessive about the strike zone. In 1923, he led the International League with 22 home runs and drew only 86 walks in 159 games. When Connie Mack bought Bishop for the Philadelphia A's, the old man told him to forget about the home runs and concentrate on the strike zone.

Bishop seemed so emotionally detached as to be without a pulse. He took a lot of criticism for that, but he also led off for three pennant winners (the 1929–31 A's). His career was broadly tied to Lefty Grove's; both he and Grove came to the A's via Mack's close connection to Jack Dunn, the owner/manager of the International League's Baltimore Orioles. Later, when Connie Mack was breaking up his A's team, he sold both Bishop and Grove to Tom Yawkey for $125,000.

Ty Cobb was Bishop's teammate in 1927 and '28. According to Norman Macht's biography of Connie Mack, Cobb told Bishop to buy stock in Coca-Cola. Bishop took the advice, "and years later was grateful that he did."

HARLOND CLIFT, 3B
1582 G, 1934–45
.272/.390/.441 (116 OPS+), 42.1 WAR

Some players conjure associations. If you think of Mike Schmidt, your first thought, ahead of the rest, might be, "Had a four-homer game against the Cubs." Then you pull back the camera and consider all his other accomplishments. For me, Clift conjures the term, "testicular mumps." Clift was stricken in 1943 and missed the end of the season. He declined to rejoin the Senators the next spring because his draft status had been changed to 1A. It was a strange decision in that he hadn't yet been drafted and never would be. He was eventually reclassified and returned to Washington having missed the first 81 games of the season. Twelve games later, his season ended due to injuries suffered when he was thrown by a horse and landed on his shoulder. Although he played every day in 1945, the injuries, both high and low, brought on the end of his career. Well, that and going from making his living in hitter-friendly Sportsman's Park to trying to do so in arid Griffith Stadium in a year of depressed offense. He hit .211/.349/.307 in 119 games in '45, and no one realized that, given the difficult environment—the Senators hit 27 home runs all season, *one* at home—Clift was roughly a league-average producer.

In his prime, he was much more than that. At his peak with the St. Louis Browns, he hit .306/.413/.546 with 29 home runs and 98 walks in 1937 and .290/.423/.554 with 34 home runs and 118 walks in '38. The latter home run total was a record for third basemen for a dozen years. He was essentially Josh Donaldson Mk I. He might be better remembered today if his teams had won any games, but, in a 12-year career, his teams finished above .500 only twice (the 1942 Browns and the '43 Senators, whom he didn't join until a mid-August trade). He had some of his best years for Browns teams that lost well over 100 games.

Clift retired to his huge Oregon cattle ranch. Due to what he called "bad management" and "a lotta mistakes," he ended his life living in a trailer. It's easy to imagine someone losing their shirt speculating on cattle—certainly Clift wasn't the first—but it's much harder to understand why someone with swollen, tender testes would decide a bouncy-jouncy horseback ride would be just the thing.

> Looking down the Browns' bench, the Babe saw only a solitary, timid-looking, baby-faced individual sitting on it, and since the youth was wearing a St. Louis uniform, Ruth assumed he was the batboy.
>
> "Hey, kid, you brought out the wrong bats for me yesterday," he barked at him.
>
> "Yes, sir," the youngster immediately replied. Then, almost as an afterthought, the young man felt moved to announce: "Mr. Ruth, I'm Harlond Clift, the third baseman for the Browns."
>
> —Milton Richman

WILLIE WELLS, SS
1038 G, 1924-39, '42, '45-48
.330/.407/.535 (152 OPS+), 51.1 WAR

Wells began his career with the St. Louis Stars of the Negro National League and stayed with them until the Great Depression killed the circuit in 1931. On paper, the schedule was about 100 games, so, as good as Wells was, he couldn't compile the same counting stats as his white counterparts in major leagues that were playing up to 154 games a year. Yet, he was so good he outpaced a good many of them in less than two-thirds the playing time. Prorating his Stars performances to a 154-game schedule gives an extra, alternative-history hint as to his capabilities:

Year	G	AB	R	H	2B	3B	HR	RBI	SB	BB	BA	OBP	SLG	OPS+
1924	70	264	45	79	19	6	2	58	3	19	.300	.353	.435	115
1925	135	526	129	152	30	11	12	82	28	82	.290	.386	.459	126
1926	131	434	103	162	19	6	20	100	25	78	.373	.470	.584	171
1927	149	562	140	204	33	8	45	168	14	87	.363	.450	.690	204
1928	121	490	128	176	44	8	34	126	20	39	.359	.414	.689	196
1929	154	586	170	213	37	9	40	199	48	82	.363	.444	.666	185
1930	140	523	174	215	53	5	26	177	28	81	.411	.492	.682	214
1931	53	190	54	61	19	5	5	42	14	37	.320	.439	.541	173

There are many contextual reasons that we can't say that *these* would have been Wells' numbers had American and National League owners been less bigoted (the Stars played in a bandbox with a short left-field line, to name just one), but if you find yourself saying, "Gosh, I always wondered how the back of Honus Wagner's baseball card might have looked if he came along 25 years later!" or, "This is probably how the back of Joe Morgan's baseball card would have looked if he had played in the 1920s and '30s," you're probably on the right track. Wells was even a little bowlegged, just like Wagner.

"The Devil" was actually a clean-living man; the appellation was about the intensity of his play, not his comportment or personality. He had to be intense, because, at 5-foot-9 and 165 pounds, he hadn't been blessed with a classic athlete's body. A native of Austin, Texas and the son of a woman who took in washing to make ends meet, Wells fell in love with baseball early and, when the professional leagues started showing interest, he defied his mother's desire for him to finish college.

An early-career arm injury, sustained while pitching, meant he couldn't get a lot of zip on his throws; he had to loop the ball to first base à la Tony Fernandez. He made up for this deficit with superior positioning. "What most people don't know is, baseball is such an intelligent game," Wells told John Holway.

"You've got to be smarter than the other fellow. Everybody says I didn't have any arm, but I still threw everybody out.... I was always in position. I didn't have to move over two or three steps. Sometimes, when you see me dive for a ball, you know I misjudged my hitter or my pitcher. That's the only way they got a ball through me. The weak arm didn't mean nothing. It was here, in my head." Buck O'Neil said Wells also pulled all the padding out of the heel of his glove to flatten it, presumably to speed up his transfer time. He also put pebbles in the fingers of his glove so he could whack incoming baserunners.

> The great third baseman and gentleman Judy Johnson was accompanied in his old age by knee scars that reminded him daily of the occasion when Wells, sliding in to attack, tried to kick the ball out of his grip and somehow missed the grip altogether. The gashes were administered despite the shin guards Johnson wore under his pants for just such an eventuality—for Willie Wells, basically.... Dink Mothell, a fine player with his own prickly edge...one day approached second base standing up in his attempt to disrupt a double play. Undeterred, Wells fired the ball in the direction of first base, a course that ran through the baserunner's face. Mothell lost a couple of teeth in the transaction. "Oh, he had the prettiest teeth you ever saw," Cool Papa lamented.
>
> —**Lonnie Wheeler,** *Cool Papa Bell*

Wells changed his equipment to thwart his limitations more than once. Because of his small stature, pitchers thought they could intimidate him, and he was skulled many times, enough times that, in his old age, the cumulative damage contributed to the loss of his vision. After being knocked unconscious in 1939, he found a miner's helmet, knocked off the lamp, and wore it up to the plate. Subsequently, he used a construction-worker's hardhat.

As with many Negro Leaguers, Wells found satisfaction playing in Mexico, where Jim Crow held no sway. "Not only do I get more money playing here," he told Wendell Smith, "but I live like a king.... I've found freedom and democracy here, something I never found in the United States. I was branded a Negro in the States and had to act accordingly. Everything I did, including playing ball, was regulated by color. They wouldn't even give me a chance in the big leagues because I was a Negro, yet they accepted every other nationality under the sun.... Here in Mexico, I am a man."

Wells was badly affected by the destruction of the Negro Leagues that accompanied the integration of the white majors. As he reached his forties, he segued into managing with the Newark Eagles. Among his players were Don Newcombe, Monty Irvin, and Larry Doby. While the white majors were willing to take those players, they weren't willing to take their managers and coaches. Thus, Wells' great baseball knowledge was wasted. The Hall of Fame began enshrining Negro Leaguers in 1971. Wells lived until 1989, but Veterans Committee voters, in their extreme, unpardonable cruelty, didn't add him until '97. He had not been good at saving his money—he liked to gamble—and the validation might have meant something to his standard of living, not to mention his pride.

> Willie Wells of 1942 was a better all-around player than he has been in any years since we first saw him in 1927. That is saying a lot, as he has been placed in the immortal class yearly. He belongs in the same class with [Pop] Lloyd, [Dick] Lundy, [Pelayo] Chacon, [Jake Stephens] and [Dobie] Moore.
>
> —**Cum Posey,** November 7, 1942

◆

> "Ignorance is pitiful," he said—loud. "If you are ignorant and stupid, you are sick—white, black or green, I don't care. It wasn't only here. It was the same thing when we played in Birmingham. Same thing in Mississippi. Something was wrong. You just couldn't understand it."
>
> —**Willie Wells,** quoted in the *Austin American-Statesman*, January 2, 1977

◆

> Willie Wells was one of the smartest ballplayers I ever saw. Understand? It didn't matter if he was on your team or the other team, Willie would sit down in the hotel lobby and talk to *anybody* who wanted to talk about baseball. Yeah. He could get inside somebody's head and make him understand better than anybody I ever knew. He was a great teacher.
>
> —**Buck O'Neil**

GEORGE BURNS, OF
1853 G, 1911–25
.287/.366/.384 (114 OPS+), 39.7 WAR

There are three George Burns we have to keep straight. Left fielder George Joseph Burns was born in Utica, New York, in 1889. First baseman George Henry Burns, whose career overlapped that of George J., was born in Ohio in 1893. Finally, George Burns, the comedian, who conquered radio, television, and motion pictures but didn't play baseball, was born in New York City in 1896. They called him Nathan Birnbaum then, but the stage name he ultimately adopted was inspired by George H. and George J., so baseball is everything and everything is baseball.

It's the Utica left fielder we're concerned with here. Burns was John McGraw's leadoff man for most of the 1910s and into the early '20s. Because his career straddled the dead- and lively-ball eras, it's hard to visualize a modern analogue for him. He was 5-foot-7 but still had some pop because he was terrifically strong—his SABR bio reports he swung a 42-inch, 52-ounce bat. His primary asset, though, was a good eye at the plate. He led the National League in walks five times. He also held the Giants' team record for stolen bases for about 50 years, albeit with the miserable percentages we would expect from the indiscriminate running of his day.

Burns began his career as a catcher. As with later players like Craig Biggio and Jayson Werth, someone (in this case, McGraw) seems to have asked, "Why the hell have we stuck this guy behind the plate when he can run so well?" Burns went to left field and became one of McGraw's favorite players, perhaps his second-favorite after Christy Mathewson. In fact, McGraw named Burns when asked that exact question. "He is a marvel in every department of play, a superb fielder, a wonderful thrower, a grand batsman and with few peers in baseball history as a run scorer. Best of all, Burns, modest and retiring to an extreme, is the easiest player to handle that ever stepped upon a field." Early baseball reportage involved Herculean feats of paraphrasing.

Here's what's wonderful about McGraw as a baseball man (and not-so-wonderful about him as a human being; these things are sometimes incompatible): McGraw traded Burns. In 1921, Burns hit .299/.386/.395 (106 OPS+), led the NL with 80 walks (not that anyone was paying attention), and scored 111 runs. That fall, Burns hit .333 (11-for-33) in a winning World Series effort. Nevertheless, on December 6, McGraw sent him, along with catcher Mike Gonzalez and $150,000, to the Cincinnati Reds for third baseman Heinie Groh. *The New York Times*' summed him up nicely in their post-trade farewell:

> Burns became a regular outfielder of the Giants in 1913 after serving a season on the bench and he immediately stepped into the ranks of stardom. For years Burns played the difficult sunfield at the Polo Grounds in masterly fashion and he has been often called the greatest outfielder in the history of the game. His quiet and unassuming ways won him a place in the hearts of New York fans such as few players ever enjoyed, and his passing will be generally regretted. For several years, Burns has been McGraw's leadoff man and he has ranked with the leaders of the sport in hitting, baserunning and heady play, while he generally excelled as an outfielder. During last season, Burns was shifted from left field to center... and he played the position as well as he had played left field during the preceding years.

The Evening World remarked that, "Burns is 32 and during the last few years, particularly in his baserunning, has been losing his 'pep.'" No doubt McGraw saw that too, and, as much as he may have liked any player, their ability to contribute mattered more. It was Branch Rickey who said "better to trade a player a year too early than a year too late," but McGraw who lived by it. Two years later, the same scenario presented itself with the player who had replaced Burns as the long half of a center-field platoon: Casey Stengel. McGraw sent him away, as well. By the time of that trade, Burns had already played his last productive season, while Stengel had just one to go.

ROY THOMAS, OF
1470 G, 1899–1911
.290/.413/.333 (124 OPS+), 40.7 WAR

Thomas, who spent almost all of his career with the Phillies, was an intelligent man who seems to have recognized where his strengths and weaknesses met the Deadball Era. Long and skinny, he wasn't a power hitter, even in the doubles and triples sense of the time, so why even bother trying to drive the ball? He'd concentrate on bat control, opposite-field hitting, bunting for hits, and strike-zone judgment. Thomas led the NL in walks seven times, passing the 100 mark in an equal number of seasons. It wasn't just that he was selective, but that he could foul off pitches almost indefinitely. That says a lot about Thomas's facility with the bat, but also about the quality of pitchers at the time and their approach: let them put it in play, because there's not much danger in that. Also, it was considered unsporting to work walks; batters were supposed to hit their way on. Thomas, along with like-minded hitters such as John McGraw and Hughie Jennings, helped provoke the foul-strike rule because while the ability to spoil good pitches is definitely a skill, the too-much-of-a-good-thing rule applies. Today, we complain about endless pitching changes but waiting through a 27-pitch at-bat while the batter slaps pitch after pitch foul must have been excruciating. It made for a bad show, and those who ran baseball were aware of it. "People like to see batters hit," Hank O'Day said. "They don't want too much waiting out." The players didn't like it either. This happened in the Phillies-Reds game of August 17, 1900:

> Today's game was marred by an incident in the eighth inning that was as uncalled for as it was unexpected. Thomas had hit up several fouls, when [Red pitcher Bill] Phillips walked up to him and said:
>
> "You're fouling those off on purpose."
>
> "I'm not," answered Thomas.
>
> "You're a liar," said Phillips
>
> "You're worse," said Thomas. And with that Phillips poked a hard one to Thomas' jaw, staggering him. Before further damage could be done, [umpire Bob] Emslie separated the men and promptly put Phillips out of the game. [Reds manager Bob] Allen claimed that Thomas had used obscene language and wanted him out of the game, but Emslie demurred.

According to one source, this was the occasion when Thomas fouled 27 pitches. To fully understand this interaction, it helps to know that there was an intermediate period between when a foul ball carried no penalty and when a foul ball counted as a strike. During this time, the umpires had to make a judgment call about whether the batter was spoiling pitches purposely. If, in their opinion, he was, they were to penalize him with a strike. Otherwise, a foul ball was a non-event. Everyone reset, and they went again. Bill Phillips seemed to have believed that Thomas was intentionally fouling off pitches, the umpire hadn't called it (over the course of baseball history, many rules have withered and died due to umpires deciding they didn't need the kind of grief enforcement would provoke), and he needed to take matters into his own hands. It was also in 1900 that Brooklyn manager Ned Hanlon, watching Thomas foul off pitches against his team, shouted, "Have your fun now, kid, because we're going to take care of you for next year."

Hanlon, you see, was on the rules committee.

Further underscoring how different baseball was 125 years ago, Thomas started out as a slick-fielding first baseman, the position he had played at the University of Pennsylvania. He moved to the outfield in part because, at just 140 pounds, he could be muscled off the bag. His isolated power (slugging percentage with batting average subtracted out) of .043 would easily have been the lowest of any first baseman of any period. Only three players in history, Sandy Alomar (the elder), Otis Nixon, and George McBride have hit for less power in a 5,000-plate-appearance career than did Thomas.

Thomas's speed allowed him to move to center and thereafter he was part of two great early outfields. First, he was flanked by Ed Delahanty in left and Elmer Flick in right. Subsequently, it was Sherry Magee in left and Silent John Titus in right. Leadoff-man Thomas scored more than 100 runs four times, peaking at an NL-leading 132 in 1900.

Not much has been written about Thomas, who seems to have been far from a quote machine, but one thing that comes up is how he refused to jump to the upstart American League—Flick (Athletics) and Delahanty (Senators) went, but he stayed, supposedly out of a sense of honor. And yet, there is this intriguing bit about meetings held by the AL in March 1901:

> Roy Thomas, the brilliant centerfielder of last year's Phillies, turned up at the meeting about 1 o'clock, and surprised everybody by announcing that he had just left [Phillies manager Bill] Shettsline, who wanted him to sign, but that he had refused to do so; furthermore, that he would probably sign within the next 24 hours with the Philadelphia American League club.... Roy is naturally sore at the National League for special legislation aimed at him to kill him as a batsman. If he signs with the American League he will not have any such handicap.

That would be the foul-strike rule. He wouldn't have escaped it long in the AL; the junior circuit adopted it in 1903. At this great remove, it's hard to see how the rule affected him. Thomas hit .321 before the rule came in and .306 in its first five years. His hitting fell off after that, but he had gotten a late start, coming up at 25, and was, by then, into his thirties. As we saw more recently with Ichiro Suzuki, when you lose a half step, you also lose the infield hits that spiked your batting average. Thomas hit .248/.366/.306 from the age of 32 onward. Given his high OBP, he still contributed.

> Thomas, personally, is a model for youngsters to copy. A polished gentleman, a splendid husband and gentle father, and in every way a credit to baseball, it is too bad that he should step out of the game—his kind should be carried on the payroll, if only to encourage the new lads to emulation and achievement.
>
> —*The Evening Star*, January 30, 1910

Appropriately, from 1909 to '19, Thomas coached UPenn baseball.

BOBBY ABREU, OF
2425 G, 1996–2012, '14
.291/.395/.475 (128 OPS+), 60.2 WAR

The all-time Venezuelan All-Star Team (through 2021):

	Pos	AVG/OBP/SLG	HR	WAR
Salvador Perez	C	.270/.301/.455	175	27.3
Andrés Galarraga	1B	.288/.347/.499	399	31.7
Jose Altuve	2B	.308/.360/.462	164	41.4
Miguel Cabrera	3B	.310/.387/.532	502	68.7
Luis Aparicio	SS	.262/.311/.343	83	55.8
Magglio Ordoñez	OF	.309/.369/502	294	38.8
Cesar Tovar	OF	.278/.335/.368	46	28.1
Bobby Abreu	OF	.291/.395/.475	288	60.2
Victor Martinez	DH	.295/.360/.455	246	32.0

Omar Vizquel, Dave Concepción, and Ramon Hernandez are on the bench. One could also bump Galarraga from the team, move Cabrera to first, and list Edgardo Alfonzo or Melvin Mora over at third. If you want a stronger center fielder, one has Tony Armas, Franklin Gutierrez, and Ender Inciarte to choose from. The rotation would start with Johan Santana and Félix Hernández, and Francisco Rodriguez would close. Were we to revisit this list in a couple of years, we'd almost certainly have to bump a player or two for Ronald Acuña, Jr. and, perhaps, Willson Contreras. It's a great country for ballplaying talent, if in unfortunate disarray in most other matters.

Abreu was one of those teenaged prospects you hear about for most of a decade before their destiny resolves. Many of those forever prospects turn out to be overhyped because projecting a 16- or 17-year-old comes with huge error bars. Abreu, who signed with the Astros at 16 and made *Baseball America*'s top-100 prospects list in 1993, '95, '96, and '97, proved to be as good as advertised, but spare a thought for fellow Venezuelan teen sensations like Jackson Melian or Kevin Maitan. They were sure to be stars but lost whatever made them special faster than a child star with a case of adolescent acne.

Abreu's career OBP of .395 clocks in at 51st on the 1901-and-up list, 26th if we limit things to the postwar years. He wasn't only patient (taking 100 or more walks in eight seasons) but could hit for average (six full seasons at .300 or higher) and power (up to 50 doubles in a season and two seasons of 30 home runs, albeit at a time when everyone hit homers) and was fast (six seasons of 30 or more stolen bases). He even won the 2005 Home Run Derby.

Defense was a different matter. He developed an odd habit of playing very shallow and pulling up well short of the wall when a ball was hit over his head, as as if he were afraid of getting hurt. This seems like a reasonable value judgment; Pete Reiser regularly ran into the wall and played 861 games in 10 seasons, whereas Abreu ranks in the top-100 for games played since 1900. A few extra doubles allowed seems a small tradeoff if it keeps the player off the 60-day injured list. It's for this same reason that, today, the Minnesota Twins have asked center fielder Byron Buxton to refrain from sacrificing himself. "The back of my head was, 'Make sure you're there for your teammates,'" Buxton told the Minneapolis *Star Tribune* after pulling up short of the wall in late May 2022. "You pick and choose your times to turn the jets on and not turn the jets on. My teammates made that very, very clear: Make sure I'm smart. I'm doing everything in my power to make sure I stay on the field and be there for them." Abreu was frustrating to watch in this regard, but, unlike Buxton, he stayed on the field.

Two teams failed to observe Abreu's potential and gave him away lightly. The Astros left him at Triple-A for two years, preferring to play outfielders such as Derrick May, Brian Hunter, Derek Bell, James Mouton, and John Cangelosi. Abreu began the 1997 season as the team's starting right fielder but slumped in May, needed wrist surgery, was benched and ignored by manager Larry Dierker when activated, and was finally demoted. When it was time to stock the November 1997 expansion draft, GM Gerry Hunsicker neglected to protect Abreu; he seems to have been convinced by Abreu's 6-for-33 showing against fellow left-handers that the kid would never be more than a platoon player. The Devil Rays took him with the sixth-overall pick. This would have been quite the coup—Abreu proved to be the best player selected by far—but the Rays and GM Chuck LaMar immediately dealt him to the Phillies in return for mediocre shortstop Kevin Stocker. Phillies manager Terry Francona put Abreu in the lineup and left him alone. Abreu hit .312/.409/.497, including .320 against southpaws, albeit with no home runs. Those would come later.

Some of the misreading of Abreu's talent might have been a misunderstanding of his attitude. At first he appeared to have a low-key personality and a low-key style of play, but his quiet exterior concealed a strong drive to succeed instilled by his father. Nelson Abreu raised six children despite being wheelchair bound. When the Astros offered Bobby his first contract, he sought his father's advice. "He told me to make my own decision," Abreu said, "But I wanted him to tell me what to do. He taught me right from wrong. He taught me how to live my life. He taught me how to be a man.... That was his dream, to see me play in the major leagues. He told me, 'I want to see you get to the major leagues. But don't do it for me. Do it for yourself.'...I wanted to play in the big leagues for him. I wanted to make him proud. I promised him." Nelson wouldn't live to see it; he died when Bobby was 18, following surgery intended to get him walking.

The Astros seemed to perceive Abreu as sullen rather than as a young immigrant who was quiet because he didn't know the words. "When guys don't speak good English, they get labeled," Francona told Kevin Roberts of the Camden *Courier-Post*. "It's not right, but it happens." Once Abreu reached Philadelphia and felt supported, he brightened up considerably and was known for his ever-present smile. He learned English, too.

"Man, I could watch him hit all day," Phillies batting practice coach Hal McRae said. "Bobby has a classic, beautiful, sweet swing. His potential is unlimited. My job would be easy if they all hit like that."…Abreu doesn't mind that he is under-appreciated. One of the running jokes in the clubhouse has the 26-year-old playfully reminding everyone that he is "very big on the streets of Venezuela."

…What would he do, if not for baseball? "Wow…I don't know. That's a tough question. This is all I ever wanted to do…I guess I'd do something…no, I just don't know. I haven't got any idea."

— *The Morning Call*, April 2, 2000

	TOP PHILLIES RIGHT FIELDERS BY WAR (THROUGH 2021)									
Rk	Player	WAR	From	To	G	HR	SB	BA	OBP	SLG
1	Bobby Abreu	47.2	1998	2006	1353	195	254	.304	.416	.513
2	J. Callison	39.4	1960	1969	1432	185	60	.271	.338	.457
3	Chuck Klein	37.1	1928	1944	1405	243	71	.326	.382	.553
4	Gavvy Cravath	31.0	1912	1920	1103	117	80	.291	.381	.490
5	S. Thompson	30.8	1889	1898	1034	95	192	.334	.389	.509
6	John Titus	26.3	1903	1912	1219	31	131	.278	.368	.379
7	Elmer Flick	21.6	1898	1901	537	29	119	.338	.419	.487
8	Jayson Werth	15.7	2007	2010	543	95	60	.282	.380	.506
9	Bake McBride	12.1	1977	1981	553	44	98	.292	.335	.435
10	Jim Eisenreich	9.5	1993	1996	499	24	32	.324	.381	.453
11	Bryce Harper	9.2	2019	2021	297	64	35	.271	.391	.522

ANDRE THORNTON, DH/1B
1565 G, 1973-87
.254/.360/.452 (123 OPS+), 24.2 WAR

There are many stories we can tell about Thornton, stories about personal tragedy and about poor communication between a dysfunctional team and its best hitter. The best *baseball* story we can tell is that four teams, and maybe even five, didn't understand they had a potential high-impact first baseman in him. He went undrafted out of high school in 1967, so maybe we can indict *all* the teams, but he was only 17, so perhaps whatever talent he had was still inchoate. The Phillies signed him off of a tryout, then left him sitting in the minors for five years before trading him to the Braves as part of a 1972 deadline swap that netted them pitchers Jim Nash and Gary Neibauer. Those two combined to go 0–10 with a 5.95 ERA as Phillies. Less than a year later, the Braves traded Thornton to the Cubs for the mortal remains of Joe Pepitone.

Thornton hit .290/.380/.547 in 95 games at Triple-A in 1972, then hit .289/.464/.681 in 40 games for the Cubs' Triple-A Wichita affiliate in 1973. This was enough, finally, to get him a cup of coffee in the majors. In 1974, he got regular work at first base and hit .261/.368/.439 (123 OPS+) in 107 games, he then improved to .293/.428/.516 (158+) in 120 games in 1975. It wasn't enough. When he started slowly in 1976, the Cubs traded him to the Expos for part-time outfielder/first baseman Larry Biittner and pitcher Steve Renko, neither of whom are in the team Hall of Fame. Thornton didn't hit in half a season with the Expos, so, that December, they dealt him to Cleveland in return for 34-year-old, sorta-replacement-level pitcher Jackie Brown.

It was in Cleveland that Thornton finally got a chance to play every day, minus an injury or two and the aforementioned tragedy, the loss of his wife and infant daughter in an October 1977 car accident. That happened after his first season in Cleveland, which was really the first season of his major-league career. No one would have blamed him if he had packed it in at that point, but he continued to perform. Never wholly consistent, Thornton didn't hit for high averages but swatted as many as 33 home runs (twice) and walked up to 109 times a year. Despite that, he was left to rot with a hapless Cleveland team that tended to second-guess him when he was slow to return from injury (think of what the guy *had* returned from) and buried him as soon as he slipped.

SUGAR CAIN, RHP
178 G, 1932–38
53–60, 4.83 ERA (96 ERA+), 5.7 WAR

Over time there have been several players who entered professional baseball as catchers but, at some point, were switched to pitching. If you're throwing the ball back to the pitcher harder than you're receiving it, and you're not likely to hit like Mike Piazza, you might as well go for it. Kenley Jansen is a recent example of that kind of transformation. Merrit Cain made the transition, too, but with more equivocal results. Part of the problem was he started late: A catcher in high school, he doesn't seem to have been very invested in baseball or anything else after leaving school. "Although a Georgia Cracker, he journeyed west and worked as a harvest hand near Albuquerque, New Mexico," explained syndicated writer Henry P. Edwards. "The crops harvested, Merritt found himself without a job, also cash. Pride prevented him from writing home for money so he hitchhiked to El Paso and signed with Uncle Sam at Fort Bliss to carry a rifle, keep his shoes shined, etc."

In the Army, Cain volunteered for the baseball team because players were given softer duty than regular soldiers. It was the All-Army team coaches who put him on the mound. The results were good enough that the St. Louis Browns offered to buy out his enlistment (that was apparently something one could do in peacetime), but Cain refused and served his full hitch, leaving the service as a corporal. As a result, he didn't get started in the minors until he was 23. It was late to learn to command his pitches, and he never did—Cain remains one of the wildest pitchers of all time with a rate of 5.2 walks per nine innings. He pitched four full seasons and passed well over 100 batters in three of them.

Connie Mack bought Cain's rights for the A's in 1930 and then farmed him out a couple of times, hoping he'd learn control. Cain started the 1932 season with the A's but struggled, and Mack sent him to Baltimore of the International League, the team that had schooled Lefty Grove. Cain pitched well, or at least better (16–5, 4.18 ERA, 4.1 walks per nine), and Mack brought him back up in September. In his first game back, Cain beat Red Ruffing and the Ruth-Gehrig Yankees 8–4. He even struck out more (four) than he walked (three) over nine innings. He hadn't really licked the problem, though, and the next summer there would be days he'd walk eight or ten or eleven batters, continuing to be, as *The Philadelphia Inquirer* put it, "wilder than a man overboard."

It wasn't wildness that ended Cain's tenure with the A's, though. After a league-average performance in 1933, he went 9–22 with a 4.63 ERA from '34 through the first six weeks of the '35 season. The A's were trending relentlessly downward as Mack broke up the 1929–31 pennant winners, so there wasn't much pressure on Cain to do better. According to the third volume of Norman Macht's Connie Mack biography, it was Cain who pushed to be dealt away. It helps to know that Cain's wife had some experience with accounting; He went to the bank to cash his paycheck while pitching for the Carrollton Champs of the Georgia-Alabama League and ended up marrying the teller who helped him.

Mack learned that Cain was telling other players that other teams wanted him and Mack wouldn't trade him. That was news to Mack. Nobody had approached him about a deal for Cain.... Mack said later that season Cain explained to him the real reason he had wanted out of Philadelphia: "Mrs. Cain was keeping the books for another player and his wife who were living with us, and there had been an argument about the bookkeeping. I didn't like that."

"Well, Sugar," said Mack, "I don't blame you. I can understand how that would kind of get under your skin."

Of course, that's not what anyone said at the time. Mack and Rogers Hornsby, then manager of the Browns, made a deal to send Cain and outfielder Ed Coleman to St. Louis in return for pitcher George Blaeholder. Writing in *The Sporting News*, James C. Isaminger reported, "Connie Mack let both Cain and Coleman go because he was convinced they needed a change of scenery. Neither player was popular with the fans here and never had a chance. This was especially true of Coleman, who was booed unmercifully every time he was sent in to pitch-hit.... They were absolutely blocked here and Mack did them a favor by sending them to a team where they could make a fresh start. Mack declared that Cain has every qualification to be a winning pitcher and he only let him go because Sugar was dissatisfied with the attitude of the fans and could not do his best." Cain, Isaminger noted, "is an odd character. From the stands it looks as if he is not trying because of an unfortunate mannerism, but as a matter of fact nobody tries harder to win." Later that season, Cain would strike out 13 A's while walking only three.

"By George, yes," said Connie, "we must get pitching or they'll positively slaughter us.... We've got some pretty good-looking fellows at that, goodness gracious, yes.... Funny thing, Mahaffey and Cain don't seem to get going for us.... They're pretty good pitchers, you know. Have to give 'em a little time."

What pitches would he use for his Big Four in the regular season?

"Big Four?" said Connie with a little chuckle. "We'll be modest and hope we get a medium-sized four."

—**John Kieran**, *The New York Times*, March 25, 1934

Chapter Nine

THE ABANDONED

They had their best years for teams that no longer exist, with the result that there is no one to perpetuate their legend.

WALLY SCHANG, C
1842 G, 1913–31
.284/.393/.401 (117 OPS+), 47.9 WAR

Selective memory unfairly punishes some great, colorful players. Wally Schang played in six World Series, three times on the winning side. He caught Babe Ruth. He was the starting catcher on the first championship team in Yankees history. He was a switch-hitter who excelled in getting on base. He was the first player to switch-hit home runs in one game (against the Yankees on September 8, 1916—no one took any notice; the story of the game was that it was played in front of only two dozen attendees and one reporter because it should have been rained out). He had the athleticism to play other positions, which, stuck on bad teams, he frequently did. He threw well and changed the outcome of one World Series with his arm. During his career, he was cited as one of the best catchers in baseball, and, for his first 10 years or so in the majors, this was true on a statistical basis. He stands 11th among catchers in career WAR; all 10 players above him have plaques in Cooperstown. Shang does not.

As first-hand impressions of Schang faded, the back of his baseball card worked against him in two ways. The typical catcher's workload of his day had him playing about three-fourths of the time, so his career high in games played was only 134, and most years he was around 115. He also suffered the usual catcher's injuries and played in two seasons shortened by the First World War. Resultantly, there is no black ink on his card. Secondly, his best stat is on-base percentage, which didn't exist until nearly 20 years after he retired and didn't become an official statistic until nearly 20 years after his death. He was patient and would have been an excellent leadoff man, but he mostly wasn't used that way (he spent about half his career batting eighth because he was in some very deep lineups; we can imagine that this played into his selectivity, as pitchers worked around him to get to the pitcher). He was part of a great deal of baseball history—just to name one small example, as Boston's catcher, it was his throw that nailed Carl Mays in the back of the head, causing the irascible hurler to walk out on the Red Sox. The ensuing controversy nearly broke the American League.

A "fat-cheeked, brown-overalled farmer's boy," Schang was from the small town of South Wales, New York, southeast of Buffalo. "In contrast to the modern jet age when players arrive quickly at their destination, Schang rode a horse to and from his baseball games when he began as a semi-pro player," *The Sporting News* wrote. His career began on a couple of Wally Pipp–ish notes. He began playing shortstop with the semi-pro Buffalo Pullmans. His brother Bob was the catcher, but a foul tip broke one of Bob's fingers, and Wally subbed for him. It was immediately apparent that this was his true position, and—except for those seasons in which strapped teams needed him to play third base or the outfield (including 64 career appearances in center)—he never looked back. The A's acquisition of Schang, which followed his hitting .333 with 10 triples in about a third of a season with Buffalo of the American Association, was attended by controversy. Per Norman Macht's biography of Connie Mack, "Schang, 23, was rated the best catching prospect in the minor leagues. Every team coveted him. The Phils' Horace Fogel thought he had a gentleman's agreement with [George] Stallings for first claim on Schang, but he didn't act on it. Mack drafted him [in the Rule 5 draft] for $2,500 and the National Commission ruled that no private agreement could make Schang immune from the draft."

Schang spent the first third of his rookie year sitting behind lesser-lights Jack Lapp and Ira Thomas. A foul tip had hit Lapp in the throat during spring training and destroyed his voice. He attempted to play through it but struggled, giving Schang room to play thereafter.

That was perhaps the third of three accidents that allowed Schang to emerge as a star with the A's. The other occurred before the 1913 season, when Mack offered Schang to Frank Chance, manager of the Yankees, in return for a pitching prospect named "Green." "I refused Schang because everyone advised me that the man Mack wanted in exchange was a far better prospect," Chance said. "He was described as a pitcher of the Walter Johnson type, a twirler sure to be a sensation in the American League.... I conferred with several supposed wise men, and all of them ridiculed the idea of a trade." Instead, Chance said, "Schang is one of the greatest young catchers that ever broke into the game.... and now Green is but a memory as a big-leaguer." He might have been referring to been Eugene Arthur Grenier, who had the *nom du baseball* "Paddy" Green. Grenier pitched for the Holyoke Papermakers. Grenier's obituary states, "Mr. Grenier pitched in the International League with a team in Montreal, Canada, and is reported to have also played at one time for the New York Giants." Nope; he never made it. He became, oddly enough, a papermaker.

Schang played on the final two pennant winners of Mack's great team of the teens. When Mack dispersed his players, he said he would rebuild around Schang. The Great War changed that; owners took it as a sign to divest of their higher-salary players. Schang was dealt to the Red Sox and played on that team's final World Series winner prior to 2004, then was swept off to the Yankees in the Harry Frazee teardown.

Along the way, he had some spectacular injuries. For example, he missed a month in 1916 after playing an overenthusiastic left field:

> Early in the game he had made a sensational catch off [Shoeless Joe] Jackson in foul territory, and when Joe lifted the same kind of a fly in the seventh, which was slightly nearer the 50-cent seats, no fan or player had any conception of what was going to happen. Wally rushed after the ball, which was descending perilously close to the wall, and just as he came within a few feet of the coping he stumbled, then plunged head-first into the concrete. He hit with a thud and rolled on his back unconscious.
>
> —*The Philadelphia Inquirer,* July 19, 1916

In 1923, the near loss of his manhood cost him about five weeks:

> The Yankees won a double victory here to-day, but they lost the services of Wallie [*sic*] Schang for an indefinite period. The husky

catcher was injured this morning and hustled off to New York for examination by a surgeon. In the second inning this morning Schang hit a grounder to Harris, and as he started to run for first base his bat bounced off the ground and struck him in the groin. Schang went to first and caught the next inning, but then had to quit. Examination disclosed a possible rupture and he was ordered to submit himself to Dr. Stewart for examination.

—*New York Tribune* (May 31, 1923)

Schang, by then 35, slumped in 1925, and Yankee manager Miller Huggins decided that Benny Bengough was the more viable player. Schang was dealt off to the Browns for a washed-up pitcher the Yankees never used. Schang continued to play very well for another three years, but he was far from the spotlight. He returned to the A's for an encore, backing up Mickey Cochrane on the 1930 World Series winners. "Just to watch him," a teammate said, "was an education in the art of catching. He had lost his reflexes but he still had all the moves. I've never seen anyone so graceful behind the plate."

Many of the pictures of Schang show him with a sad little mustache. This was an affectation of one spring early in his career that attracted a great deal of attention and ridicule; it wasn't the fashion then. He ultimately gave in to peer pressure and shaved it.

After the 1913 series, Schang was given a testimonial dinner emceed by Elbert Hubbard, which must be the only time a ballplayer had a socialist/anarchist/soap-salesman writer as a toastmaster.

Rooming with Wally on a trip one offseason, Bobby Schang awoke to find Wally trying to strangle him while shouting, "He's out! He's out! I touched him when he was two feet off the bag!" He had been dreaming of Ty Cobb trying to take home on a double steal and was arguing with the umpire.

"When I was his age," said Wally, pointing an accusing finger at Bob Feller, "I was a pitcher. I worked on a farm and pitched Saturdays, Sundays and holidays. I'd go out and pitch a game and the next day my arm'd be so stiff I couldn't comb my hair; had to eat left-handed; couldn't raise my food to my mouth with the old right wing." That possibly explained why he became a catcher.

—John Kieran, *The New York Times*, June 18, 1937

"I need him to help me splitting wood and milking cows. He's got to keep his muscles harded up for next year, and I'm going to see that he does it. He'll be better off right out there on the farm than anywhere else in the land."

—Schang's father, Frank, October 22, 1913

We need many more Wally Schangs in the United States. We have them, but they are in the minority. We need men who can come back from a triumph at any world's series of life's endeavor and, with laurels bedecking their brows, revert to the plough and the potato field.

—*Buffalo Sunday Morning News*, October 26, 1913

"The catcher is the jockey. The pitcher is the horse. A good horse will lose with a bad rider. The catcher must not let the pitcher lose his courage, confidence, control."

—Wally Schang

JOE KUHEL, 1B
2104 G, 1930–47
.277/.359/.406 (104 OPS+), 30.2 WAR

In 1940, White Sox first baseman Kuhel had what looks like a very typical season for a first baseman, hitting .280 with 27 home runs in 155 games. It's an amazing season in its way, because Kuhel, who appeared in 18 major-league seasons, hit about a fifth of his career homers in that season alone. Kuhel rarely had a chance to show off his power because he spent his entire career playing in two tough hitter's parks: Griffith Stadium in Washington and Comiskey Park in Chicago. During the latter's long existence only seven players hit more than 16 home runs at the ballpark in a single season: Zeke Bonura, Gus Zernial, Al Smith, Bill Melton, Dick Allen, Ron Kittle (twice), and Carlton Fisk (twice).

Griffith, which hosted the original Senators from 1911 through their departure for Minnesota after the 1960 season, was even harder on power hitters. Before the foul poles were pulled in between the 1953 and '54 seasons (the left-field line dropped from 405 feet to 388 and right from 328 to 320), no Senator had hit more than 22 home runs in a season, overall, and only one, the unfairly maligned Bonura again, hit more than seven homers in the park in a single season. In the seven seasons the team remained in Washington after the alteration, Bonura's 11 home runs at home in 1938 were tied or exceeded 11 times, with Roy Sievers hitting 26 home runs there in 1957.

Kuhel (pronounced "cool") was born too soon to take advantage of those reduced dimensions. He had two stints with the Senators (1930–37 and 1944–46) with his White Sox phase in between. He hit 56 home runs in 1,205 games in Washington drag and 75 in 899 games with Chicago. With the Nats, he hit .284/.363/.392 with 16 home runs at home—tied for the most of any Senator from 1930 through '46—and .293/.365/.432 with 40 home runs everywhere else.

Having been purchased by the normally-abstemious Senators from the Kansas City Blues for $65,000, Kuhel took over the Senators' first-base job from Joe Judge. Judge had had the job since 1916 and was pushed aside in '31 only because he was sidelined by appendicitis. Except for Kuhel's six years with the White Sox (what we might call the Zeke Bonura Interregnum—Kuhel and Bonura were traded for each other in March 1938), the Senators had nigh statistically-identical first basemen named Joe for most of 30 years. You could tell them apart because Kuhel was the Joe who did card tricks. "If I am a better first baseman now than when I joined Washington late in 1931," Kuhel said in 1932, "it is because of Joe Judge. Not only have I learned by watching him, but Joe is such a great fellow he took me in hand and coached me."

Like many Clark Griffith–era players, Kuhel was reacquired after Griffith regretted sending him away and subsequently got to manage the team. Whereas the Senators were still a good team when Kuhel was a player, by the time he got to run the club (1948–49) they were irredeemably broken. He took over for former Senators third baseman Ossie Bluege and was replaced by former Senators second baseman Bucky Harris.

◆

Charles Schulz's Snoopy first appeared on October 4, 1950, but he would not manifest his collegiate Joe Cool aspect (the gods have many guises) until May 12, 1971: "Here's Joe Cool hanging around the student union…. Joe Cool can't worry about chemistry when he's hanging around the student union." Whereas the Joe Kuhel model of first baseman is largely extinct, the Joe Cool model of college student, whose goal is less to get an education than to spend four years making the scene, is still alive and well. For some "students," that has long been the purpose of college. As Christopher R. Browning wrote in *The New York Review of Books* regarding the "anti-democratic, anti-middle-class, anti-capitalist, anti-modernist, and anti-Semitic" German nobility of the years before the Great War(s), "The university was a place to experience dueling, drinking, fraternities, and masculine rituals, not to attain an education in the sense of knowledge and expertise." *Those* Joe Cools disproportionately went into the officer corps. Our Joe Cools run for Congress.

◆

Major league writers say that Kuhel stuck at first base because he knew how to shift his feet, one of the most important assets of a good first baseman. Lots of first basemen can hit. Only a few can use their feet around the bag while fielding and receiving throws.

—*The Atlanta Constitution*, May 21, 1931

SKI MELILLO, 2B
1377 G, 1926-37
.260/.306/.340 (64 OPS+), -1.0 WAR

Oscar Melillo was a very light-hitting Browns gloveman whose fielding prowess kept him in the lineup for a decade. By one measure, he was the worst hitter in the history of his position:

	WORST-HITTING SECOND BASEMEN (1000 G MIN.)						
Rk	Player	Years	G	BA	OBP	SLG	OPS+
1	Oscar Melillo	1926-37	1,377	.260	.306	.340	64
2	Sandy Alomar	1964-78	1,481	.245	.290	.288	69
3	Gary Sutherland	1966-78	1,031	.243	.291	.308	70
4	Billy Gardner	1954-63	1,034	.237	.292	.327	70
5	Jackie Hayes	1927-40	1,091	.265	.318	.344	70
6	José Lind	1987-95	1,044	.254	.295	.316	70
7	Mark Lemke	1988-98	1,069	.246	.317	.324	71
8	Julio Cruz	1977-86	1,156	.237	.321	.299	71
9	Hughie Critz	1924-34	1,478	.268	.303	.352	74
10	Jimmy Bloodworth	1937-51	1,002	.248	.292	.358	75

Many contemporaneous reports about Melillo acknowledged that he couldn't hit but tried to hand him a fig leaf by talking about how dangerous he was in the clutch. It's always hard to know what is meant by this, but whether one looks at Melillo's performance with runners in scoring position or in "late and close" situations, his performances were largely indistinguishable from what he did the rest of the time. There were outlier seasons—for example, in 1929 he hit .374 with runners in scoring position—but these fleeting variations represent luck more than skill.

It is arguable that his glove should have persuaded anyone to let him play as much as he did. In the old days, by which we could mean any time from the stone age to about 2000, Very Serious Baseball men could say of such players, "Sure, he doesn't hit, but he saves 100 runs a year with his glove." It should have been obvious then—by dint of very basic mathematics or just simple observation—that there aren't enough balls distributed around the playing field for that to be true. It was *closer* to true in eras when batters made more contact, but it still was nothing like 100 runs. Contrast him with

Frankie Frisch, who was playing in St. Louis for the Cardinals at the same time Melillo was with the Browns. Per Baseball-Reference, Frisch had the best defensive season of his career in 1927, saving 37 runs more than the average player. He also hit .337/.387/.472, making him 23 runs above average at the plate. Melillo's best defensive season came in 1929, when he saved 15 runs more than the average player would have. He also had one of his best offensive seasons, hitting .296/.337/.401. It looks like a decent performance, but the average AL player hit .284/.349/.407 that year, so Melillo, below average in the ways that mattered, was 10 runs below average with the bat. He had given back two-thirds of what he had achieved with his glove. In most years, the contrast was more stark. In 1934, he saved five runs above average but was -46 runs at the plate, having hit .241/.279/.297. No matter how good your glove is, it's almost impossible to post a 45 OPS+, as Melillo did that season, and still contribute to the winning effort.

He did that for the Browns, so possibly no one cared (they averaged 1,500 spectators a game). That said, Melillo, called "a Napoleonic figure in defensive warfare today" in his rookie year, by *The Philadelphia Inquirer*'s James Isaminger, did things in the field that sometimes cut through the universal Brownie apathy and got him noticed: In 1929, he turned a triple play against the Senators, (the pitcher deflected the ball, so it was not unassisted, but Melillo made all the putouts himself). In 1930, he made 572 assists, breaking an AL record set by Nap Lajoie (Melillo's record still stands), and, in 1933, he made just seven errors in 130 games for a .991 fielding percentage, also a record (since surpassed many times). The latter two achievements are perhaps functions of, respectively, the sheer number of balls put in play against the Browns in a high-offense year and generous scoring, but he was a good fielder. "It is unfortunate that he is not a better batter," mourned *The Sporting News* in 1933, "for if he were he would rank as the outstanding all-around second baseman of the game."

> The two men who have robbed me of more hits than any other pair are that spinach fiend Melillo and that little [Rabbit] Warstler. Those two devils play short right field for me and have thrown me out on many a legitimate base-hit. There ought to be a law against it.
>
> —Babe Ruth

In addition to "Ski," inspired by Melillo's appreciation for International Harvester company-team football player Frank "Ski" Fiske, Melillo's baseball nickname was "Spinach." He earned this because he was, at least for a while, obsessive about eating the stuff. This may have been exaggerated, and, at least early on, he pushed back against the story from which it derived. Melillo fell ill in early August of his rookie season and was initially reported to be suffering from a bad case of tonsilitis. Three months in the hospital ensued. In reality, he had been diagnosed with Bright's disease (today referred to as nephritis), or failing kidneys. Upon his release, he was reported to have been cured, which is not something that happened to people with Bright's disease. *The St. Louis Star* noted that Bright's disease, "in cases where older patients are concerned, usually proves fatal. But Melillo's youth saved him and made his cure possible." Tell that to Giants outfielder Ross Youngs, who died of Bright's disease at the age of 30 the following August.

Despite his supposed cure, Melillo struggled to stay in the lineup over the next couple of seasons as the aftereffects of his illness wore on him. "There is no assurance that Melillo will be of much value," *The Sporting News* reported in March of 1927. "He is following a strict diet and does not look bad externally, but it is not easy to say he is equipped internally to stand the rigors of a major league season." He barely played in spring training and then went a worrisome 1-for-21 (.048) in the first six games of the season.

Melillo had been told to go vegetarian, or more accurately, spinach-with-the-odd-serving-of-carrots-etarian:

> They told me I'd have to eat nothing but spinach for the next few months if I wanted to live. I tried to talk them into letting me have a steak, spaghetti, ravioli or goulash once in a while, but they said nothing doing.
>
> When I told them I couldn't stand the monotony of spinach three times a day, they told me I could have some variety by boiling it for breakfast, making a salad of it for lunch and baking it for dinner.
>
> **—Ski Melillo**

Melillo was able to play only 107 games in 1927 and just 51 in 1928, but played more or less every day beginning in 1929. The diet got the credit for his recovery.

> Late in March of this year, Bill Killefer, manager of the Browns, was seen walking back to his hotel in West Palm Beach. He stopped at a vegetable market and purchased two bunches of carrots.
>
> "Why those, Bill? Do you feed 'em to your automobile?"
>
> "No, they're for Melillo. I'll take them out to the ball field and he will make his luncheon on them."
>
> "Is he as much a vegetarian as that?"
>
> "Nope, that's his fodder. He's on carrots and spinach—carrots raw—and he can get as much out of a bunch of carrots in his diet as I can get out of an orange."
>
> —*Worcester Evening Gazette*, June 9, 1931

Melillo pushed back on the notion that rabbit food was responsible for his newfound endurance. "Don't spill that spinach yarn. I didn't get a lot of base hits on one Eastern trip because I ate a lot of spinach," he said after an uncharacteristically hot streak at bat in 1931. "That's a lot of bologney [*sic*]. I guess I had the right bats, that's all." That same year, he confessed to *The Milwaukee Journal* that, "I hate the damned stuff. It's poison to me out of those hotel cans. I haven't touched spinach in two weeks." The *Journal* clarified that Melillo, "sticks strictly to home brew turned out by Mrs. Melillo in her St. Louis kitchen." Given the muddy glop that is canned spinach, one could hardly blame him. "Say, I knock off the biggest breakfast on the club," he added. The only items he *didn't* consume at breakfast, he said, were eggs—and spinach. The real point was not so much the spinach but what today we would call lifestyle improvement. "I just stored away the vegetables—mostly spinach," he said in 1938, "ate no fried foods, quit smoking and chewing and did what I thought best for my health." Like most of us, despite the benefits dieting brought him, he wasn't having any fun. "I hated it worse than to pop out to the catcher," Melillo said, "but I determined to learn to like it."

Melillo's SABR biography, written by Bill Nowlin, speculates that Melillo's spinach habit might have influenced *Thimble Theater* comic strip creator Elzie "E. C." Segar to make the leafy vegetable the source of strength of his character Popeye the Sailor Man. It almost certainly did not. It is true that Popeye first appeared in Segar's strip roughly 18 months after Melillo's spinach diet was first publicized, but the character didn't begin his long association with spinach for more than two years after. More to the point, Popeye's reliance on the canned stuff so despised by Melillo was an artifact of the long, repetitive series of Popeye theatrical cartoons initiated by the Fleischer Studios in 1933 (six years after Melillo's spinach consumption was a sports-page novelty), not Segar's strip.

Segar's Popeye did advocate for children to consume spinach, but he didn't make constant recourse to it. From the outset, the character's appeal and source of humor was his preternatural strength and indestructability, no green stuff required. As Jules Feiffer wrote, "The daily and Sunday newspaper strip Popeye was perfectly capable of winning fights without strength-enhancing, vegi-based steroids." That wasn't what the strip was about, in any case; the focus was on character-driven comedic adventure, not formulaic repetition. As newspaper-comics historian Bill Blackbeard wrote, "Segar was only interested in gimmicks when they offered story or gag possibilities, and spinach was a dead end." That doesn't rule out Melillo as an inspiration, but to default to him ignores the broader cultural moment.

From the beginning of the century, America was understood to be in the midst of a nutrition crisis generally and a childhood nutrition crisis specifically. Prior to the 1910s, the concept of vitamins did not exist. It took biochemists like Elmer McCollum to discover and proselytize for them before Americans began to realize there was a direct correlation between what they ate and how they felt. Greens, heretofore dismissed as "cow food," took on a sudden importance. "The United States Food Administration began distributing literature to American schools, encouraging the consumption of milk and leaves of plants and other vegetative products in 1918," wrote Richard Pillsbury in *No Foreign Food: The American Diet in Time and Place*, "even though the actual amounts needed for good nutrition were not known." Americans learned the idea of "protective foods,"—foods that warded off illness. Prior to the 1920s, very little spinach was grown in the United States. Then McCollum endorsed it as a protective food, and suddenly it was on everyone's table. Thus, by the time both Melillo and Popeye were promoting it, "the social norm surrounding the nutritional value of spinach did not have to be restated." That is, everyone had already heard about it and had an understanding of its supposed properties.

Thus, spinach was having a moment. On December 8, 1928, *The New Yorker* published a single-panel cartoon drawn by Carl Rose and captioned by E. B. White. It depicted a mother and daughter at table; the mother says of the items on the child's plate, "It's broccoli, dear." The recalcitrant child replies, "I say it's spinach, and I say the hell with it." To the extent something could go viral in the late 1920s, this expression did and became part of the American vernacular. As late as 1932, Irving Berlin wrote a hit song musicalizing the words. Thus, when Segar's Popeye shrugged off bullets, knife-wounds, and poison and credited spinach, it was primarily satire in the form of mockery of a popular fad.

Segar subsequently transformed comedy into advocacy. Popeye was very popular with children, and Segar seems to have tried to reach them. On February 28, 1932, Popeye receives a strength upgrade after consuming a heaping bowl of spinach—one of the only times this happened during the Segar years—and the strip concludes with an open letter to parents:

> "Notice to the Mothers of Chil'ren: Please tell yer youngstirs I said they should eat spinch an' vegetables on account of I wants 'em to be strong an' helthy—I will be persnal fren of all chil'ren who eats what their maw says to eat. Yers trulie, Popeye."

By then the United States was plummeting towards the nadir of the Great Depression. A great many children were malnourished, and there were harrowing scenes of both adults and children crawling over piles of newly deposited refuse at city dumps looking for edible scraps.

> In 1933 the Children's Bureau [part of the federal government] reported that one out of every five children in the nation was not getting enough of the right things to eat. A teacher in a coal-mining town asked a little girl in her classroom whether she was ill. The child said: "No. I'm all right. I'm just hungry." The teacher urged her to go home and eat something. The girl said: "I can't. This is my sister's day to eat."

In that sense, Segar's well-intentioned imprecations to mothers and sportswriters' concurrent celebration of Melillo's miraculous spinach cure were ill-timed. Baseball provided Melillo with employment through the Great Depression and after. Segar's art had made him wealthy. It's well and good to popularize "an odious" vegetable, as a syndicated obituary for Segar put it, but only if people can afford to buy it. Similarly, a cure for a serious disease has no utility if you can't afford to obtain it.

People liked Melillo enough that, after retirement, he spent 13 years coaching in the majors with the Browns, Cleveland, the Red Sox, and A's. The last three assignments came courtesy of Lou Boudreau, who took Melillo wherever he went. From 1938 to '40, the Indians were managed by a hypercritical guy named Ossie Vitt. (Like Melillo, his real name was Oscar.) At midseason, a faction of Cleveland players decided they had had enough verbal lambasting and went to management demanding a change. The general manager, a seemingly eternal baseball man named Cy Slapnicka, tried to cow them into backing down, saying that if the story became public they would all be humiliated. It did, and they were; Cleveland finished a game out that year, and the loss was blamed on the "Cry-Baby" portion of the team. Nevertheless, when the season was over, Vitt was fired for losing the clubhouse. Melillo was one of his coaches and resigned in protest. A year later, Boudreau became player-manager and brought Melillo back. "I hired Ski Melillo not only for his immense knowledge of baseball," he said, "but also for that quality of loyalty." Melillo was still there, six years later, when Cleveland won its last World Series to date.

"Children are often slow to learn and intellectually simple because they have not eaten the right kind of breakfast."

—**Ad campaign for Cream of Wheat hot cereal,** 1920s.

"I hate myskeries on account of I kin not understan' 'em."

—**Popeye,** ad for E.C. Segar's *Thimble Theater,* June 8, 1932

ART DEVLIN, 3B
1313 G, 1904-13
.269/.364/.338 (109 OPS+), 36.1 WAR

John McGraw managed the New York Giants for 29 full seasons plus fractional bookend seasons in 1902 and '32. As you know, he remains among the most successful managers of all time, winning 10 pennants and three World Series over that long run. Devlin was the starting third baseman on his first two pennant winners (1904 and '05) and is emblematic of the way he built rosters. While he had stars, most of them (with a couple of notable exceptions) were of the lower-magnitude variety or shone only transiently. Devlin was one of those.

In an era before the farm system became the primary supplier of new talent to a major-league team (and limited a team to the minor-league talent under its immediate control, as opposed to allowing its scouts to range over the free minors as a whole), McGraw maintained a restless acquisitiveness and a confidence in his own eye for talent that allowed him to find what players he needed as he needed them, get what he wanted out of them, and repeat the process when it was time to move on. Devlin was playing at Newark when he impressed McGraw during an exhibition against the Giants; the manager signed him then and there. That was not unusual for him.

McGraw's willingness to take talent when and where he found it allowed him to take a holistic approach to the roster. While he did have some true stars in the nearly three decades he ran the Giants—Christy Mathewson, Frankie Frisch, and Mel Ott among them—the depth and breadth of his rosters was more impressive than their peaks; if he had been a king in the 1200s, he would have built walls instead of towers. Decades after the manager had passed, Frisch would make a point of packing the Hall of Fame with the better players from McGraw's 1920s teams, but, in doing so, he demonstrated a misapprehension about what made those teams great. Here's a quick rundown of McGraw's top players, by position (300 or more games played, in rough order of playing time):

C: Chief Meyers, Frank Snyder, Shanty Hogan, Roger Bresnahan, Frank Bowerman, Bob O'Farrell, Earl Smith

1B: George Kelly, Fred Merkle, Bill Terry, Dan McGann

2B: Larry Doyle, Frankie Frisch, Billy Gilbert

3B: Art Devlin, Freddie Lindstrom, Heinie Groh, Heinie Zimmerman, Frankie Frisch

SS: Art Fletcher, Travis Jackson, Bill Dahlen, Dave Bancroft, Al Bridwell

LF: George Burns, Irish Meusel, Sam Mertes, Josh Devore, Freddy Leach, Spike Shannon

CF: Fred Snodgrass, Benny Kauff, Cy Seymour, Edd Roush, Roger Bresnahan, Mike Donlin

RF: Ross Youngs, Red Murray, Mel Ott, George Browne, Dave Robertson, Mike Donlin

There are 10 Hall of Famers in there, but they're mostly the sentimental Frisch-picks, not the true (pardon the expression) giants of the period. The rest remain obscure, even as they went to the afterlife with many championship rings (or the equivalent). Consider the McGraw years from the perspective of Wins Above Replacement:

McGraw's Best Position Players (1903-32)						
Rk	Player	WAR	Rk	Player	WAR
1	Larry Doyle	42.7	11	Freddie Lindstrom	23.3
2	Art Fletcher	42.3	12	Dave Bancroft	22.9
3	Bill Terry	39.9	13	George Kelly	22.8
4	Travis Jackson	38.7	14	Chief Meyers	21.6
5	Frankie Frisch	38.8	15	Al Bridwell	15.1
6	George Burns	36.4	16	Dan McGann	14.9
7	Art Devlin	33.9	17	Bill Dahlen	14.6
8	Ross Youngs	32.7	18	Benny Kauff	14.5
9	Mel Ott	32.2	19	Fred Merkle	13.9
10	Roger Bresnahan	27.8	20	Mike Donlin	13.7

We can gain one insight into McGraw's strategic vision at the top of the left-hand column: Four of the top five players are middle infielders. First basemen like High Pockets Kelly were good rather than great, but McGraw balanced that off with above-average production at positions that were usually sacrificed to defense. None of these were bad players, not even Kelly, who is often cited as one of the weakest of the Frisch Famers (both can be true), but they were also not the Trouts of their time (Ott was closer, but this table doesn't fairly capture him as he was only 23 when McGraw stepped down). With the exception of one fraught season with Rogers Hornsby and the late-arriving

Ott, he didn't have the stars of the period, but had lesser players who could, for brief periods, play like stars for him.

We can do the same thing with pitchers, McGraw had one certified God of the Game in Christy Mathewson (like Ott, Carl Hubbell had his best years under Bill Terry) but most of the rest were bricolage:

MCGRAW'S BEST PITCHERS (1903-32)						
Rk	Player	WAR		Rk	Player	WAR
1	Christy Mathewson	88.2		11	Art Nehf	11.9
2	Iron Man McGinnity	30.0		12	Jesse Barnes	11.0
3	Hooks Wiltse	27.3		13	Jack Scott	10.3
4	Jeff Tesreau	22.6		14	Virgil Barnes	10.2
5	Carl Hubbell	21.9		15	Larry Benton	10.0
6	Red Ames	18.5		16	Luther Taylor	9.7
7	Rube Marquard	17.0		17	Hugh McQuillan	8.2
8	Freddie Fitzsimmons	16.4		18	Doc Crandall	8.1
9	Fred Toney	12.2		19	Pol Perritt	7.8
10	Bill Walker	11.9		20	Rube Benton	6.8

Stats were less important to McGraw than being good at every position. That's why he took so many chances on players who were flawed, whether in on-field or off-the-field ways.

A native of Washington, DC, Devlin played baseball and football at Georgetown. He was a fullback due to his good size and speed. You can see that speed in his stats. Not many third basemen have been prolific basestealers, even in the Deadball Era. Devlin was one of the few. He led the National League with 59 steals in 1905 (tying with Cubs outfielder Billy Maloney). That stands as the second-highest total by a third baseman of all time (Fritz Maisel stole 74 for the Yankees in 1914). Devlin's career total of 285 steals is second all-time among third baseman to Hans Lobert's 316 (the postwar leader is Carney Lansford with 224).

Quickness on the bases and in the field was Devlin's main skill. For example, on May 23, 1908, he tied the record for most clean chances accepted by a third baseman in one game when he fielded 13 balls. He also made two errors in the game, which the Giants lost to the Cardinals 6–2. "Heavy hitting by the Cardinals and stupid fielding by the Giants" accounted for the loss, said the *New York Tribune*. Adding injury to insult, Devlin was badly spiked on the hand by Cardinals right fielder John Barry, and the game was stopped for 15 minutes while he was bandaged. Sometimes a record just isn't worth it. Then again, both of his errors came after he was spiked, and neither was decisive, so maybe we should cut his ghost some slack.

On June 23, 1910, the Giants visited the Dodgers. Devlin was heckled throughout by a group in the boxes. "You yellow dog," they shouted. During the change of sides, as the Giants took the field for the top of the seventh, one Philip Schmidt continued to shout abuse at Devlin, daring him to come fight. He did. Schmidt got the worst of the altercation, while Devlin was fined $50 and suspended for a week. Schmidt wanted to press charges, but nothing came of that.

Devlin had a short career. He had very little power even by the standards of his day, and when, at midseason 1911, McGraw "found that his legs would not stand big league championship speed"—that is, Devlin was slowing down—the manager benched him in favor of Buck Herzog. Devlin was sold to the Braves the following spring. If he was losing his speed, there would have been little reason to play him, and it's telling that in 1912 the Braves often played him at first base in deference to the now-forgotten Ed McDonald. They sold Devlin down to the minors in late August 1913, ending his major league career. Devlin went off to Fordham, coached a young Frankie Frisch, and recommended him to McGraw, who listened.

Devlin sounds as if he were a bit on the annoying side. He wouldn't have been the only player in history to be ruled by superstitions, but, according to Mathewson, he would hit you if you hummed in the dugout, could only sit in certain places therein, and once had to be benched because he had been jinxed by a cross-eyed woman in the stands.

> "Mac," he said one night in the club-house, "it's that jinx. Have you noticed her? She sits behind the bag every day, and she has got me going. She has sure slid the casters under me. I wish we

could bar her out, poison her, or shoot her, or chloroform her, or kill her in some nice, mild way because if it isn't done this League is going to lose a ball-player. How can you expect a guy to play with that overlooking him every afternoon?"

—**Christy Mathewson**, *Pitching in a Pinch*

◆

Who was the greatest third baseman in Giants history, New York or San Francisco? The answer may still be Devlin. Baseball-Reference has it as Matt Williams with 34.1 WAR, Devlin with 33.9. WAR is not literal but an approximation, and the fraction of a point separating the two is well within the margin of error.

◆

"I'll tell you one queer turn in my work at third.... I played against Hans Wagner for ten years in more than two hundred games, and in all that time he never tried to bunt against me. Yet I had to watch him all the time, fearing he would cross me. One day I guessed wrong. I was sure he was going to bunt; I saw him start the motion and I rushed in. He hit one through me so fast I haven't seen it yet. After that I decided to let him beat out a bunt before I came in again, but he never put one down my way, although he is a fine bunter."

—**Art Devlin**, April 1916

◆

Arthur Devlin suffered a strange fate. On August 25 [1913], the Boston third baseman made a ninth-inning hit to beat Pittsburgh, and that night was released to Rochester for George Davis, a pitcher. "I wonder where they would have sent me if I'd struck out instead of making a hit—Medicine Hat?" mused Devlin.

—**Harold Kaese**, *The Boston Braves*

CECIL TRAVIS, SS
1328 G, 1933-41, '45-47
.314/.370/.416 (108 OPS+), 30.3 WAR

One reason the designation "Hall of Famer" is so inadequate is that it can't account for players like Travis, greats derailed by an externality, in his case World War II. That didn't make him any less great—arguably it makes him greater—it just means that the voters penalized him for his service to his country.

Travis, who came up with the Washington Senators just as they were about to go into their long, fatal decline, was the kind of high-contact, high-average, line-drive hitter that is mostly extinct. He came up young, at just 19, and although he was capable of hitting .300 from day one—literally; he went 5-for-7 in his major-league debut—it took him a while to become an above-average run-producer. One of the very small, infinitesimal tragedies of the Second World War was that Travis was peaking just as his career was, for all intents and purposes, ended by Germany. He turned 26 in 1940 and hit .322/.381/.445 (120 OPS+) then followed that with an MVP-level season in 1941, hitting .359/.410/.520 with a league-leading 218 hits. He got some notice for that, but all the attention justly went to those DiMaggio and Williams fellows. Then the war came.

Like most major leaguers in the service, Travis initially played ball for Uncle Sam, but he saw combat during the cold, post–Battle of the Bulge winter of 1944–45 and suffered frostbite on two toes. Absent from the majors from September '41 to September '45, Travis couldn't get going again after his return; he hit only .241/.307/.302 in 226 postwar games. "I'm not so sure Cecil Travis doesn't belong in the Hall of Fame," Ted Williams said in 1994. "He was just as good a hitter as John Olerud is today, only he did it longer. But in World War II, he got frozen feet and his career went boom."

Travis always disputed the frozen-foot thesis of his postwar struggles. To him, it was just the lost time and the added age. "You didn't have to be off but just a hair," he told Dave Kindred, "and you couldn't play." Interviewed in 2000, he said, "There are a lot of players with records as good or better than mine who are not in [the Hall]. I just don't think it would look right.... Now, if I had several seasons like 1941, it might be different. But the war came along, and when I got back, it was gone." There's no way of knowing if Travis would have had anymore 1941s on his baseball card had fascism not reared its genocidal head. We can't know if he would have suffered a career-ending injury on the first day of the 1942 season. We can only hypothesize that he would have had more than 2,000 hits and continued to hit over .300. He gave up those achievements for his country. That would seem to be more than enough for recognition, but numbers outweigh valor in the minds of Hall voters.

> The black fans came to see the best of the Senators, Travis, square off against the best of black baseball, [Satchel] Paige and the Grays. Travis won the initial showdown. In the second inning, he ripped Paige's slow curveball up the middle for a single.... In his final duel with Travis, Paige gave Washington's late-arriving fans a thrill.... The Senators star worked the count to three balls and one strike. Paige threw an inside fastball. Travis swung and missed. Paige threw another inside fastball, this one higher and more inside. Travis swung and missed again. Paige had struck him out.... By striking out Travis, Paige refuted any notions of inferiority and gave people hope that the integration of baseball...was not far off.
>
> —**Brad Snyder**, *Beyond the Shadow of the Senators*

CHUCK HINTON, OF/UT
1353 G, 1961–71
.264/.332/.412 (109 OPS+), 13.6 WAR

Hinton was a Ben Zobrist, but, since that concept didn't exist during his career he was undervalued. Being a Zobrist in a pre-Zobrist era was kind of like being Liberace in the 1950s. Sure, everything about Liberace's deportment shouts out his sexuality to us *now*, but during an era when there were no out gay men in the media, it simply didn't occur to a significant portion of the public that he could be anything other than an eccentric straight man. Similarly, before baseball men fully accepted the value of the all-around player who could stretch one roster spot, a Hinton was a player who needed to be nailed down to one position. As with many things in life, first you have to imagine the concept, then accept it, and only then can you see it.

Hinton got a late start on his pro career, not signing with the Orioles until he was 22, then was further delayed by a two-year hitch in the Army. He started out as a catcher but was moved to the outfield because he was too fast and athletic to waste behind the plate. By the time he got to play, he was 25 and a man among boys (a career .346/.441/.554 hitter in the minors). The Orioles liked him, didn't know what to do with him, and ultimately didn't protect him in the 1960 expansion draft. They nosed it about that he was injured, but, despite the rumor, the Washington Senators took him with the 44th pick (he fell between Faye Throneberry and a 36-year-old Ted Kluszewski). An afterthought, he spent the first month of the Senators' inaugural season in the minors, again tore up the pea patch, and was finally called up.

For five years, beginning in 1962, Hinton was a versatile regular, hitting .275/.343/.434 (116 OPS+), stealing 97 bases, appearing at every position except pitcher and catcher, and starting games everywhere but shortstop and behind the plate. That doesn't give the whole picture, because injuries damaged his final numbers in more than one season. On September 5, 1963, he was hitting .280/.348/.447. In the top of the third inning that day, he was hit just above the right ear by Ralph Terry of the Yankees. "The ball hit Hinton's head with a sickening thud," *The Evening Star* reported. "He went down but did not lose consciousness. The ball bounced back to the mound and the helmet flew halfway to the dugout." He was carried off on a stretcher and hospitalized with a concussion. He came back only eight games later—despite a buzzing in his ears that he was still talking about late the following *January*—and went 4-for-38 through the end of the season.

"It hurt!" Hinton told author James R. Hartley. "I probably shouldn't have played the rest of the season. In fact, when I started to play, I was sort of seeing double." Almost a year later, in late July 1964, he was hitting .291/.354/.451 when he was hit on the left hand by Cleveland's Gary Bell. Despite his hand being too sore to grip a bat, Hinton persevered through the pain, never sitting for long enough to heal. He hit a powerless .222 over the remaining third of the season.

Hinton made the All-Star team in 1964 but never received the acclaim he might have had he made his way to a playoff team. Sadly, when the Senators dealt him away in December 1964—because he, "simply wasn't [manager Gil] Hodges' type of ballplayer" —they sent him to Cleveland, a team that had seemingly tendered its resignation to the league. He played at a high level for another couple of seasons, and then age started to work its dark magic. He had strong pinch-hitting seasons in 1969 and '70, but he was no longer the player who provoked *The Evening Star* to mourn the loss of "a fleet outfielder with almost unlimited potential" when the Senators traded him away.

Hinton seems like he was a smart, self-aware man, funny but also serious and community-minded. After Cleveland stashed him on the bench to begin the 1966 season, he said, "Then everybody got hurt and so they let me play. And isn't the world wonderful today?" From July 5 to August 6, 1966, he hit .315/.387/.613 with eight home runs in 30 games, but he only hit 12 home runs total that year, including none in September. There was something in the man's bat that was allergic to autumn; he was a career .239/.319/.350 hitter in September, though his many late-season injuries no doubt played a part in setting that pattern.

> I hit so many homers in July it scared me. I only average about 15 a year, and there it was…eight in one month. I was thinking about Babe Ruth's record, but then I came to my senses. I mean, after all, I got such a late start. I guess I'll have to wait until next year to catch Ruth.
>
> —Chuck Hinton.

During the offseasons, he stayed in Washington and worked with children. "I got into the…well, I guess you'd call them ghettos, and find a bunch of kids doing nothing. Then I try to organize them. We meet once or twice a week and play baseball or do something constructive. Now, these kids are… well, people everybody is a little afraid of. Tough. You know the type. It's hard to get through to them. You have to work at it." After retiring, he coached baseball at Howard University for 28 years and founded the Major League Baseball Players Alumni Association, a charitable organization through which former players can "promote the game of baseball, raise money for charity, inspire and educate youth through positive sport images and protect the dignity of the game through former players." It currently boasts more than 8,600 members.

HI MYERS, OF
1310 G, 1909, '11, '14-25
.281/.312/.378 (96 OPS+), 8.8 WAR

Myers is one of countless players who might have reached the Hall of Fame had they been able to bottle whatever it was that allowed them to play well for just a season or two at a time. He had a long career spent mostly with the Dodgers, and, for all but two years, he was a fringe regular with a fourth-outfielder's profile, hovering between being a platoon player and a starter. The exception came from 1919 to '20, when he was 30 and 31. In the former season, he hit .307/.339/.436 (130 OPS+) and led the NL in triples (14), RBI (73—the season had been shortened due to the Great War), and slugging percentage. In the latter year, he hit .304/.345/.462 (127 OPS+) and again led the league in triples (22). Although he had a couple of .300 seasons in the years after that, they were hollow, reflecting the inflationary offensive times rather than true productivity on his part. His gap power was gone, and he was such a hacker that he only drew 20 walks in a good season. A .300 batting average is never a bad thing, but if it's a player's entire offensive contribution it won't get you too far.

"Hi Myers—an outfielder who used to play 'em off the wall," teammate Casey Stengel remembered. "He never let a fellow start an inning with a triple." That defensive ability kept Myers in the lineup for years before and after his brief peak. He was one of the few Dodgers prior to 1941 who could say he played in two World Series for the team, starting in center for both of Uncle Robbie's World Series losers (1916 and '20).

Myers was a key part of one of the great postseason ballgames in 1916, the kind we will never see duplicated in our own time. The Dodgers drew the Red Sox as their opponent in that year's World Series. On October 9, Game 2 was played at Braves Field in Boston (the Red Sox, who had just moved into Fenway Park four years earlier, wanted to play in the higher-capacity NL park). The game was to be a battle of southpaws: Sherry Smith started for Brooklyn, and the 21-year-old Babe Ruth pitched for Boston. Myers batted third. With two outs in the top of the first, Myers drove a 1–0 "outshoot on the end of his bat for a home run to right-center. It might have been only a triple, but [right fielder Harry] Hooper was not fast enough in his effort to back up [center fielder Tillie] Walker, and the ball got clean away."

That was the first run the Dodgers scored and, though the game went 14 innings, also the last. Ruth and Smith went the whole way, with Myers helping out in the pastures. "His fielding twice saved the day for Brooklyn," according to a wire report, "once in the sixth, when he dived head foremost after a line drive off Hooper's bat and snared it, and again in the ninth, when he captured [first baseman Dick] Hoblitzel's fly after a hard run. He whipped it to the plate while still running, nailing [second baseman Hal] Janvrin, who was trying to score after the catch." Despite Myers' efforts, Boston won the game, 2–1, and the Series in five.

In 1923, Branch Rickey, then with the Cardinals, traded first baseman Jacques Fournier to the Dodgers in return for Myers. This was a spectacularly bad trade—Fournier was a clunky glove redeemed by a great bat—but it did give Rickey a story he enjoyed telling after-dinner audiences for the rest of his life. It seems that the Cardinals were playing an exhibition game in an unfenced field. A batter hit a long drive to the outfield, and Myers faded back, back, back…and since there was no fence, there was nothing to block Myers or definitively turn the fly into a home run. Gravity would eventually get involved, but this was apparently a very powerful clout, and it was taking its time plunging back to earth. Myers continued his retreat, and Rickey, while admiring his effort, was starting to wish he would just let it go already. At that point, the ball descended, and, as it did, it struck a tree and rebounded hard into Myers' mitt. Myers whirled and threw home just in time to catch the runner at the plate. And so, Rickey concluded, one should never give up, because you never know about trees—or something like that.

There is another story about Myers that sounds a little too elaborate to be true, but, if it is true, it demonstrates the lengths to which players had to go to cadge a few extra bucks from the team owners prior to the advent of agents and the Players Association. The spring after the 1916 World Series, Myers held out. As with most players of the period, he had no leverage, so he made some up. He had some stationary printed bearing the legend, "MYERS' STOCK FARM," and wrote Dodgers owner Charlie Ebbets that he was doing so well raising animals that, if the Dodgers didn't up their offer, he'd be happy to stay home. This was a lie. As a sitcom might have had it, had such a thing existed at the time, Ebbets was so impressed with Myers' enterprising spirit that he decided to head out to Ohio to see this livestock operation in action. Myers then had to beg, borrow, or steal every sheep, cow, horse, duck, and possibly alpaca in the county so that Ebbets didn't catch him out. Ebbets appeared, was duly impressed with Myers' menagerie, and gave him his raise. Myers subsequently returned all the animals, but it would be nice to think that he held on to the alpaca, he and it having become too attached to each other during their brief association to endure parting. In fact, it should be a rule that every fourth outfielder with an above-average glove and light bat gets to have a comfort animal.

TOMMY HOLMES, OF
1320 G, 1942-52
.302/.366/.432, 36.5 WAR

So much of our lives are determined by chance interactions with others, or the lack thereof. We can do much to influence our own destinies, but we can't control the opinions of other people, or who does or doesn't take an interest in our progress. Tommy Holmes grew up in the Borough Park section of Brooklyn, not terribly far from Ebbets Field. He was a known prospect as an amateur, posting .600 batting averages in high school. He never broke any store windows with his hitting, said his neighbors, "for the simple reason that Tommy used to hit 'em over the stores and out onto Bay Parkway.... He had the motorists proceeding with caution as they drove by the ballpark when he was playing." Nevertheless, the Dodgers, Holmes said, "never did show much interest." Possibly they looked at his dimensions—he was only 5-foot-10 and was frequently described as "chunky"—and decided he lacked the physique of an impact player. But like later Braves outfield great Henry Aaron, Holmes had strong wrists; Casey Stengel, who gave Holmes his first chance in the majors, called him, "the greatest wrist hitter since Paul Waner." As it turned out, Waner would have a role to play in Holmes' career, too. So much of life is who you run into.

Yankees scouting great Paul Krichell was more avid to sign Holmes than the Dodgers were. So, having already passed up a scholarship to Duke University in favor of semi-pro ball, Holmes began his professional career in the New York organization. He hit well from the start. Had the Dodgers felt differently about him and taken him into their more fluid, more talent-hungry organization, he might have been playing for Leo Durocher as of 1939 or '40. As a Yankee, he made it to the International League and came to a dead stop, his path blocked by Charlie Keller, Tommy Henrich, and Joe DiMaggio. And so there he sat, getting to know Newark, New Jersey, far better than anyone should.

During his five-year sojourn in minor-league flannels, Holmes' approach at the plate underwent a transformation that would later need to be undone so that he might have his greatest major-league season. A left-handed hitter, his initial approach was to try to pull the ball for home runs. His first minor-league manager, former major-league first baseman Johnny Neun, discouraged that. Neun was Holmes' manager all the way up the Yankees ladder and kept reinforcing the lesson. "Johnny watched my batting average wilt to

.185," Holmes said, "and I saw finally that I was doing myself and my club a lot of harm trying to kill the pitch. So I took to meeting the ball and my average started climbing again." Ironically, his improvement, which resulted from an up-the-middle approach, gave the Yankees further reason to bury him—manager Joe McCarthy preferred his left-handed hitters be able to take advantage of Yankee Stadium's short right-field porch.

As of the early 1940s, George Weiss, the New York Yankees' farm director, and Casey Stengel, the manager of the Boston Bees/Braves, had been friends for nearly 20 years. With the Yankees still trying to find a long-term successor to Lou Gehrig at first base and the Braves still trying to find *anybody* after bottoming out in 1935, the two pals helped each other out. On December 9, 1941, the Yankees dealt Holmes to the Braves for two players to be named: first baseman and former Yankees farmhand Buddy Hassett and oft-injured outfielder Gene Moore. There are a number of counterfactuals invited by the trade. There's a fascinating alternate history in which, as soon as Lou Gehrig got sick, the Yankees moved Henrich to first base (he would play there on and off in the future, but they never really committed to it) and brought Holmes up to plug the resultant hole in the outfield. There's also the question of the attack on Pearl Harbor, which had occurred two days before the trade. Did the Yankees (meaning Weiss and general manager Ed Barrow) not understand the implications of a world war for baseball? In short order, all three of their great outfielders would be wearing other uniforms, while Holmes, who was married and had a young daughter, played on.

Holmes went into center field for the 1942 Braves, replacing the aged Johnny Cooney, one of his childhood favorites from the Dodgers (Cooney's improbable major-league career spanned 23 years). His right-field wingman was Paul Waner, 39. Waner began to tutor Holmes on his philosophy of shooting the ball down the foul lines. To that point, Holmes tended to bunch his hits in the center of the field. "The Phils apparently had heard that Holmes seldom hits the ball down either foul line," the *Boston Herald*'s Arthur Sampson observed in early April. "They bunched their outfielders close together leaving wide open spaces behind the first and third base men." That was still the case that September, when the *Boston Traveler*'s John Drohan noted of a game against the Cubs that "Tommy got all [three of] his hits 'right through the box.'" That would soon change.

Holmes hit only .274 with little power his first two seasons, but, in 1944, he commenced a five-season run of hitting over .300 with more robust production.

Now, yet another outside force exerted itself over him: The bankrupt Braves were sold, and the new owners, looking to drive attendance, brought in the right-field fence from 340 feet to 320 in April 1943. Suddenly, what had been a very difficult park to homer in became quite giving. The change didn't affect Holmes' power output right away, perhaps because the wartime balata ball suppressed home runs. When the possibility of power was restored with the return of the standard ball, Holmes was ready to meet it with a change of philosophy, which he described to *The Sporting News* in May 1945:

> This may sound a little odd, but I think I'm hitting better this year because I spent most of the 1943 season learning to pull the ball to right field. I probably sacrificed 50 batting points in the process, but I think the method is paying off. I used to hit a lot of line drives at the left fielder, who wouldn't have to move, and I thought I was just hitting in tough luck. But one day Casey Stengel…said to me: "You're not hitting in tough luck. They're pitching to you and you're hitting the ball right where they want you to. Now what you've got to do is help yourself by learning to pull the ball, and they won't know how to play you or how to pitch to you."

That season, the old Dodgers first baseman Del Bissonnette was coaching with the Braves. He gave Holmes an ancient yellow bat, hardened with age, that had once belonged to Johnny Frederick, an outfielder who had played for Brooklyn during Holmes' youth. Bissonnette had kept it in his attic since 1928. Holmes adopted the 34-ounce model as his own, "raving" about its "quality of wood, seasoning, and balance." "The wood's as hard as steel," Bissonnette said, "so I don't think it'll ever break." It did, but not until after it had helped put Holmes in the history books.

Now it all came together: Holmes' innate skill and new open-mindedness, Waner's and Stengel's lessons, the right bat, the shortened fence. The result was a season almost unprecedented in Boston Braves history: Holmes hit .352/.420/.577, led the league in doubles (47), and home runs (28), and struck out only nine times. (For his career, Holmes struck out once every 41 at-bats, the fifth-best rate among modern players.) He was the first (and still only) hitter ever to lead simultaneously in most home runs and fewest strikeouts (among qualified batters). He also set a modern NL record with a 37-game hitting streak. The streak, which began on June 6 with Holmes going 10-for-21 over a two-day doubleheader orgy, ended on July 12, just a few days after the "ironwood" bat finally broke. When Pete Rose surpassed the streak in 1978, Holmes was there to shake his hand.

\multicolumn{8}{c}{TOP OFFENSIVE SEASONS IN BOSTON BRAVES HISTORY}							
Rk	Player	Year	Pos	WAR	BA	OBP	SLG	OPS+
1	Rogers Hornsby	1928	2B	8.9	.387	.498	.632	202
2	Tommy Holmes	1945	OF	8.4	.352	.420	.577	175
3	Jimmy Collins	1898	3B	6.9	.328	.377	.479	140
4	Wally Berger	1933	OF	6.9	.313	.365	.566	172
5	Hugh Duffy	1894	OF	6.8	.440	.502	.694	173
6	Bob Elliott	1947	3B	6.5	.317	.410	.517	147
7	Sid Gordon	1950	OF	6.3	.304	.403	.557	156
8	Bob Elliott	1948	3B	6.3	.283	.423	.474	143
9	Dan Brouthers	1889	1B	6.2	.373	.462	.507	165
10	Ezra Sutton	1884	3B	6.2	.346	.384	.455	165

Holmes should have been the National League MVP that year, but he lost to Chicago's first baseman Phil Cavarretta, who edged Holmes for the batting title by .003 during a pennant-winning effort—the Braves, as was their wont during this listless period, went 67–85. One would think Holmes' breakthrough would have led to other chances at the major awards, especially with the club's rapid improvement after the war. In actuality, he didn't have a lot of time left. "My own inclination is to keep swinging for the fences," he said during spring training 1946, but the owners had second thoughts about the right-field fence and pushed it out again. Holmes never again hit more than nine home runs in a season. He was also ebbing physically and, by 1949, had slipped into a part-time role. "How much Holmes will play this season is problematical," Bob Holbrook wrote in 1950, when Holmes was 33. "The speed is gone.... The arm is gone.... All that's left of Tommy Holmes is a 'seeing eye' bat and a burning desire to win."

> "To be sure, in recent seasons he has been maligned on occasion for his poor throwing. One player made the statement this Winter that opposing team players were fined automatically if they didn't go from first to third on a single to [Holmes]."

—*The Boston Globe*, 1950

Holmes played briefly for his hometown club in 1952, and managed the Braves almost as briefly after Billy Southworth burnt out. He finished up his baseball career with more than 20 years as a community-relations director with the Mets, running a youth sandlot program he had initiated. It was an appropriate end for a player who was so relatable. "'Never took a drink in his life and never smoked,' said Lou Grottola, proprietor of the grille on Holmes' [Brooklyn] corner. 'And yet he was always one of the most regular guys you'd ever want to meet.'"

Holmes was probably the Braves' second-best player (after Wally Berger) of the long down period which lasted roughly from 1917 through 1945, and he was easily the most beloved. Al Hirshberg devoted an entire chapter to Holmes' popularity in his 1948 book, *The Braves: The Pick and the Shovel*, describing how he fended off several potential position changes and challenges to his starting position because, once he had moved to right field, the Braves' bleacherites would make life pure hell for any player who played there in his stead. When Southworth tried to switch Holmes, who had a notoriously weak arm, to left field and play new acquisition Johnny Barrett in right, "Fifteen hundred indignant fans rose in angry wrath.... they peppered [Barrett] with bleating invective...boos and insults which became louder each inning.... It was too much for Barrett. 'I'll never go out there again' he remarked." He did, but not for another three weeks, and then only once.

> That Brooklyn-born Irishman has made most of the public forget all about Ted Williams, Boston's last .400 slugger. Tommy never is too busy to halt and chat with his admirers. Williams generally regretted that he didn't have his favorite bat to hold them off.
>
> —*Springfield Republican*, July 6, 1945

DUTCH LEONARD, RHP
640 G, 1933-36, '38-53
191-181, 3.25 ERA (119 ERA+), 48.9 WAR

This is Emil, the second Dutch Leonard. The first was Hub, the Deadball-Era pitcher with the 0.96 ERA in 1914 (memorably referred to as "Dutch the Accuser" by Bill James for his role in the 1926 Ty Cobb–Tris Speaker scandal). Emil is the more interesting of the two in that he provokes questions about destiny, causality, and the way chance works for and against our plans. Leonard, a first-generation American, was not unlike today's immigrant players from the Dominican Republic; whereas they can either succeed in baseball or risk poverty, Leonard's choice was baseball or the coal mines.

He had to confront that danger at least three times: First, because Leonard was working his way up during the Great Depression, he had his minor league fold under him and became a man without a team. He regrouped, hooked on again, and pitched his way to the majors with a super-miserable, bankrupt Dodgers team that only survived on the largesse of the other National League owners and the local bank. A rookie in 1934, Leonard was used as a swing man by manager Casey Stengel (also a rookie) and went 14–11 with 5 saves and a 3.28 ERA (119 ERA+). The next several years were frustrating because (a) Leonard was a knuckleball pitcher and no one wanted to deal with that, and (b) he had arm problems. Leonard wound up back in the minor leagues. He made it back up in 1938 with the Washington Senators, and that was when his career finally began in earnest. He was 29. He ended up staying in the big leagues until he was 44.

The Senators were a strange team willing to try anything to avoid spending money, and so they not only picked up Leonard but kept adding knuckleballers. This climaxed in 1944, when Leonard headed up a rotation that also included Roger Wolff, Mickey Haefner, and Johnny Niggeling, all of whom threw the fluttering ball. The team went 64–90. Leonard had terrific control, walking few batters and keeping the ball in the park. In the late 1940s, particularly during a two-year stint with the Phillies, he was as good as any pitcher in baseball, posting a 2.60 ERA in 460 ⅔ innings. The Phillies traded him to the Cubs just as they were getting good, and, but for 1945, when the Senators finished 1 ½ games behind the Tigers, he never did come particularly close to pitching in the postseason. It's easy to imagine a version of Leonard's career in which he landed with the Yankees and was now in the Hall of Fame. In fact, let's try a little experiment:

Pitcher	Years	Record	ERA (ERA+)	FIP	IP	SO	Pennants	WAR Peak	WAR Career
Leonard	1933–53	191–181	3.25 (119)	3.34	3,218.1	1,170	0	6.7	51.7
Brand X	1930–43	189–102	3.34 (125)	3.88	2,503	1,468	7	9.2	43.1

Brand X is Lefty Gomez. The point here isn't that Leonard was better, or that Gomez was unjustly enshrined, or even that Leonard should be in (that's irrelevant to everyone but the player's family, should any still be living), but rather that he was quite good and that, with some cosmetic differences, he might be better remembered.

Chapter Ten

IT'S COMPLICATED

Some of them were very good, some very bad, but all of them caused consternation.

SPUD DAVIS, C
1458 G, 1928-41, '44-45
.308/.369/.420 (110 OPS+), 22.4 WAR

A catcher can be one of the best hitters ever at his position and still be totally forgotten. It might have helped Virgil Davis if the good teams hadn't made a habit of trading him away. He spent most of his career with a carefully managed workload, sharing his team's backstopping chores with another player. Keep that in mind when you evaluate the following statement: Davis hit .300 in seven consecutive seasons. From 1929–35 he hit .327/.382/.472, which was inarguably good, but here come the caveats: (1) He did it in only 799 games, or about 114 per season; (2) it was a time in which .300 averages came more cheaply than they do today; (3) he played for the Phillies for five of those seven seasons, which meant his numbers were boosted by the Baker Bowl (he hit .372 at home, .296 on the road); (4) "the big, bald-pated catcher" was not considered to be a good glove.

Davis came up with the Cardinals in 1928 under defense-minded manager Bill McKechnie and general manager Branch Rickey. That same season, Davis was dealt to the Phillies for Jimmie Wilson, more of a traditional catch-and-throw receiver. In 1933, the two teams reversed the trade (McKechnie was long gone by then), and Davis got to be part of the Gashouse Gang championship team of 1934, although manager Frankie Frisch had young Bill DeLancey do all the postseason catching. In the winter of 1936, the Cardinals sold Davis to the Reds despite DeLancey having developed serious health problems that kept him out of baseball. McKechnie took over the Reds in 1938, and soon Davis was on the move again, this time going back to Philadelphia as part of the package for Bucky Walters, who would become the Reds' ace.

Despite repeatedly being deemed dispensable, Davis was special in his way. He hit .300 in 10 different seasons, although you have to define a "season" as anything between 103 and 540 PAs for that to be true. Even granted that liberal definition, not many catchers have done it:

Rk	Player	Years
1	Bill Dickey	11
t2	Ivan Rodriguez	10
t2	Ernie Lombardi	10
t2	*Spud Davis*	10
t5	Mike Piazza	9
t5	Mickey Cochrane	9
t7	Mike Redmond	6
t7	Jason Kendall	6
t7	Don Slaught	6
t7	Ted Simmons	6
t7	Walker Cooper	6
t7	Gabby Hartnett	6
t7	Bubbles Hargrave	6

CATCHERS WITH MOST SEASONS HITTING .300 OR BETTER: (100 PA MIN.)

According to John Skipper's *Baseball Nicknames*, Davis was called "Spud" because, as a kid, his preferred food was potatoes. The carbo-loading would put him at risk for excessive avoirdupois as a player.

> If you don't win, you don't make the money in the majors. Fancy batting averages don't get you the money unless they help a club

to win ballgames. I know ballplayers hitting less than .260 with winning clubs that get more money than players hitting better than .300 with losing clubs. It is hard for a ballplayer to live down the reputation of loafing or not seeming to care when his team is losing. Ballplayers have to hustle, not on one play but on every play, to hold their jobs in the majors. Scouts are looking for aggressive players. I don't mean rowdy ballplayers. They are passing out of the picture. What I mean by a fighting player is one giving his best efforts every minute, hustling to beat out a hit, taking that extra base on the outfielder and going for a base with the full intention of keeping it. We have been hearing a lot about minor league players from the scouts, complaining they see very few hustling players. My advice to any player is to hustle. Managers will overlook a lot of faults if the players convince them they are trying to win. No hustling ballclub is ever going to look bad in defeat.

—**Spud Davis,** *The Birmingham News,* July 10, 1941

Retrade Winds
For Jimmy Wilson
The Phillies gave us
A former Redbird,
Virgil Davis.

But neither one
Will be downhearted;
They're going back
From where they started.

As major stars
They both are graded.
The trouble is
They won't stay traded!

—**Leo Davis,** *St. Louis Post-Dispatch,* November 17, 1933

RUDY YORK, 1B
1603 G, 1934, '37-48
.275/.362/.483 (123 OPS+), 31.7 WAR

York came up as a catcher (sort of). Like later players such as Brian Downing, Carlos Delgado, Josh Willingham, Carlos Santana, and Kyle Schwarber, it's tempting to wonder how history would have ranked him had he been considered adept enough to remain behind the plate. In York's case, it isn't a straightforward evaluation, because he got in his own way and shortened his career through dissipation. This was a problem throughout his life.

As they did with Danny MacFayden's glasses, writers of the day felt a compulsion to mention that York was part Cherokee; he was fortunate to get through life without ending up as "Chief" York in the encyclopedias. See, for example, Furman Bisher's column, "The Cherokee Has No Regrets." Actually, Bisher called him "Chief," too.

We can't say for sure who would have won any Rookie of the Year award in the many seasons prior to its institution, but York would have had a very good case in 1937. He played 104 games that year, hit .307/.375/.651 (151 OPS+), and set a record with 18 homers in August alone (he slugged .920 on the month). That was the record for any month until Sammy Sosa hit 20 in June 1998, and it's still the record for August, though York now shares it with Giancarlo Stanton. York never surpassed the 35 home runs he hit that year, but he had other seasons in which he hit just as well. When a rookie takes off like that, people notice. "That DiMaggio boy sure looks like a natural to become the No. 1 hitter in the game," said Babe Ruth, "but you can't overlook that young Tigers catcher, Rudy York."

Defense was a different story, one of malpractice by York's coaches. Whether he was an amateur, a minor leaguer, or a major leaguer, his managers could never decide where to play him. He cycled through six positions in the minors. During spring training 1936, the Tigers auditioned him at third base, sent him down to Milwaukee to play first base, and, in 1937, returned him to the majors and used him as a catcher. Part of the indecisiveness resulted from congestion: The Tigers had future Hall of Famers installed at catcher and first base in Mickey Cochrane and Hank Greenberg. York hit .334 with 37 home runs for Milwaukee in 1936 and won the American Association MVP award. Most teams would have happily made room for him. For the Tigers, it wasn't so simple. Eventually, they incentivized Greenberg (with $10,000) to move to left field so York could play first (the opposite was also tried, but

York protested he was "liable to get killed out there" by a fly ball). Forever after, York's position was blamed on his inadequacies—one racist detractor (an almost obligatory presence in the sports media of the 1930s) said he was "half-Indian, half-first baseman"—rather than on long years of bad coaching and a roster crunch.

> Rudy had good cause to be peeved because this year he was a better first baseman than Greenberg was the first year he came up.... The big difference between Rudy and Hank is ambition. Hank had it to the nth power. Rudy would like to succeed. But he is not so concerned about his future as Hank was in 1933.
>
> —**Detroit newspaper,** 1936, quoted in *Famous American Athletes of Today (1939)*

York's teammates tended to remember two things about him: He could hit ("He studied pitchers, spotted giveaways, was uncanny in outguessing the opposing batteries," said Bobby Doerr), and he could drink. York had a habit of getting drunk, lighting a cigarette, and lying down in bed. If he woke up before the hand holding the butt dropped to the bed, great. If he didn't, there was a fire. He roomed with Charlie Gehringer for a while. In *Cobb Would Have Caught It*, he remembered, "I don't know how many mattresses he burned up. We always said he led the league in burned mattresses. I finally moved in with someone else. I wanted a little better chance of getting out in case he burned the hotel down." Late in life, York worked fighting forest fires; maybe he was making amends.

The mattress memories weren't just hyperbole. Here's an account of one such conflagration from *The Boston Globe* on April 27, 1947, when the A's were in town to play York's Red Sox:

> "My curtains were on fire," reported Rudy York, "I was fighting them with a pillow. The night clerk knocked on my door and hollered, 'Your rooms on fire.'" It was the only laugh Rudy got out of the fire which routed 100 guests in his Back Bay hotel about 3 am Saturday.... Rudy lost everything he had in the room.... [A's coach] Earl Mack was telling Rudy how he heard about the fire. 'The newsboys were yelling, "Rudy York's on fire!" Well, I was beginning to think it would be a good idea if we didn't show up today.'"

He was traded to the White Sox that June. An equal-opportunity arsonist, he once again generated fiery headlines that August: "RUDY YORK'S ROOM IN FLAMES AGAIN." This time he had left a lit cigarette in contact with the drapes.

In 1954, Bisher turned a series of interviews with York into the first-person "Letter to My Son" for *Sport*. Young Joe York was then trying to make it as a ballplayer, and the "Letter" contains advice that would still be valuable to any player today—not just, "Son, leave that liquor alone," but, "Don't be shortsighted. Remember there's a future after you're through playing ball. If you make a good name and a good reputation for yourself, you can always stay in baseball. There'll always be a good job as a manager, or a coach, or in some end of the game, for a fellow who conducts himself wisely while he's a player." After his retirement, he blew through his baseball earnings and, in the mid-'50s, when he was putting out fires instead of making them, was making $150 a month. A late stint as Red Sox hitting coach helped, but it didn't erase the pain of a life poorly thought out. "I've no regrets," he told Bisher, "except I wish I'd saved my money."

Any criticism of York seems beside the point. He grew up poor in Alabama and Georgia, his parents broke up, and he left school to work when he was in the third grade. That would have been circa 1920; that's what life was like in pre-safety-net America and could be like again. Having gone to work early to help make up for his father's desertion of his family, York found his way onto a mill team, and that saved him. "From that time on," he said long after his career was over, "all I ever knew was baseball, and I'm thankful for it, for baseball was my ticket out of the mill." We have too few such tickets today.

◆

On October 6, 1946, York was responsible for one of the few Red Sox highlights of that year's World Series. His long shot to left in Sportsman Park ("deep among the hot dogs and mustard in the left field concessions stands," wrote Red Smith) off of Cardinals pitcher Howie Pollet in the top of the 10th inning in Game 1—a measure of revenge given that, "Several times Pollet brought laughter from the crowd by tossing up a tantalizing change of pace that left Rudy all snarled up like a kitten in yarn"—gave the Red Sox the lead and eventually a 3–2 victory.

◆

"A hell of a player," recalls Johnny Pesky.... "We all respected his judgment. He never squawked on a pitcher. And if one of us had a question—was the pitch too high, too low, or whatever?—we'd go to Rudy for an opinion. 'John,' he'd say, 'I think it was all right.'"

GARY SUTHERLAND, 2B
1031 G, 1966-78
.243/.291/.308 (70 OPS+), -3.8 WAR

Sutherland was ubiquitous throughout the 1970s. He's an artifact of a miserable decade, like stagflation, gasoline rationing, Tony Orlando, Watergate, multi-purpose stadia, and…It occurs to me that, if I try to list all the miserable things that happened during the 1970s, we'll be here for a hundred pages, possibly 150. Suffice it to say that, even if one doesn't like disco, one can find enough good things in it to understand why many people did. If one doesn't like punk rock, one can find enough good things in it to understand why many people did. With Sutherland, you really had to be there.

Maybe all of baseball had been corrupted by the same malaise that gripped the country. As per Baseball-Reference, there have been only 10 players who have lasted at least 1,000 games with a WAR as far underwater as Sutherland's. Four of them played during the '70s. In reverse order:

Rk	Player	Pos	Years	G	Rates	WAR
10	Ken Reitz	3B	1972-82	1,344	.260/.290/.359	-3.1
9	Eddie Miksis	UT	1944-58	1,042	.236/.288/.322	-3.4
8	Myril Hoag	OF	1931-45	1,020	.271/.328/.364	-3.5
7	*Gary Sutherland*	2B	1966-78	1,031	.243/.291/.308	-3.8
6	Joe DeMaestri	SS	1951-61	1,121	.236/.274/.325	-4.0
5	Tommy Thevenow	SS	1924-38	1,229	.247/.285/.294	-5.3
4	Johnnie LeMaster	SS	1975-87	1,039	.222/.277/.289	-5.4
3	Juan Castro	IF	1995-2011	1,103	.229/.268/.327	-5.4
2	Dan Meyer	1B/LF	1974-85	1,118	.253/.293/.379	-6.4
1	Doug Flynn	2B	1975-85	1,309	.238/.266/.294	-6.9

In the wrong hands, Sutherland could be a suicide weapon. He spent much of his career batting second. From 1969–70, Expos manager Gene

Mauch gave him 91 starts in that spot. We can cut Mauch some slack given that the Expos were an expansion team (Sutherland had been Montréal's fourth pick in the 1968 expansion draft) and the second baseman wasn't yet a known quantity. There is no such excuse for Ralph Houk, who put him in the same slot every day for *two years* with the Tigers when Sutherland was already well-established.

Sutherland played more than 100 games in seven seasons. Just one of those seven teams had a winning record; two lost more than 100 games. "Sutherland makes the double play as well as anyone who ever played," said Tigers scout Jack Tighe, "and that includes Bill Mazeroski, Frankie Frisch, and all the rest." Tighe added that whatever Sutherland gave you with the bat would be a bonus. To the extent we can trust retroactive fielding stats, the evidence isn't there: Frisch was +140 fielding runs in his career, peaking at +37 in 1927; Maz was +147, peaking at +23 in '58 and '63; Sutherland was -53, peaking at…well, he didn't peak. Even if we defer to Tighe and the others who saw Sutherland and deemed him worthy of playing time, we still have to balance offense and defense: If a player is 20 runs above average on defense but 20 runs below average on offense, is one 20 somehow greater than the other 20? That was the argument for playing Sutherland and countless other glovemen throughout time. There was *no* argument for batting him at the top of the order.

RED SMITH, 3B
1117 G, 1911–19
.278/.353/.377 (119 OPS+), 27.0 WAR

Baseball subcategory: Players who went on a tear after being traded. Lou Brock '64 is the iconic example, but there are many others, including Doyle Alexander '87, David Justice 2000, and this fellow, James Carlisle "Red" Smith, who was dumped on the Braves by the Dodgers ("Robins," if you want to be historically accurate) on August 10, 1914, as the result of some sort of tiff with manager Wilbert Robinson—Uncle Robbie thought Smith was an "underminer." Boston got Smith—who went by J. Carlisle, not Red, in civilian life—for the waiver price of $1,500. "The deal came as a complete surprise, although it had been freely reported that Smith was to be benched because of [his sloppy play].… There have been rumors that Smith was flirting with the Federal League, but they have not been substantiated." Smith had hit .296/.358/.441 (125 OPS+) in 1913, but, in 90 games for the 1914 Dodgers, he hit only .245/.310/.361 (97). Freed of the generally jolly but hypercritical old Oriole Robbie, Smith sprang to life, hitting .314/.401/.449 (148) the rest of the way. The Miracle Braves had already begun their historic climb out of eighth place by the time he arrived, but they only got better once Smith joined the club and replaced Charlie Deal: 51–46 (.526) and six games out on the day of the trade, they went 43–13 (.768) the rest of the way and won the pennant, then the World Series.

Smith didn't get to participate in the October sweep of the A's. The Braves' season ended with a doubleheader back in Brooklyn. Attempting to leg out a potential opposite-field double in the top of the ninth, Smith slid late on "long and new spikes." His right foot stuck in the dirt, while the rest of his body kept going. Result: "Anterior dislocation of the ankle joint; right leg fracture of the fibula (small bone of the leg) three inches above the ankle joint; fracture of the tibia (large bone of the leg) near the external malleolus (knuckle of the fibula); rupture of external and lateral ligaments." Thus we are reminded of one of the best of Joe McCarthy's Ten Commandments of Baseball: "When you start to slide, slide. He who changes his mind may have to change a good leg for a bad one." Smith's injury was the inverse of that—if you're not going to slide, don't. He who changes his mind, etc. The ending of Smith's 1914 season shows how cruel the universe can be. For two months, he was Cinderella at the ball, but he didn't so much turn back into a pumpkin as he was crushed by one. So much for having the last laugh on Uncle Robbie.

Smith recovered and played well for several years, but, much as Robbie had done earlier, Braves manager George Stallings soured on him as soon as he slumped. On his way to a .245/.359/.282 season in 1919—not terrible by the standards of the deadball day—Smith was benched and subsequently sold at the waiver price. The Yankees bought him first. Manager Miller Huggins didn't want him but thought he could flip Smith to another team. That deal failed to come together, and the Yankees, too, put Smith on waivers. He was picked up by the Senators, but failed to catch on with them and ended up in the minors, playing his way back down from the PCL to the Southern Association to Peoria. It was never Smith's bat that was the true problem, but his capacity for errors, both of the defensive and interpersonal kind.

BILL DAHLEN, SS
2444 G, 1891–1911
.272/.358/.382 (110 OPS+), 75.2 WAR

"Bad Bill" presents a dilemma for those who defend the beauty-pageant Hall of Fame gallery as somehow essential to telling the story of baseball. Dahlen ranked among the great shortstops of his day. He was a terrific fielder who was also an above-average hitter. That's not something that became clear only in retrospect, it was apparent to observers at the time. One of John McGraw's first big moves after taking over the Giants was to trade two players and $6,000 to acquire the then-34-year-old shortstop from Brooklyn. McGraw would later say that Dahlen was the key to the Giants' pennant winners of 1904 and '05. No doubt the team's improvement had multiple causes, not all of which were attributable to Dahlen's presence, but the record shows why McGraw was so chuffed by the move: The Giants jumped from 84–55–3 with Charlie Babb at short to 106–47–5 in '04 and 105–48–2 in '05. They also went from turning 67 percent of balls in play into outs to 71 percent. The deal "gave me just what I wanted—a great defensive shortstop," McGraw said in *My Thirty Years in Baseball*. "There were mighty few better than Dahlen."

> Local baseball enthusiasts will be far from pleased to hear the latest deal which has been put through by Manager Hanlon of the Brooklyn Club, while their opinion of that gentleman will be apt to take a tumble. Hanlon has exchanged "Bad Bill" Dahlen, the idol of the Brooklyn club for Happy Jack Cronin, the pitcher, and Infielder Babb of the Giants.... While it is conceded that Babb will be a good addition to the local team...it is also certain that he cannot under any circumstances be better than Dahlen, who is without a peer in baseball as a shortstop, all things considered. This may not be shown in the "dope" sheets, but it can readily be seen in his play. The chances which he takes and the work which he can do cannot be duplicated by any man in the business to-day.
>
> —*The* (Brooklyn) *Standard Union*, December 14, 1903

Yet, Dahlen is without a plaque. His baseball card largely lacks blank ink (the 1904 NL RBI title is the sole exception), but a larger part of his exclusion is surely that his on-field career, which extended through 1913 as manager of the Dodgers, ended long before the Hall of Fame came into being. Even that explanation only goes so far: Dahlen, who lived until the end of 1950, was noted in Hall elections in both 1936 and '38, and any number of his contemporaries have been inducted since, including fellow shortstops Hughie Jennings (1945), Bobby Wallace ('53), and George Davis ('98). (Honus Wagner, whose career overlapped with Dahlen's, was one of the inaugural group at Cooperstown; he's in his own category.)

TOP SHORTSTOPS 1890-1910									
Rk	Player	WAR	Years	G	BA	OBP	SLG	OPS+	Fielding Runs
1	Honus Wagner	101.7	1897-1910	1,902	.344	.406	.492	163	60[1]
2	George Davis	84.9	1890-1909	2,372	.295	.362	.405	121	146[2]
3	Bill Dahlen	75.3	1891-1910	2,443	.272	.358	.382	110	139
4	Bobby Wallace	67.2	1894-1910	2,014	.274	.336	.371	111	129
5	Hughie Jennings	42.3	1891-1910	1,282	.312	.391	.406	118	60

The true reason may be inherent in that "Bad Bill" nickname and Dahlen's most incredible statistic: 70 ejections, 34 as a player, 36 as a manager. In *Pitching in a Pinch*, Christy Mathewson (or his ghostwriter) says that Dahlen would purposely provoke the umpires so he could get to the racetrack in time to place a wager. Mathewson specifically cited umpire Hank O'Day as someone from whom Dahlen could get a sure reaction. Unless Dahlen explained himself to Mathewson, this was hearsay: O'Day ejected Dahlen four times in his career, but never when Dahlen was with the Giants. That's not to say that Mathewson was wrong, but it opens up the possibility of exaggeration. Closer to our own time, Rickey Henderson was frequently accused of not wanting to play, and yet his actions belied his reputation: Henderson held on until he was 44 and would have kept going if anyone had let him; the man who didn't want to play currently stands fourth all time in games played. Similarly, Dahlen retired as the all-time leader in games played and still is 12th on the all-time list of games played at shortstop. There's something inherently contradictory in saying that a player who exhibited such sticktoitiveness was uncommitted.

That's not to say Dahlen wasn't a provocateur. On September 25, 1907, he had another player deliver flowers to Bill Klem at home plate in the midst of

---

1. Wagner didn't become a fulltime shortstop until 1903.

2. Davis played 529 games at third, 303 in the outfield, and 113 at second base.

Dahlen's at-bat. On April 20, 1912, when Dahlen was managing the Dodgers in a game at the Polo Grounds, Brooklyn took a 3–2 lead into the bottom of the ninth, at which point New York's Heinie Groh singled, and Art Wilson hit a shot down the line into the right-field grandstand for an apparent walk-off home run. As fans flooded onto the field, Dahlen charged out to argue to umpire Cy Rigler that the ball had gone foul. The reports of what happened next have a *Rashomon*-like variance, but, given Dahlen's reputation, the version reported by *The Brooklyn Citizen* seems credible: Dahlen "was within four feet of the umpire when the latter turned and, without a word, shot out his fist." *The Brooklyn Daily Eagle* put it similarly: "The perturbed Dahlen had no time to work his vocabulary up to the exploding point and was merely gesticulating and uttering general words of inquiry and condemnation when the aggrieved umpire struck him upon the right cheek." Dahlen hit back, of course, and, with fans already on the field, there was a near-riot. *The New York Times* summed Dahlen up nicely in 1912: "Keeping Bill Dahlen in the game is like trying to keep a sparrow in an open lot." That was just a few days before Rigler had punched him—Rigler had thumbed him out that day, as well, then pulled a watch out of his coat when Dahlen was slow to depart.

Rigler's threat of a delay-of-game forfeit was not idle. There was a memorable moment in 1901 when the Dodgers, trailing the Giants 7–6 in the bottom of the ninth, loaded the bases with two outs and Dahlen coming to bat. "'Bill can't do it,' yelled back a New York fan," according to *The Brooklyn Daily Times* account. "But Bill did do it. The memory of those old Chicago days, when he was the hardest hitting shortstop in the profession seemed to return to him and he squared himself off for a mighty effort." Dahlen "swat the ball a mighty lick" to left-center for an apparent two-run, game-winning single. Umpire O'Day ruled that the left fielder, Kip Selbach, had nailed Brooklyn's Tom Daly as he tried to go from first to third on the hit, recording the third out before the second run had scored. The inning was over, the second run taken off the scoreboard, and the two teams would play on tied 7–7. Dodgers first baseman and team captain Joe Kelley argued, threw his mitt, and was ejected; Dahlen threw himself to the ground and lay on his back as if in a faint. O'Day pulled out his watch, let the Dodgers argue for another two minutes, and then forfeited the game to the Giants.

Dahlen had broken into the majors with the Cubs (then called the Colts) under Cap Anson in 1891 and was later elected team captain. On the opposite end of his career, he scouted for the Dodgers and Giants. His approach to self-discipline was problematic for his teams, but it's also true that, upon trading him from the Dodgers to the Giants, manager Ned Hanlon said, "I've parted with Dahlen, and somehow I feel that I have just parted with half of my team," while McGraw said, "His ears go up when the bell rings and thereafter is always in the game until the last man has been retired." Dahlen's 70 ejections represent just two percent of the 3,055 games he played or managed in the majors.

So where is Dahlen's plaque? If he's not in due to his performance, that stance is impossible to defend. If he's not in due to his character, then voters are selectively editing history to conform to their expectations rather than the reality of the player and his time. If he's not in because a plaque is just a career-achievement award and there's no point in giving one of those to someone who has been dead since 1950, it just points up the hollowness of the whole enterprise. Regardless of the reason, the facts of Bill Dahlen are impervious to such small-minded concerns.

> "It has always been my ambition to play in New York City. Brooklyn is all right, but if you're not with the Giants you might as well be in Albany."
>
> **—Bill Dahlen,** 1904

> You used to be Bad Bill Dahlen
> In the old Chicago days:
> You used to lie on your back and cry
> When the "ump" decided plays.
> You used to jeer ant Cantillon
> And furrow Tim Hurst's broad brown,
> You used to be Bad Bill Dahlen,
> But you're Good Bill Dahlen now.
>
> **—From "To Bill Dahlen,"** William F. Kirk, 1911

My first time at bat we had a man on first and Dahlen gave me the bunt sign. The pitch wasn't good and I let it go by.... Hendrix threw another and I singled to right-center. When I got to the bench after the inning Dahlen stopped me. "Didn't you see the bunt sign?" he asked. I told him yes, but that down south we had the privilege of switching on the next pitch if we wanted to. "I don't want you to carry too much responsibility, kid," he said, "so I'll run the team and that way all you'll have to worry about is fielding and hitting." My ears were red when I got to center field.

—**Casey Stengel**, on reaching the majors with Dahlen's Dodgers.

"Now, Manager Dahlen," began the interviewer, "will you please tell us how you formed your team and how you consider its prospects?"

A jackknife closing up didn't have anything on the way Dahlen's jaws contracted. The manager forgot himself for a second when he said he didn't care to talk baseball and had nothing to say about his players.

—*The Evening World,* May 17, 1913

Towards the end of Stengel's rookie year a popular rumor had Dahlen not returning in 1914. A member of the press caught Dahlen leaving the ballpark after a game that September. "Well, Bill, I hear you're losing your job," the writer said.

"I dunno," Dahlen muttered, "but you ain't gonna get it, you slob."

—*Forging Genius*

RICO CARTY, OF
1651 G, 1963–79
.299/.369/.464 (132 OPS+), 32.7 WAR

One of the earliest stars out of the Dominican Republic, Carty came up with the Braves in 1963. Henry Aaron did *not* like the self-styled "Beeg Boy":

> The Braves were successful in maintaining good relations with the black community.... the fans had [outfielders] Mack Jones and Rico Carty. Jones was popular because he was a native of Atlanta and had his own radio show, and Carty because he craved it. Rico was always signing autographs and throwing baseballs to the kids and playing up to the reporters. The players saw a different side of Carty, but Atlanta loved him. And everything else aside, there's no denying he was a gifted hitter, although personally I had much more respect for the other Dominican on our team, Felipe Alou.
>
> —**Hank Aaron (with Lonnie Wheeler)**, *I Had a Hammer: The Hank Aaron Story*

Aaron raises a question about performative stardom versus actual stardom, or actual stardom for what is perceived to be impure motives. To get the negatives out of the way first, Carty was a poor defensive left fielder (as soon as the designated hitter came along, the Braves traded him to the Rangers, and he played about 650 of the last 700 games of his career sans glove), and he got hurt a lot, including missing all of 1968 due to tuberculosis and all of '71 because of a leg injury incurred when he collided with Matty Alou during winter ball. Carty also had more shoulder dislocations than one can easily count on their fingers. And, as Aaron makes abundantly clear, he tended to annoy people. He alienated a long list of managers, including Cleveland skipper Frank Robinson, whom Carty once ripped while speaking at a banquet in his own honor—with Robinson on the dais.

For all of that, Carty could be a masterly hitter. As a 24-year-old rookie in 1964, he hit .330/.388/.554 and finished second to Dick Allen in the Rookie of the Year balloting. He won the NL batting title in 1970, hitting .366/.454/.584 with 25 home runs. (He finished 10th in the MVP voting, well behind award winner Johnny Bench, which was fair.) Aaron thought even the high averages represented Carty's selfishness: "Carty was a big guy with plenty of power, but if he came up in the ninth inning with us down by a run, he'd be choking up on the bat trying to punch the ball to right field for a hit. Some of the guys on the team called him El-Chokee."

For his career, Carty hit .297 with runners in scoring position, .320 with men on, and .309 in late and close situations. In his big 1970 season, he slugged .645 late and close, and, for his career, he hit 24 home runs in 663 at-bats, or one every 27 times up—exactly the same as his overall career rate. How much more did Aaron want? More intriguingly, even if Aaron was right that Carty hit .317 (his Braves career average) and signed balls for selfish reasons, how is that *functionally* different from doing those things for the right reasons? A selfish .317 is still .317; a signed ball is still a gift to the fan.

Here's another thing Aaron said about Carty: "The strange thing about Carty was that he was as dark-skinned as any of us, but he didn't consider himself black and would go around calling the black players [the N-word] and other things." He and Aaron got into a fistfight over that.

Late on the night of August 21, 1971, Carty and his brother-in-law, one Carlos Ramirez, were driving in Atlanta when two white men pulled up next to them and said, "There're are some of those [N-words] who've been killing our policemen." Seeing a patrol car nearby, Carty pulled up and sought assistance from the policeman in it. The two white men also pulled up, and a fight ensued. Rather than aiding Carty and Ramirez, the cop called for backup and then joined the white men in the assault. Two off-duty plainclothes officers jumped in on the side of the racist agitators. Carty and Ramirez had the hell beat out of them and then were arrested on charges of "creating a turmoil and simple battery," while Ramirez, who had to be treated for scalp lacerations, was charged with "obstructing an officer."

Atlanta's mayor and police chief didn't politicize the incident at all. The former called it "blatant brutality," and the latter the "worst case of misconduct of a police officer I've ever seen." The charges were dropped, the three policemen were fired, and Carty, who worried that a punch that had blackened his eye would damage his vision, didn't suffer long-term harm. (A week later, someone set fire to Carty's barbecue restaurant. Coincidence? Maybe.) One wonders if—assuming Aaron's portrayal was accurate—Carty had a different perception of his place in the American racial hierarchy after that incident.

Carty was signed as a catcher. Actually, he was signed as a catcher, depending on the source, seven to 10 times, as he apparently put his signature to every contract put in front of him.

> Rico always played with his wallet in his back pocket. He didn't trust the valuables box in the dressing room, so he kept the wallet with him on the field and you could see the bulge. Besides, he

never slid, so it wasn't like something would happen to him on the field and his money would fall out.

—Duane Kuiper

◆

Carty was aided considerably during his hospital stay by fan response in the form of get-well cards and letters. Rico estimates he received 2,000 pieces of mail, over 100 per day. "That gives you a lot of determination," he said. "I am very grateful to the fans."

—*The Atlanta Constitution*, January 9, 1971

DUSTY COOKE, OF
608 G, 1930-36, '38
.280/.384/.416 (105 OPS+), 7.3 WAR

Cooke, Ben Chapman, and Dixie Walker were, at least briefly, teammates on the 1931 Yankees. Sixteen years later, they'd be the tip of the spear of the anti–Jackie Robinson cabal—Walker from within the Dodgers, Chapman and Cooke as Phillies manager and coach, respectively. One can only imagine what their conversations were like back in the 1930s, when *those people* knew their places. There's a 1974 Randy Newman song, "Rednecks," in which he imagines the thinking of the sort of people that Chapman (born in Tennessee, died in Alabama), Walker (born in Georgia, died in Alabama), and Cooke (born in North Carolina and ended there too) apparently were:

> We talk real funny down here
> We drink too much and we laugh too loud
> We're too dumb to make it in no Northern town
> And we're keepin' the [N-words] down

The song functions on two levels, both mocking the kind of racist who knows he lacks status but can still pat himself on the back because there's always this other group he can look down upon, and (subsequently) indicting northern liberals whose holier-than-thou attitude towards those same racists elides their own marginalization of blacks, which is just as severe despite its greater subtlety. We might call the latter set the Al Campanis group.

Chapman and Walker actually had status, in that they were highly accomplished major leaguers, but one suspects they felt exactly this way nonetheless, just by virtue of received culture. Cooke was a little different; he had the innate skills to play at Chapman and Walker's level but was derailed by injuries. Nonetheless, as a group, theirs was the kind of unthinking, pathetic racism that then dominated the South, the virulent version that said that, if a Black person was spotted in the local swimming pool, you had to drain the thing and sterilize it before it was fit for use by whites.

Cooke, "the big, grinning, good humored outfielder," first played in the affiliated minors in 1927 as a 20-year-old with the Durham Bulls of the Piedmont League. He hit .319 and slugged .563 on 32 doubles, 11 triples, and 15 home runs. He moved up to the Asheville Tourists of the Sally League the next year and hit .362 and slugged .611 on 30 doubles, 30 triples (!), and 13 home runs. Finally, he joined the St. Paul Saints of the American Association and hit .358/.458/.660 (on-base percentage is approximate due to the absence of hit-by-pitch numbers) with 39 doubles, 16 triples, and 33 home runs, scoring 153 runs and leading the league in RBI (148) and walks (105). This was a *prospect*. The Yankees signed him and brought him to the majors; he was the Opening Day right fielder in 1930, with Babe Ruth (who refused to play the sun field in any given ballpark) playing left on the road against the A's and Chapman at third.

A star wasn't born—Cooke had a cold start and slipped into a part-time role behind veteran Harry Rice and another youngster, Sammy Byrd. (Ruth and center fielder Earle Combs, weren't going anywhere.) The 1931 season brought another opportunity for Cooke to prove himself; this time he was the Opening Day left fielder (the game was at home, so Ruth was in right). On April 26, 1931, just 11 games into the season, Cooke was playing right field at Washington (Ruth was out with a leg injury). In the bottom of the third, Senators third baseman Ossie Bluege hit a sinking liner to right. Cooke dove after it. It was a rainy day, and the field was slick; Cooke missed the ball and landed on his head and right shoulder. Bluege circled the bases for a home run as Cooke "lay on the ground writhing." He had "displaced the outer end of his right collarbone and several ligaments were torn, but an x-ray showed no bones were broken."

Actually, his collarbone *was* broken, but it took almost a year to figure that out. "Yesterday, it was learned that there is a disturbing protuberance on his shoulder," the New York *Daily News* reported the following January. It's never a good thing when your doctor says you have a disturbing protuberance. One Dr. F. H. Albee grafted a ligament from Cooke's leg to his right shoulder. Cooke mended for roughly eight weeks, couldn't get back in the lineup when he returned, and was sent down to Newark. The game in which Cooke was hurt has gone down in history, not because of Cooke, but because Yankees shortstop Lyn Lary failed to touch home plate on a Lou Gehrig home run. Gehrig was called out for passing the runner and credited with a triple, thereby finishing in a tie with Ruth for the home-run title rather than winning it outright.

Cooke got one more chance in New York in 1932, though, even early in spring training, Yankees manager Joe McCarthy was saying, "Allen Cooke's arm is not right, and I may have to put him on the ineligible list." Cooke opened the season on the bench. As a measure of Cooke's intelligence, he reinjured his arm pitching batting practice before an exhibition game. Then he broke his leg in May, and that was his season. The broken leg was seemingly not reported at the time, and the way it has subsequently been described, as having been suffered while he substituted for Combs in some sense, doesn't seem to have happened, either. More likely, the primary cause for his extended absence was the damage done to his throwing arm at the exhibition game.

Cooke subsequently got a chance to play for the Red Sox and was serviceable, but no star. There had just been too much damage to his body, too much time off. Even away from the Yankees, he was subject to misadventure, spending time in a Cleveland hospital after being skulled by Oral Hildebrand, and, in 1936, dislocating his own knee during an over-enthusiastic stretching session. Thus thwarted, all that was left for Cooke to do was coach for Chapman's Phillies (he was first hired as the trainer following his World War II work as a pharmacist's mate) and join the manager in shouting racist invective at one of the greatest of American heroes.

On July 9, 1932, *New York Times* columnist John Kieran wrote a column about Cooke titled, "The Forgotten Man." The piece is full of painful parodies of Cooke's Southern accent: "Ah was doin' all right until we went to Cumbahland to plan an exhibition game.... Ah pitched in battin' practice and—blam!—Mah ahm is gone again." The reason Cooke was Kieran's forgotten man was that, "The big fellow is on what he calls the 'voluntarily retard list.'" Kieran meant to indicate a Scarlett O'Hara-like *retahd* to indicate "retired," and the unfortunate similarity to a slur of our own time is purely coincidental. What is more troubling, especially from a writer as knowledgeable and erudite as Kieran was, is his appropriation and cheapening of "forgotten man," a politically loaded term that had a specific meaning at that time.

On April 7, 1932, at the very beginning of his first term as president, Franklin Roosevelt gave a radio address in which he invoked, "the forgotten man at the bottom of the economic pyramid." His intention was to highlight those who had been economically devastated by the Great Depression but had yet to receive aid, and to suggest that a recovery should start with them rather than the banks, railroads, or industry. This was derided by his critics as demagoguery, but it happened to be an accurate diagnosis of the problem, which was—among many things—a crisis of overproduction and underconsumption. It was also humane, seeking to prioritize those who needed the most help the most urgently. Cooke was a bigot, and therefore the farthest thing from a forgotten man, an oppressor, not an underdog. Kieran was being far too cute. Then, and for many years after, the forgotten man was the player of color who Cooke wanted to keep out of a major leagues made only for people who looked like him.

MATTY MCINTYRE, OF
1072 G, 1901, '04–12
.269/.346/.343 (110 OPS+), 20.7 WAR

Many of us want to be remembered after we're gone, but will it be for something good or something bad? One theme of Stephen Sondheim and John Weidman's 1990 musical *Assassins* is that the debased souls who murder presidents are motivated less by politics than a desperate need to *become*. They are so shrunken and inadequate in their own lives that they can only satisfy their narcissism by killing someone who is their opposite in accomplishment. The sad thing is that it works.

McIntyre was a decent-enough player. In 1908, he was more than that, hitting .295/.392/.383 (149 OPS+), leading the AL in runs scored (105) and starting in left field and leading off for the pennant-winning Detroit Tigers. That's not why we remember him, though. He still exists, if he is called to mind at all, as Ty Cobb's antagonist. Cobb, a teenager when he joined the team and soon to be grieving the accidental murder of his father (yes, "accidental murder" is a contradiction in terms, but it's not clear how else to characterize what happened at this late date), was mercilessly harassed by McIntyre, who was about six years his senior. More than 100 years later, it's impossible to know if McIntyre's hazing was motivated by a first-generation Irish-American's dislike of a Southerner, if Cobb seemed like more of a target because he was so young, if McIntyre thought his job was threatened, or some combination thereof. What seems certain is that the hostility Cobb received over a period of years was more than that experienced by the typical rookie. "You have to look at the other side, too. We weren't cannibals or heathens," Cobb's frenemy Wahoo Sam Crawford said in *The Glory of Their Times*. "We were all ballplayers together, trying to get along. Every rookie gets a little hazing, but most of them just take it and laugh. Cobb took it the wrong way."

That was easy for Crawford to say; it's the language of the abuser, not the abused. Today, Crawford might have called Cobb a snowflake or those who would defend him "woke." In both cases, what is being derided is empathy. At the beginning of the twentieth century, as at the beginning of the twenty-first, a pernicious individualism animated a nervous class hegemon, whether veteran ballplayers Cobb might have put out of work (he could only displace one, but, as they couldn't know *which* one, he was a threat to all) or a predominantly white middle class whose economic status has become so shaky and hollow they cling on via "values," which is to say they cohere over the people they don't like. Thus does punching down become a virtue.

As long as baseball is allowed to operate as a meritocracy (that is, the best players play regardless of other considerations, be they racial or contractual) a wonderful Darwinian justice rules. By June of 1906, Cobb was hitting about .350 and McIntyre was hitting .267. Manager Bill Armour seems to have had an epiphany: Maybe his best young player shouldn't be pushed to the point of mental breakdown. McIntyre was suspended. "McIntyre is now posed as a deep dyed villain," wrote *The Washington Times*. "He has not been one of the bold noisy disturbers who can be heard for blocks, but a quiet schemer who talks words of discontent in a soft voice." The day McIntyre was suspended, Cobb went 3-for-4 with a walk.

> Matty McIntyre, erstwhile outfielder, is now appearing in a new role. He is the Horrible Example. Suspended by the club several days ago…it was officially announced yesterday that the suspension, instead of being merely indefinite, is to be indefinite and then a

little longer, if such trifling with English is permissible. In other words, the Detroit club will not use him, and will not let any other team do so. All offers to trade or purchase are respectfully declined, and McIntyre, drawing no stipend, is to be given a long think.

—*The Detroit Free Press*, June 26, 1906

McIntyre was eventually allowed to apologize to the team and was reinstated. Some sources suggest he and Cobb came to some sort of understanding, but, if Al Stump's ghosted bio is to be believed (a huge, honking *if*) the Peach still held a grudge 50 years later. McIntyre spent another four seasons with the Tigers but declined rapidly after his big '08 season and was sold to the White Sox in 1911. He played well for them, but slumped to open '12 and was trade down to Milwaukee of the American Association. He hung on in the minors until 1917, finishing as player-manager with Mobile of the Southern Association. There are stories that Cobb gave him financial support after that. McIntyre took ill in 1920, getting hit by the flu and then kidney disease, and died that April at the age of 40.

The 1908 Tigers outfield was very, *very* good. McIntyre had his career year, Cobb hit .324/.368/.476 (170 OPS+), and Crawford averaged .311/.355/.457 (160 OPS+). That's not how McIntyre survives in history, though; he comes down to us as someone who did his best to make someone else's life harder. Possibly, he even set the course for the rest of Cobb's life by taking a paranoid streak and justifying it—they really were out to get him. Numbers are just a record of your hits and outs and speak of character no more than the balance of your bank account; how you treat people is who you *are*, and it will define your memory forever.

PETE ROSE, OF/1B/3B/2B
3562 G, 1963–86
.303/.375/.409 (118 OPS+), 79.6 WAR

When Rose transgressed baseball's prime directive, "Thou shalt not bet on ballgames," it was hardly his only sin against the game. He was also guilty of a selfishness that motivated him to play long enough to eclipse Ty Cobb's record for total hits. Cobb's hit total is just a number, a big pile of things that are largely imaginary. Cobb had 4,189 hits, Rose 4,256. Where are they? Where can you find them? Hieronymus Bosch has been dead for more than 500 years and left behind just a few paintings, but we have more solid mementos of his career than we do of Rose's. If you've got some time and a plane ticket or two, you can go see them. You can see films of some fraction of Rose's hits, but they lose something with the subtraction of immediacy. There are select at-bats in a player's career that are special works—perhaps he fouled off 11 pitches before making a hit—and those linger impressionistically in the memory, but one cherishes the athletic *how* of the hit rather than the hit itself. Most of them are jejune in their execution and irrelevant even in context (Rose hit 538 singles with two outs and no one on, the "why'd ya even bother?" of base hits). Thus, you can't experience a hit for much longer than a quark lingers in a particle accelerator. And if you think it's just the pile that's an accomplishment, let's consider other transient events, such as meals, or orgasms. They weren't all equally accomplished. What matters is quality.

Rose was a very good player, and sometimes a great one, through the age of 40. He had only two true off-years in that span, one at 23, the other at 39, and, in the latter season, he was still close to being a league-average offensive player. He reached the big 4-0 in 1981. To that point, he'd already made 3,697 hits and scored 1,915 runs. His career rates were .310/.380/.426, which are good on the surface but get even better when you add in context—Rose played through the worst offensive era since the Deadball years. It was a lot. It could have been enough. Now, in fairness to Rose, his age-40 season was pretty good. He hit .325, so it's hard to blame him for failing to retire on the spot. There were clues, perhaps, such as his .368 slugging percentage from 1980–81; his power had vanished. No one wants to acknowledge a growing impotence, professional or otherwise. And so, he carried on with the Phillies, moved to the hapless Expos, and then back to Cincinnati (dealt there, pathetically, for Whitey Herzog's eventual perpetual 25th man, Tom Lawless), where he was made manager and allowed to write his own name into the lineup. Rose played 625 games in the years from 1982 through '86, hitting .261/.348/.315—as a first baseman.

Oddly, his nadir came in 1983, when he hit .245/.316/.286 (69 OPS+) for a Phillies team that went all the way to the World Series. In a soft year for the NL East, the Phillies didn't so much overcome Rose's –2.1 WAR as no one else bothered to show up. It also must be admitted that Rose hit .334 in the postseason (11-for-32). Phillies manager Paul Owens had benched Rose for Game 3 of the World Series after he went 1-for-8 in the first two games. It was a sensible thing to do given that he had given every impression of being done. Rose was deeply offended. "It's just not the way baseball is played, and this is the third game of the World Series," he said. Add this to the legend of Pete Rose: He pulled himself together, and, possibly fueled by resentment, went 4-for-7 after that.

The day Owens sat him, Rose sang paeans to the game. "Imagine getting $10,000 a day to do something you'd do anyway. It is like having a license to steal." He took that license all too literally in the ensuing years by writing his own name (and that of fellow geriatric ballplayers Dave Concepción and Tony Pérez) into the lineup at the expense of the younger players who would push the Reds into the World Series the moment he was banned. Eric Davis, he once said, was like having an atomic bomb sitting next to you in the dugout. It never occurred to him to ask why said A-bomb was sitting and not playing. Rose's Reds finished second in the NL West from 1985 through '88. His solipsism was a big reason why. *He* got an empty record. The fans got nothing.

PASCUAL PEREZ, RHP
207 G, 1980-85, '87-91
67-68, 3.44 ERA (110 ERA+), 18.9 WAR

Even more so than most players, Perez's stats don't remotely tell his story. It's hard to know where to begin, so let's just jump around a little. A native of the Dominican Republic, Perez was gangly and looked as if someone had put a uniform on the letter I and given it a fastball and an overbite. He came up with the Pittsburgh Pirates in 1980 and was traded after pitching just two games for them, possibly because he was too weird for a clubhouse in which everyone else was already on drugs—which is not to say that he wasn't on drugs, too. In 1984, he spent three months in a Dominican jail for cocaine possession. Baseball suspended him 35 games for that (later reduced to 27 games by an arbitrator). Perez's take: "Jail is no good. No more jail." He had a good fastball and a highly effective slider, but, every now and again, he lobbed an eephus, and he had no unwritten-rules hesitation about cheering for himself when he got a batter to miss. He burst on and off the mound at the start and end of innings, sometimes making it back to the dugout before the final out had been recorded. He had no consistency whatsoever and could spend half a season pitching like Cy Young and the other have pitching like Cy Schwartz.

Perez's 1989 season with Montréal was his career in miniature. He opened the season in the rotation and went 0–6 with a 4.97 ERA in nine starts (the league ERA that year was 3.49). Exiled to the bullpen for about three weeks, he returned to the rotation in June and finished the season pitching to a 2.54 ERA in 20 games (19 of them starts) covering 138 ⅓ innings. When the Yankees signed him that November, Expos manager Buck Rodgers called Perez "a sick man, and a time bomb that the Yankees will have to monitor closely. I wouldn't be surprised if he has a relapse, but I'd hate to see it. We never let him go anywhere on his own, even to the dentist, because he wouldn't be there. We checked him for drugs twice a week." He went 1–13 with a 6.14 ERA (62 ERA+) for the 1985 Braves amidst occasional disappearing acts. He stopped throwing his fastball that year, and because he was a man to whom communication was anathema, the Braves didn't know if he had an arm injury or had just decided to junk it.

The following spring, Perez impressed the Braves with his newly found dedication. "This is like getting a front-line pitcher without having to give away half your club," said general manager Bobby Cox. They released him two days later. He vanished for 10 months. He next appeared in the majors in August 1987. He failed a drug test in 1992, was suspended for a year, and that was the end of his career. He was brutally murdered by robbers in 2012; he was only 55 years old.

The number most associated with Perez is 285, the interstate beltway around Atlanta. Upon first joining the Braves, he tried to drive to the ballpark and couldn't figure out how to get there. He circled the city like a moth until he ran out of gas. This has been the source of much laughter over the years, but given Perez's other odd failures to appear, not all of which have been recounted here, it's possible that there was something more troubling behind his absence than a stranger on a strange highway.

ACKNOWLEDGEMENTS

Writing is a solitary exercise, but making a book requires collaboration. This one wouldn't exist without the inspiration and contribution of literally thousands of people, starting with the listeners of the *Infinite Inning* podcast. Listeners (you know who you are), without your support, attention, and interest in hearing me tell stories about the intersectionality of baseball, I would not have been inspired to tell even more stories, such as those contained within this volume. When I started the program, I no longer knew where I fit in what had become a very large universe of baseball coverage. Now I do—in this special place we made together. You will forever have my gratitude.

The statistics in this book, which add color and vital facts to the anecdotes and arguments, exist via the indispensable brainchild of Sean Forman: Baseball-Reference. What used to take hours paging through *The Baseball Encyclopedia* or *Total Baseball* (or wasn't possible at all) now takes seconds. And while the stories contained in this volume are based on my own primary-source research and a lifetime of reading, the many contributors to the Society for American Baseball Research's Baseball Biography Project provided countless articles against which I could check my work. I am indebted to them.

Every word and punctuation mark in this book was checked by my long-time friend and collaborator Cliff Corcoran, not only the show's "Man of 1,000 Baseball Caps" but an ace writer and editor, an empathetic and generous personality, and a hawkeyed reader with a pointillist's insistence on detail. He improved everything he touched with his edits and suggestions, and there is very little here that did not benefit by his scrutiny. Any errors that remain are solely mine.

David Roth and I were first thrown together some 10 years ago when we were both hired by a sports-content mill that had no idea what to do with either of us. Not only did the job immediately become more bearable, but I learned a new seven-word expression, one I have not only said hundreds of times since but have also heard an equal number of times from our mutual acquaintances: "I wish I could write like David." That praise undersells the humanity which undergirds his artistry. I am honored by his friendship, collegiality, and his presence in this book.

Steve Kuhn designed the cover and the book's interior. This is my first experience with self-publishing, and no doubt he has already saved me from many mistakes. Had I been left to my own devices, these pages would better resemble an eye chart than a book. I recommend him to anyone considering this sort of endeavor.

I suspect that Bret Sayre and Craig Goldstein of Baseball Prospectus do not wholly appreciate what their support has meant to me. They gave me a home. During my long first run at BP, when a prodigal writer would express interest in returning, I would say, "Once a BPer, always a BPer." They made it true for me by having me back in both a writing and advisory role that allows me to feel like I still have a lot to contribute. The BP branding on this book is a tribute to them as much as the honorable old publication itself. I would also like to express my appreciation to fellow BP writers and editors Marc Normandin, Ginny Searle, and Patrick Dubuque. Special thanks go to Jeffrey Paternostro, who not only has edited many of the show's long interview segments but is willing to field my queries about marginal (but selective!) semi-prospects like Trevor Hauver.

There are others who have been indispensable colleagues and fast friends: Regular *Infinite Inning* rotation member Jesse Spector; the generous Mike Ferrin, collaborator multiple times in the past and, I hope, again in the future; Craig Calcaterra, a kindred spirit; Ben Lindbergh, who I have had the privilege of watching grow well beyond me; the great Rob Neyer, whose work helped create the odd niche I inhabit, and whose frequent postcards are always a pleasure; the ever-erudite Lincoln Mitchell; my old BP comrade Kevin Goldstein; and my brother in the now-obscure, Alex Belth. May we all someday lunch at the Algonquin Hotel—in 1925.

I have never published a book without thanking the two friends of my childhood who are also the pillars of my adulthood: Dr. Richard Mohring and Andrew Baharlias. Dr. Mohring not only coauthored the show's "Infinite

Man" theme song and other topical tunes on the show throughout the years but gives me valuable feedback on every single episode. Mr. Baharlias, Esq., has also provided invaluable support and enthusiasm over the five-year run of the program. Without them, this book would surely not exist.

My parents, Reuven and Eliane Goldman, never let a conversation end without asking, "What are you working on now?" This is the best sort of parental expectation to try to meet. My sister, Ilana Goldman, holds me to the even-higher standards set by siblings. As Joe DiMaggio always played his best because he couldn't bear to disappoint anyone who might be watching, you must always endeavor to be your best self because your sibling is paying attention.

My daughter, Sarah, who created the initial logos for *The Infinite Inning* while still a teenager, has grown into a creator in her own right. Sarah, now it is your turn to bring something new into the world with pen and paper. My son, Clemens, amazes me each day. I hope I have provided a positive example by toiling away each day at this manuscript and other works.

My wife, Stefanie, has been my companion for 30 years, through good times and bad, elation and depression, inspiration and discouragement. She has never wavered in her faith, support, and love, even when I gave her good reason. I hope, in some small way, this book justifies her confidence in me; continuing to do so will be the work of the rest of my life.

NOTES

FOREWORD

"We don't like [ballplayers] as much" Roger Angell, *The New Yorker*, February 16, 1992.

INTRODUCTION

"A classical understanding" Robert Pirsig. *Zen and the Art of Motorcycle Maintenance* (1974), 70.

"He's my idol" Joel Bierig, *Chicago Sun-Times*, June 5, 1983.

Inscription on the tomb of Martin of Tours: Peter Brown. *The Cult of the Saints* (1981).

"Don Drysdale isn't in" Bill James. *Whatever Happened to the Hall of Fame?* (1995). Italics in the original.

"If I had to do it over" *The Cincinnati Enquirer,* January 21, 1978.

"He's the best player" *Tallahassee Democrat,* March 12, 1978.

CHAPTER ONE

"Mackey has probably caught" *The Pittsburgh Courier,* November, 13, 1937.

"Oooh, my goodness" John B. Holway. *Blackball Stars.*

"I probably learned" Monte Irvin, foreword to *Biz Mackey: A Giant Behind the Plate* by Rich Westcott.

"More than once" Westcott, *Biz Mackey.*

"He was a good storyteller." Irvin, foreword to *Biz Mackey.*

"Often he played while drunk" Mark Ribowsky. *A Complete History of the Negro Leagues.*

"In the Game against the Tomon club" Kazuo Sayama and Bill Staples Jr. *Gentle Black Giants: A History of the Negro Leaguers in Japan.*

"This is the man that gave me" John Holway, "Cool Papa, Biz and Satch," *LA Weekly,* May 21, 1992.

"You got to scold some" *The Baltimore Sun,* April 30, 1990.

"Mr. Horace Stoneham, President" Chester Washington, *The Pittsburgh Courier,* October, 16, 1937.

"I'm starting 1931" J. Roy Stockton, *St. Louis Post-Dispatch,* January 14, 1931.

"By that late in the training season" Leo Durocher. *Nice Guys Finish Last.*

"Herman will help us" Tommy Holmes, *Brooklyn Eagle,* May 7, 1941.

"It's going to be fun" *The New York Times,* May 7, 1941.

"Casey Stengel, the phrase-coiner" Arthur Daley, *The New York Times,* March 2, 1947.

"Finally they wrote a deal" Donald Honig. *The Man in the Dugout.*

"Hitting for average, line-drive power" Bill James. *The Bill James Baseball Abstract* (1985).

"We can't stay in business" Bob Logan and Rick Talley, *Chicago Tribune,* February 12, 1977.

"They're trying to make me" Ibid.

"What I said was" Dan Donovan, *The Pittsburgh Press,* May 2, 1980.

"What about the safety" Charles Feeney, *Pittsburgh Post-Gazette,* May 3, 1980.

"Everything has been said" Charles Feeney, *Pittsburgh Post-Gazette,* June 7, 1980.

"The traditional number-five" Bill James. *The Baseball Book 1990.*

"Playing for the Yankees" L. Robert Davids, "Sewell was a Real Fox at the Plate," *The Baseball Research Journal* (1976).

"If Speaker continues to bat" F. C. Lane, *Baseball Magazine,* 1913.

"Prickly son of the Confederacy" Timothy M. Gay. *Tris Speaker: The Rough-and-Tumble Life of a Baseball Legend.*

"Sold into slavery" Ibid.

"This is why I had to go away and play ball" Ibid.

"The embrace and kiss" *Cleveland Plain Dealer,* October 13, 1920.

"I never let him know" *St. Louis Post-Dispatch,* December 9, 1958.

"That morning, as thousands gathered" Mike Sowell. *The Pitch That Killed.*

"In what we call the reality-based" Ron Suskind, "Faith, Certainty and the Presidency of George W. Bush," *The New York Times,* October 17, 2004.

"We've shaken Andre's hand" *Sports Illustrated,* June 15, 1987.

"I accomplished some things" John Weyler, "Downing Reigns as Angels' Self-Made Survivor," *Los Angeles Times,* April 9, 1990.

"Right off a mustache cup" Jim Murray, "Downing Takes a Stance," *Los Angeles Times,* March 16, 1980.

"If I played 10 more years" Weyler, "Downing Reigns."

"The pitcher has to find out" Dave Anderson, "Don Drysdale's 'Inside' Pitch, *The New York Times,* July 9, 1979.

"Drysdale led us in wins" John Roseboro with Bill Libby. *Glory Days with the Dodgers and Other Days with Others.*

CHAPTER TWO

"Kitty did not prove" *Poughkeepsie Eagle-News,* February 18, 1918.

"I just like to hear" Clarence J. Cassin, "'Kitty' Bransfield Takes the Helm," *Hartford Courant,* April 17, 1927.

"A reporter with bad hearing" David W. Anderson, "Kitty Bransfield," https://sabr.org/bioproj/person/kitty-bransfield/.

"When I was a youngster" Cassin, "'Kitty' Bransfield Takes the Helm."

"A baseball man" Ibid.

"If I get a good jump" Tom Friend, "Bip Roberts," *Los Angeles Times,* March 8, 1926.

"'Roberts 2B'" Tom Groeschen, *The Cincinnati Enquirer,* April 8, 1993.

"I guess I was embarrassed" Bob Nightengale, "Improved Relations," *Los Angeles Times*, March 10, 1991.

"Bip, what question" Friend, "Bip Roberts."

"A sensational story" *The Buffalo Enquirer*, July 23, 1896.

"Second Baseman Robert Lew" *Louisville Courier-Journal*, June 18, 1904.

"The first sight that Miller Huggins had" John Kieran, "Wanninger Takes Firm Grasp on His Chance with Yanks," *New York Herald Tribune*, June 14, 1925.

"Ruth's Homer Fails" Harry Cross, "Ruth's Homer Fails as Tigers Win, 7 to 3," *The New York Times*, July 19, 1925.

"The story of this particular Sabbath" "Yankees Lose, 7–6, as Road Trip Ends," *The New York Times*, August 31, 1925.

"Frank is tired of chasing" Ring Lardner, *Chicago Tribune*, May 19, 1909.

"He said he figured" Cynthia J. Wilber. *For the Love of the Game: Baseball Memories from the Men Who Were There.*

"The guys on my team" *Sports Illustrated*, July 4, 1955.

"I figure it's mostly up to Musial" Tommy Holmes, "Musial Set to Join Game's Best Hitters," *Brooklyn Eagle*, September 11, 1951.

"I know one time" Wilber, *For the Love of the Game*.

CHAPTER THREE

"The truth" Roger Kahn. *The Era 1947–1957: When the Yankees, the Giants, and the Dodgers Ruled the World.*

"I never play a game without my man" Steven Goldman. *Forging Genius: The Making of Casey Stengel.*

"Maybe. Was your mother" Ibid.

"All this came about" Jackie Robinson. *Baseball Has Done It.*

"There never was any thought" Art Rust Jr. *Get That N----- Off the Field.*

"We always thought that" Larry Moffi and Jonathan Kronstadt. *Crossing the Line: Black Major Leaguers, 1947–1959.*

"Managers are hired to be fired" Arlene Howard and Ralph Wimbish. *Elston and Me.*

"**Another fella deserves credit**" "That Fella," *Time*, October 3, 1955.

"**Weren't working hard enough**" CBS News Miami, "Tino Martinez: Young Marlins Players Were 'Very Soft,'" March 27, 2014, https://www.cbsnews.com/miami/news/tino-martinez-young-marlins-players-were-very-soft/.

"**One day early this season**" Dick Young, "The Hoss That Nobody Bets," *New York Daily News*, August 18, 1972.

"**Nobody can blame this defeat**" Dick Young, "Hoss-Trading Yanks Whipped By Tony O, Carew & Twins, 5–2," *New York Daily News*, June 1, 1974.

"**I don't care what you do**" Young, "The Hoss That Nobody Bets."

"**If we had one of those lumberjacks**" Harold Rosenthal, "Stengel Views McDougald as Likely to Stick," *New York Herald Tribune*, March 15, 1951.

"**Daffy-looking**" United Press International, "Gil McDougald May Lead Yank Hitting as Rookie," *Greensboro Record*, July 27, 1951.

"**He fielded the ball way back**" Charlie Metro. *Safe by a Mile*.

"**He's the lousiest-looking ballplayer**" Joe Reichler, Associated Press, "McDougald 'Does Everything Wrong'—But He Produces, Beams Stengel," *Baltimore Evening Sun*, October 10, 1951.

"**How d'suppose you**" Red Smith, "Views of Sport," *Baltimore Evening Sun*, October 10, 1951.

"**I'm not fence happy**" Scott Baillie, United Press International, "McDougald Didn't Know His Slam Tied a Record," *Stockton Record*, October 10, 1951.

"**I used to spray**" James P. Dawson, "McDougald's New Batting Stance Launches First Yank Experiment," *The New York Times*, February 26, 1953.

"**If the pitch was on the outside**" Dom Forker. *The Men of Autumn: An Oral History of the 1949–53 World Champion New York Yankees*.

"**If you don't change**" Forker, *The Men of Autumn*.

"**If he loses his sight**" Arthur Daley, "A Frightening Injury," *The New York Times*, May 9, 1957.

"**What I said last night**" "Herb Score Waits for Word on Eye," *The New York Times*, May 9, 1957.

"**I came close to decapitating him**" Forker, *The Men of Autumn*.

"You need *me* to make a living" Ibid.

"You don't see color" Milton Richman, United Press International, "Color No Barrier to McDougalds," *Boston Herald*, December 29, 1978.

"The stance was as wide" Red Smith, *New York Herald Tribune*, January 22, 1961.

"One of these days now" Associated Press, "Casey's Got Problem: Where to Play Gil," *Daytona Beach Morning Journal*, March 18, 1958.

"For gosh sakes" Joseph M. Sheehan, "Phil Rizzuto's 'Day' Full of Warm Tributes," *The New York Times*, September 19, 1955.

"If I did that in our league" J.G. Taylor Spink, "Pluck Wins Over Percentage," *The Sporting News*, October 8, 1942.

"Hit the umps' protector" Harry Forbes, "Ruffing, Sundra Blank A's 2–0," *New York Daily News*, August 10, 1940.

"Crosetti stormed into Summers" John Drebinger, "69,123 See Cards Defeat Yanks, 2–0, For 2–1 Series Lead," *The New York Times*, October 4, 1942.

"Crosetti pulled Summers" Arthur "Bugs" Baer, "Bug's View on Big Games," *The Cincinnati Enquirer*, October 4, 1942.

"The only ring I have" Mike Hornick, "Crosetti remembers Ruth, Gehrig & baseball," *Lassen County Times*, September 29, 1992.

"Sonny boy" Charles Dunkley, Associated Press, "Yankees In Good Mood After Game," *The Evansville Courier*, October 12, 1943.

"Frank Crosetti, 37 years" Joseph Durso, *The New York Times*, October 5, 1968.

"The Agile Albino" W. O. McGeehan, "Yankees Pound Johnson And Regain Lead As Browns Lose," *The New York Herald*, September 9, 1922.

"Whitey will be a great aid" Thomas W. Meany, "Uncle Robby Signs Whitey Witt, Ex-Yankee Outfielder, In Record Time," *The Brooklyn Daily Times*, December 8, 1925.

"The less people know" Jon Heyman, "Laid Back," *Newsday*, July 14, 1992.

"All I wanted" Joe Sexton, "Kelly Uneasy at Center of Debate," *The New York Times*, August 11, 1989.

"Teammates occasionally refer to Roberto Kelly" Jon Heyman, "Laid Back."

"Kelly…had a gun" Michael Martinez, *The New York Times*, March 23, 1990.

"**I've always stood close**" Associated Press, "Baylor Achieves Record," *Oroville Mercury Register*, June 29, 1987.

"**Don can hit**" *Los Angeles Times*, February 15, 1980.

"**The first day he got here**" Bill Lyon, Knight Ridder, "Veterans help Boston, California reach playoff," *St. Joseph News Press*, October 7, 1986.

"**Don gives us something**" Ibid.

"**I don't seem to concentrate**" Associated Press, "Baylor, John spark Angels by Brewers," *News Journal*, October 6, 1982.

"**Don Baylor, the new manager**" *Miami Herald*, March 18, 1993.

"**There's nobody**" Claire Smith, "Winfield Baylor take names to Ueberroth," *Hartford Courant*, June 27, 1987.

"**I thought trading Ted Lilly**" Joe Torre and Tom Verducci. *The Yankee Years*.

"**I had no options**" Ibid.

"**It's baseball**" Mike DiGiovanna, "Angels Exchange One Weaver for Another," *Los Angeles Times*, July 1, 2006.

"**Jered's human**" Ibid.

"**Jackson is unknown**" Doug Brown, "Jackson a Stone Wall as Oriole Fireman," *The Sporting News*, January 18, 1975.

CHAPTER FOUR

"**I'm committed, at this point**" Steve Rock, "Sweeney finds a home at first with Royals," *The Wichita Eagle*, August 13, 1999.

"**Chewing on cookies**" Dick Kaegel, "The Lean Years," *Kansas City Star*, May 1, 2002.

"**If I hurt anyone's feelings**" Bob Dutton, "Muser apologizes for comments; gets support from players," *St. Joseph News-Press*, May 5, 2001.

"**I've said many times**" Ibid.

"**He's going to be a good player**" Dan Shaughnessy, "Team running a bit short," *The Boston Globe*, April 30, 2001.

"**I know people are happy**" Joe Posnanski, "It's like this: There weren't enough wins," *Kansas City Star*, April 30, 2002.

"Mike Sweeney says" Ibid.

"Is playing shortstop" Harry Grayson, "Coscarart 'Thrown In' by Dodgers in Deal for Vaughan, is Pittsburgh Find," *Wisconsin Rapids Daily Tribune*, May 19, 1942.

"$340,000" Steve Love, "Grand (?) old game's golden years," *Akron Beacon Journal*, July 21, 2000.

"What's so exceptional" Jack Smith, "Lavagetto's Hit Nips Yanks in 11th, 2–1," *New York Daily News*, March 26, 1941.

"Early to bed, early to rise" *The Sporting News*, July 25, 1940.

"If I get hit again" Peter Pascarelli, "Phillies defeat Cards," *The Philadelphia Inquirer*, June 27, 1988.

"I told him he doesn't have to look" Ibid.

"I know I can hit" Frank Dolson, "Vukovich: 0-for-30, Then a Joyous Hit," *The Philadelphia Inquirer*, July 18, 1971.

"I've offended enough people" Frank Dolson, "Vukovich is a good man wherever," *The Philadelphia Inquirer*, Oct. 4, 1987.

"He was probably my second dad" Todd Zolecki, "John Vukovich, tough Phil with soft side," *The Philadelphia Inquirer*, March 9, 2007.

"He's a showboat" Will Doerge, "Speaking of Sports," *The Indiana Gazette*, March 25, 1955.

"It wasn't something I wanted to do" Associated Press, "Hunter Not Bad, Says Stengel," *Fort Worth Star-Telegram*, August 5, 1955.

"I think Billy is the type of guy" Phil Rogers. *The Impossible Takes a Little Longer: The Texas Rangers, from Pretenders to Contenders*.

"We were a team that was waiting" Russ Cohen. *100 Things Rangers Fans Should Know & Do Before They Die*.

"Seldom showed more personality" Rogers, *The Impossible Takes a Little Longer*.

"May be Hitler" Jim Reeves, "No apparent resolution for Hunter-Ellis tiff," *Fort Worth Star-Telegram*, May 27, 1978.

"I scared all the old-timers" Donald Hall with Dock Ellis. *Dock Ellis in the Country of Baseball*.

"We had a bitter team" Bob Lindley, "Corbett's firing of Hunter a well-kept secret to most," *Fort Worth Star-Telegram*, October 2, 1978.

"**Maybe because Hunter's hands were tied**" United Press International, "Rangers Fire Billy Hunter," *Longview Daily News*, October 2, 1978.

"**I felt I had accomplished**" James Briggs, "Former Orioles Billy Hunter is an example for the career-obsessed," *Baltimore Business Journal*, April 16, 2013, https://www.bizjournals.com/baltimore/news/2013/04/15/former-oriole-billy-hunter-is-an.html.

"**Everyone in Triple-A**" John Eisenberg. *From 33rd Street to Camden Yards: An Oral History of the Baltimore Orioles*.

"**Sometimes I wonder myself**" Shirley Brown, "Billy Hunter—a great coach," *The Baltimore Sun*, July 21, 1972.

"**Was he sorry**" Randy Galloway, "Rangers fire Hunter; Corrales gets nod," *The Dallas Morning News*, October 2, 1978.

"**The Yankees traded Chase**" Frank Graham. *The New York Yankees: An Informal History*.

"**Did not seem anxious**" "Hal Chase Lost to the Yankees; Traded to the Chicago White Sox," *New York Tribune*, June 2, 1913.

"**Rollie Zeider, the Chicago Cubs' old second sacker**" "One Joke Rollie Zeider Did Not Greatly Enjoy," *The Laclede County Republican*, August 17, 1923.

"**Many of the officials**" "Rollie Zeider, Auburn Player, Victim of a Joke," *The Garrett Clipper*, October 10, 1921.

"**Lukon's father helped him**" Sue Goodwin, "Skirting the Field," *The Cincinnati Enquirer*, August 18, 1941.

"**Brown was not a success**" Tommy Holmes, "Superba Fielder Makes His Debut With Pinch Hit," *Brooklyn Eagle*, June 6, 1924.

"**Throughout his career**" "Eddie Brown, Baseball Star, Dies at Vallejo," *Nebraska Signal*, September 27, 1956.

"**The greatest catcher of long flies**" Thomas S. Rice, "Brooklyn Lands O'Neil In Desperate Effort To Energize Robins," *The Brooklyn Daily Eagle*, October 7, 1925.

"**I'm 31.**" Holmes, "Superba Fielder Makes His Debut."

"**Lumped [him] in with Casey Stengel**" Chris Rainey, "Sumpter Clarke," https://sabr.org/bioproj/person/sumpter-clarke/.

"**He also caused his team, the Birmingham Barons**" Zipp Newman, "Dusting 'em off," *The Birmingham News*, February 5, 1953.

"I was afraid it wasn't going to go" Bob Hertzel, "Stewart's Shot Gains Reds Split With Mets," *The Cincinnati Enquirer*, August 24, 1970.

"They both saw life as" Scott Eyman. *Hank & Jim: The Fifty-Year Friendship of Henry Fonda and James Stewart*.

"He ain't got no neck." Clifton Blue Parker. *Fouled Away: The Baseball Tragedy of Hack Wilson*.

"Tall, supple, strong" "One of M'Graw's Real Hopes," *The Sporting News*, December 31, 1925.

"Raised in the hills" Cullen Cain, "The Rookie," *The Saturday Evening Post*, April 3, 1926.

"Greenfield has about everything" "M'Graw Banks On Greenfield," *The Sporting News*, November 19, 1925.

"Neither McQuillan nor Greenfield" "Farrell is Traded; Giants Get Benton," *The New York Times*, June 13, 1927.

"Pirates Humbled" Harry Cross, "Pirates Humbled By a Giant Rookie," *The New York Times*, May 24, 1925.

CHAPTER FIVE

"Kids in the playground" Marybeth Sullivan, ed. *The Scouting Report: 1985*.

"I found the homers still will come" Gregg Hoffmann, "Schroeder unsure of role, but certain hitting will help," *Kenosha News*, March 28, 1988.

"It's like the chicken-and-the-egg theory" George A. King III, "Brewers' Schroeder struggling," *Trenton Evening Times*, July 27, 1988.

"I'm not a home run hitter" Jim Murray, "Joyner proved he's All-World," *The Tampa Tribune*, August 30, 1986.

"I could drag bunt" Jim Murray, "Looks Are Deceiving: Joyner's Sweet Face, Mean Swing Prove It," *Los Angeles Times*, September 22, 1986.

"He reminds me of a young Keith Hernandez" Mike Penner, "Angels Took Some Big Stumbling Blocks Out of Joyner's Path," *Los Angeles Times*, March 11, 1986.

"It's almost a case of false representation" Murray, "Looks Are Deceiving."

"After Wally Joyner shaved his head" Dan Good. *Playing Through the Pain: Ken Caminiti and the Steroids Confession That Changed Baseball Forever*.

"If Jody accepts" Fred Claire. *My 30 Years in Dodger Blue.*

"A powerful economic move" Jeff Blair, "Swap 'strictly baseball deal': Brochu," *The Gazette*, November 24, 1993.

"This is a kid with a great arm" Jeff Blair, "Expos trade DeShields For L.A. hurler Martinez," *The Gazette*, November 20, 1993.

"This is the Expos' one big deal" Michael Farber, "Deal is rotten to the core," *The Gazette*, November 20, 1993.

"A similar statement by Claire" Steve Dilbeck, "Dodgers Send Pedro Martinez to Expos for DeShields," *The San Bernardino County Sun*, November 20, 1993.

"Society's changed a lot" Jeff Blair, "Growing up fast," *The Gazette*, April 29, 1990.

"That is just my way" "Role model material," *The Arizona Republic*, December 18, 1993.

"Diaab means" Victor Lee, "DeShields' main aim is to be there," *The Palm Beach Post*, August 3, 1993.

"Bob Horner can break any home run record" Ken Leiker, "Braves' Horner hopes for trade," *The Arizona Republic*, April 23, 1980.

"Man, am I gonna" Eric Girad, "Horner Takes to His Corner for His Big Debut," *The Atlanta Constitution*, June 16, 1978.

"I don't like Horner" Rick Hummel, "Herzog: Thumbs Down On Bob Horner," *St. Louis Post-Dispatch*, January 8, 1988.

"Horner is only 26" Bill James. *The Bill James Baseball Abstract* (1984).

"I'll never forget Opening Day" Whitey Herzog. *You're Missin' a Great Game.*

"Paul Molitor had three seasons" Steven Goldman and Christina Kahrl, eds. *Baseball Prospectus 2006.*

"We joke about it" Ron Kroichick, "Already in a groove," *The Sacramento Bee*, August 23, 1994.

"When local baseball talent" Eric Zarate, "Grieve is top of local crop," *Fort Worth Star-Telegram*, June 5, 1994.

"His lack of speed" Phil Rogers in *The Scouting Notebook 1999*, ed. John Dewan, Don Zminda, and Jim Callis.

"When a ball is hit to Ben Grieve" *Baseball Prospectus 2001.*

"I played eight years." Rick Herrin, "One meteoric rise, fall," *Fort Worth Star-Telegram*, July 10, 2007.

"I always believed" Art Spander, "Dan Gladden a big hit," *San Francisco Examiner*, June 27, 1984.

"Will Gladden start tomorrow" Terence Moore, "Rookie show in center field Gladdens Giants," *San Francisco Examiner*, September 9, 1983.

"I didn't know anything about the Twins" Associated Press, "No doubting Dan Gladden and intense desire to win," *San Francisco Examiner*, March 19, 1988.

"What kind of guy" Greg Hoard, "Cards can't keep up with Jones," *The Cincinnati Enquirer*, May 23, 1986.

"Several weeks ago" John Erardi, "Rookie Jones gets a surprise," *The Cincinnati Enquirer*, April 8, 1986.

"Has gotten the reputation" John Dewan, ed. *The Scouting Report: 1990*.

"I always thought I was a pretty good ballplayer" Associated Press, "Jones regrouping," *The Cincinnati Enquirer*, July 1, 1990.

"I'm very high strung" John Erardi, "All's not Rose-y with the Reds' Jones," *The Cincinnati Enquirer*, April 20, 1987.

"He does things I never thought of" Tim Sullivan, "Jones won't stand still for success," *The Cincinnati Enquirer*, July 2, 1987.

"Glenn Davis had come over" Ian Browne, "HRs, compassion made Horn a Sox cult hero," MLB.com, December 5, 2019, https://www.mlb.com/news/sam-horn-red-sox-cult-hero.

"Thurston was a junkballer" The indispensable *Neyer/James Guide to Pitchers* argues that Thurston's "fadeaway" should be read as a changeup rather than as a screwball.

"Everything I threw" Associated Press, "Thurston Dies at 74," *Miami Herald*, September 17, 1973.

"According to the available information" J. C. D., "Bee Skipper Suspends Hollis Thurston for Defiance of Authority," *The Salt Lake Tribune*, March 31, 1922.

"Perhaps the most talented" "Gets His Big Chance," *Deseret News*, December 14, 1922.

"Hollis Thurston's ding-dong delivery" John J. Peri, "In-Between Peri-Graphs," *Stockton Daily Evening Record*, April 4, 1934.

"There's no question in my mind" Dave Van Dyck, "Drug Woes In Baseball, Too?" *The Tampa Tribune*, July 25, 1982.

"**Celebrate**" Tracy Ringolsby, "Caudill Inspecting His Inconsistency," *The Sporting News*, August 15, 1983.

"**In addition to his repertoire**" E. M. Swift, "Need Help? Call the Inspector," *Sports Illustrated*, August 16, 1982.

CHAPTER SIX

"**Somebody thought of that**" Kenneth Ascher and Paul Williams, "Rainbow Connection"

"**Edna St. Vincent Millay**" See, for example, Maggie Doherty, "Burned Out," *The New Yorker*, May 16, 2022.

"**Brother or no brother**" Kerrie Ferrell, "Rick Ferrell," https://sabr.org/bioproj/person/rick-ferrell/.

"**In the words of the world-renowned Popeye**" Bob Murphy, "Bill Terry Thinks Cubs Will Be Great Threat; Praises Hubbell and Ott," *The Knoxville Journal*, December 21, 1933.

"**Bill Terry was approached**" Ibid.

"**One spring when I did not sign**" Ira L. Smith. *Baseball's Famous First Basemen*.

"**Terry will be of little use**" Jimmy Powers, "McGraw-Terry 'Mad' On!" *New York Daily News*, March 5, 1932.

"**When I joined the Giants**" Bob Broeg. *SuperStars of Baseball*.

"**Bill managed like he played**" Ibid.

"**Baseball is too cheap for me**" Associated Press, "Baseball Too Cheap, Says Terry, Quitting for Cotton," *New York Daily News*, January 9, 1944.

"**One of the country's biggest**" Arthur Daley, "Visit With Bill Terry," *The New York Times*, April 7, 1957.

"**I have nothing at all to say**" Broeg, *SuperStars*.

"**I didn't know I'd ever feel like this**" Louis Effrat, "Terry and Dickey Inducted Into Hall of Fame," *The New York Times*, August 10, 1954.

"**It is impossible to reconcile**" Arthur Daley, "Bidding Farewell to Bill Terry," *The New York Times*, January 11, 1944.

"**Bill hasn't the glamour**" Sidney Skolsky, "Tintypes," *New York Daily News*, June 15, 1932.

"Flushed with success" Harold Rosenthal, "Baseball's Most Famed Quote Recalled in Book on Giant," *New York Herald Tribune*, May 18, 1952.

"Look, I'm doing the best" Milton Richman, "'Not Everybody Can Be a Nellie Fox,'" *The Daily Freeman*, December 2, 1975.

"He's a rip-snorting" Irving Vaughan, "When Is Fox Not a Fox? When It's Nellie of the Sox," *The Sporting News*, July 4, 1951.

"Nellie Fox isn't real fast" Les Woodcock, "Two for the Pennant," *Sports Illustrated*, August 10, 1959.

"I'm no ballet dancer" Ibid.

"I just loved him" Richman, "Not Everybody."

"He's got a new system" John P. Carmichael, "The Barber Shop," *Chicago Daily News*, June 11, 1951.

"He gets into high gear" Woodcock, "Two for the Pennant."

"In some tellings" Al Hirshberg and Joe McKenney. *Famous American Athletes of Today* (Tenth Series).

"Letting the Boston players know" Tom Meany, "Jackie's One of the Gang Now," *Sport*, August, 1949.

"A really nice man" John Lardner, "Reese and Robinson: A Team Within a Team," *The New York Times*, September 18, 1949.

"A familiar scene around Ebbets Field" Hirshberg and McKenney, *Famous American Athletes of Today*.

"Pee Wee Reese should go on" Zipp Newman, "Dusting 'Em off," *The Birmingham News*, July 10, 1941.

"When I finally decided" Peter Golenbock. *Bums: An Oral History of the Brooklyn Dodgers*.

"He played shortstop" Roger Kahn. *The Boys of Summer*.

"I just can't bring myself" Hank Aaron with Lonnie Wheeler. *I Had a Hammer*.

"Tommy stood in the corner" Murray Polner. *Branch Rickey: A Biography*.

"Lefty Grove called Simmons" Harold Kaese, "Few Could Carry Simmons' Glove, Even Fewer Could Carry His Bat," *The Boston Globe*, May 28, 1956.

"In his excitement" Bob Considine, "Mister Mack," *Life*, August 9, 1948.

"His ankle wasn't so bad" Harold Kaese, "Blackwell Will Need More Than New Record to Outrank Bob Grove," *The Boston Globe,* July 21, 1947.

"There were long periods" Leroy Atkinson and Austen Lake. *Famous American Athletes of Today* (Third Series).

"In mid-July" Goldman, *Forging Genius.*

"This kid was a big leaguer" Grantland Rice, "Mel Ott Still A Star, After 15 Seasons In Big Time," *Tampa Bay Times,* May 28, 1940.

"I shall always remember" "Fans Honor Ott," *New York Daily News*, Jack Mahon, August 8, 1940.

"I told both men" Claire. *My 30 Years in Dodger Blue.*

"Pedro was rated" Don Hartack in *The Scouting Report: 1992,* ed. John Dewan.

"Wandered out of the mountains" James Goodwin, "Kitty League Pitching Ace Will Likely See Action In Series with Mayfield Browns," *The Jackson Sun,* June 8, 1941.

"Slipped off back of box" Roger Birtwell, "The Story of Kinder, Pitcher Unusual," *The Boston Globe*, January 24, 1956.

"We came out of the train" Peter Golenbock. *Fenway: An Unexpurgated History of the Boston Red Sox.*

"To the degree Ellis trained at all" David Halberstam. *Summer of '49.*

"Bless his heart" Ibid.

"Me old?" Steve O'Leary, "Wonder-Kid Kinder 'Just Starting' at 35," *The Sporting News*, September 28, 1949.

"Arthur Richman" John Steadman, "Sox' Kinder: Drink Hard, Throw Harder, *Valley News,* June 25, 1995.

CHAPTER SEVEN

"Our catching needs" Jerome Holtzman, "Burns to Yanks; Fisk Next?" *Chicago Tribune*, December 13, 1985.

"We got him to pull" Murray Chass, "Hassey Returns to Yankees," *The New York Times,* February 14, 1986.

"I heard they were looking" Murray Chass, "Inertia Is Unusual for Hassey," *The New York Times,* March 13, 1987.

"More than halfway through the season" Tracy Ringolsby, "Mets' Decision to drop Foster as clear as black," *Fort Lauderdale Sun-Sentinel*, August 10, 1986.

"'Clyde,' said Madden" Bill Madden and Moss Klein. *Damned Yankees*.

"Still, the news shocked Hassey" Craig Wolff, "Yanks Trade Hassey and Obtain Kittle," *The New York Times*, July 30, 1986.

"The first six years" Jim Murray, "His Bat Does His Talking," *Los Angeles Times*, June 21, 1983.

"I would hate" Ibid.

"I should have known better" Bruce Nash and Allan Zullo. *The Baseball Hall of Shame*.

"No longer will I congratulate" Dan Castellano, "Lots of bleeps as Jim fries during interview," *Staten Island Advance*, August 4, 1985.

"I thought I'd be treated special" Ross Newhan, "Sax Goes to Yankees for 3 Years, $4 Million," *Los Angeles Times*, November 24, 1988.

"In time, Steve Sax" David Leon Moore, "Meet Steve Sax, the Dodgers' Mr. Enthusiasm," *The San Bernardino County Sun*, April 7, 1982.

"Steven Louis Sax" Jim Murray, "Steve Sax: a Budding Pete Rose," *Los Angeles Times*, April 1, 1983.

"Blessed with an easy temperament" United Press International, "Ex-Yankee Great Red Rolfe Dies," *The Times Recorder*, July 9, 1969.

"I always hoped" Steve Cady, "A Yankee at Heart," *The New York Times*, July 9, 1969.

"Hank Bauer used to say" Forker, *The Men of Autumn*.

"Sure, I got mad" Larry Moffi. *This Side of Cooperstown: An Oral History of Major League Baseball in the 1950s*.

"During one clubhouse meeting" Peter Golenbock. *Dynasty: The New York Yankees, 1949–1964*.

"The year that Casey and I" Forker, *The Men of Autumn*.

"Woodling used to fuss" Danny Peary. *We Played the Game*.

"Gene Woodling is a fellow" Gordon Cobbledick, "Plain Dealing," *Cleveland Plain Dealer*, January 21, 1958.

"Each new player" Hank Greenberg, "How We Got Into the Series," *Life*, September 27, 1954.

"I've never even seen the boy" "Klieman to Hurl in Boston Series," *Cleveland Plain Dealer*, September 23, 1943.

"Net result of the transaction" Vince Johnson, "Eastern Trip Stern Test For Pirates, *Pittsburgh Post-Gazette*, April 26, 1947.

"Everyone says" Joe Trimble, "Casey Spots Woodling In Joe's Niche—Pro Tem," *New York Daily News*, March 11, 1949.

He hit .493 with five home runs against the Oaks. Bill James. *Bill James Historical Baseball Abstract*.

"He is not the Yankee type" Joe Trimble, "Bomber Rookies Top A's, 4–2," *New York Daily News*, September 30, 1948.

"This guy Throneberry" "Woodling Put On Waivers After Hassle With Mets," *The Journal Herald*, March 4, 1963.

"The whole situation with Woodling" Associated Press, "Mets Let Veteran Player-Coach Go," *The Clarion-Ledger*, March 4, 1963.

"You know, when I was playing" Tom Melody, "Woodling content with past, present," *The Akron Beacon Journal*, October 14, 1977.

"I'd quit the Indians" Jim Schlemmer, "Lane Acting Like Dictator—Woodling," *The Akron Beacon Journal*, February 12, 1958.

"I had good parents" Norman L. Macht. *They Played the Game: Memories from 47 Major Leaguers*.

"I led four leagues in hitting" Moffi, *This Side of Cooperstown*.

"I escaped all right" "Torre having too much fun to retire from Yanks," *The Cincinnati Enquirer*, September 03, 2000.

"I just want to remain professional." David Heuschkel, "Brawls Don't Bode Well for Series Finale," *Hartford Courant*, August 30, 2000.

"Under the momentum" James P. Dawson, "Selkirk Hurt in Circus Catch As Yanks Rout Athletics, 12–7," *The New York Times*, July 2, 1937.

"You had to hustle" Lewis F. Atchison, "Selkirk, Never One to Worry, Shrugs Off Talk of Yankee Job," *Washington Evening Star*, September 15, 1952.

"Ruth has signed" Henry McLemore, "Ruth Has Signed—Pity Poor George Selkirk," *Casper Star-Tribune*, March 17, 1932. Another headline chosen for this UPI story: "Sigh for George Selkirk, His Dream Goes Haywire."

"**No terms were announced**" "Yankees Buy George Selkirk, Outfielder, From Jersey City," *New York Herald Tribune*, November 5, 1931.

"**The press tried to put pressure**" Paul Patton, "Selkirk decries tag; Ruth 'irreplaceable,'" *The Globe and Mail*, August 4, 1983.

"**Only one thing has Selkirk**" Associated Press, "Ruth Torments Ticklish Player," *The Spokesman-Review*, January 25, 1934.

"**There was always something wrong**" William Barry Furlong, "The Senators' Prize Castoff," *Saturday Evening Post*, August 14, 1954.

"**A sinker that didn't sink**" Jack Hand, "Porterfield Hit By Sinker That Didn't Sink," *Battle Creek Enquirer*, June 10, 1950.

"**He fell to the ground**" Louis Effrat, "Yanks Beaten by Tigers," *The New York Times*, June 10, 1950.

"**Porterfield is much improved**" Dan Daniel, "Yanks Wrap Up Package Deal for Pitcher," *The Sporting News*, May 9, 1951.

"**Nats Fans Disappointed**" "Nats Fans Disappointed Over Kuzava Trade for 3 Yanks Has-Beens," *Washington Evening Star*, June 15, 1951.

"**Nats Pick Up Three Losers**" "Nats Pick Up Three Losers From Yankees," *The Washington Post*, June 16, 1951.

"**He jumped into France**" Tom Meany. *The Boston Red Sox*.

Poterfield's SABR biography Warren Corbett, "Bob Porterfield," https://sabr.org/bioproj/person/bob-porterfield/.

"**In a short baseball career**" Meany, *The Boston Red Sox*.

"**I didn't throw the ball**" Ibid.

"**PORTERFIELD OVERCOMES EARACHE**" Bob Addie, "Porterfield Overcomes Earache, Tigers, 4–1," *The Washington Post*, August 6, 1954.

"**Billy Martin…was loath to use him**" Madden and Klein, *Damned Yankees*.

CHAPTER EIGHT

"**Frank Fernandez went to bat**" Gerald Eskanazi, "Fernandez Walks 4 Straight Times," *The New York Times*, September 1, 1969.

"**I was only about nine**" Jim Ogle, "Fernandez 15-year Wait Finally Ends," *Jersey Journal*, September 13, 1967.

"I just did it" Leonard Koppett, "Yankees Beat Angels, 1–0, on Homer by Fernandez in Season Opener Here," *The New York Times*, April 11, 1968.

"He didn't deny" Ibid.

"The defensive play of the day" Joseph Durso, "Yanks Beat Orioles, 3–1, on Stottlemyre's 4-Hitter, Then Lose, 3–2, in Ninth," *The New York Times*, July 8, 1968.

"Perhaps I didn't use Fernandez" Jim Ogle, "Yanks to Let Fernandez Duel Gibbs for No. 1 Backstop Post," *The Sporting News*, December 21, 1968.

"How can anyone hit" Jim Ogle, "Fernandez' Plea—More Work in '69," *The Sporting News*, February 22, 1969.

"Now that Fernandez" Ron Bergman, "Fernandez Hates N.Y.—That Suits the A's," *The Sporting News*, March 21, 1970.

"Catcher Frank Fernandez" "Fernandez' Anger Costs Him Money," *Oakland Tribune*, August 28, 1970.

"A sort of 'rump legislature'" Bill James. *The New Bill James Historical Baseball Abstract*.

"Fletcher is a fine boy" Gerry Moore, "Bees Ship Out Elbie Fletcher in Pirate Deal," *The Boston Globe*, June 16, 1939.

"And so mornings" Brent Kelley. *The Early All-Stars: Conversations with Standout Baseball Players*.

"Bad management…a lotta mistakes" Milton Richman, "Often Overlooked Clift Has His Pride," *St. Louis Post-Dispatch*, July 21, 1984.

"Looking down the Browns' bench" Ibid.

"What most people don't know" John B. Holway. *Voices from the Great Black Baseball Leagues*.

"The great third baseman" Lonnie Wheeler. *The Bona Fide Legend of Cool Papa Bell*.

"Not only do I get more money" Wendell Smith, "Introducing 'El Diablo' Wells of Mexico," *The Pittsburgh Courier*, May 6, 1944.

"Willie Wells of 1942" Cum Posey, "Posey Selects 19th All-American 'Dream' Team," *The Pittsburgh Courier*, November 7, 1942.

"Ignorance is pitiful" John Kelso, "Willie Wells: It was a good time," *Austin American-Statesman*, January 2, 1977.

"**Willie Wells was one of the smartest**" Ray Buck, "Giving 'The Devil' his due," *Fort Worth Star-Telegram*, July 6, 2003.

"**He is a marvel**" Al Munro Elias, "George Burns Leads National League In Run-Scoring Streaks," *The Hartford Courant*, February 25, 1918.

"**Burns became a regular**" "M'Graw Gets Groh In Deal With Reds," *The New York Times*, December 7, 1921.

"**Burns is 32**" Robert Boyd, "George Burns Goes to Cincinnati, *The Evening World*, December 7, 1921.

"**Today's game was marred**" "Phillies Almost Win a Game on Blunders," *The Philadelphia Inquirer*, August 18, 1900.

"**Have your fun now**" Bill Lamberty in *Deadball Stars of the National League*, ed. Tom Simon.

"**Roy Thomas, the brilliant centerfielder**" "Baseball on April 24," *The Baltimore Sun*, March 21, 1901.

"**Thomas, personally, is a model**" "Various Veterans Due To Be Released," *The Evening Star*, January 30, 1910.

"**The back of my head was**" Megan Ryan, "Twins winning streak snapped by Tigers; Buxton's 0-for-26 slump continues," *Star Tribune* May 26, 2022.

"**When guys don't speak**" Kevin Roberts, "Promise kept, dream realized," *Courier-Post*, April 3, 2000.

"**Man I could watch him hit**" Don Bostrom, "Sweet Swing," *The Morning Call*, April 2, 2000.

"**Although a Georgia Cracker**" Henry P. Edwards, "Like Crowder, Sugar Cain Found Army Baseball Easy," *Brooklyn Times Union*, December 6, 1936.

"**Wilder than a man overboard**" James C. Isaminger, "A's Jar Browns, 8–7," *The Philadelphia Inquirer*, July 23, 1933.

"**Mack learned that Cain**" Norman Macht. *The Grand Old Man of Baseball: Connie Mack in His Final Years, 1931–1956*

"**Connie Mack let both**" James C. Isaminger, "Mack Gets His Man After 5-Year Wait," *The Sporting News*, May 30, 1935.

"**By George, yes**" John Kieran, "Connie Mack, the Cheerful Man," *The New York Times*, March 25, 1934.

CHAPTER NINE

"Fat-cheeked, brown-overalled" "Putting Wales on the Map," *The Buffalo Sunday Morning News*, October 26, 1913.

"In contrast to the modern jet age" "Schang, Yanks' Star Catcher, Dead at 75," *The Sporting News*, March 20, 1965.

"Schang, 23, was rated" Macht, *The Grand Old Man of Baseball*.

"I refused Schang" Billy Evans, "How Chance Lost Schang," *The Illustrated Buffalo Express*, November 2, 1913.

"Mr. Grenier pitched" "Paddy Green Dies in Lee," *The Berkshire Evening Eagle*, August 15, 1952.

"Early in the game" "Schang Badly Hurt Chasing Foul Ball," *The Philadelphia Inquirer*, July 19, 1916.

"The Yankees won a double victory" "Schang Out of Game For Indefinite Time," *New York Tribune*, May 31, 1923.

"He's out! He's out!" "Schang Some Dreamer—'Licked Umpire' in Sleep," *Altoona Times*, March 31, 1914.

"When I was his age" John Kieran, "Talking About a Young Feller," *The New York Times*, June 18, 1937.

"I need him to help" "Schang Will Stick to the Farm," *The Buffalo Times*, October 22, 1913.

"Just to watch him" Al Hirshberg. *Baseball's Greatest Catchers*.

"We need many more Wally Schangs" *The Buffalo Sunday Morning News*, October 26, 1913.

"The catcher is the jockey" Harry Grayson, "Catcher Schang Made Great Hurlers' World Series Followed Wally Around," *The Tribune*, June 13, 1943.

"If I am a better first baseman" Henry P. Edwards, "Joe Kuhel's Baseball Saga," *The Nebraska State Journal*, December 25, 1932.

"Here's Joe Cool" Charles M. Schulz, *The Complete Peanuts Vol. 11: 1971–1972*.

"Anti-democratic, anti-middle-class" Christopher R. Browning, "Blue Bloods and Brownshirts," *The New York Review of Books*, July 1, 2021.

"Major league writers say" Ralph McGill, "Success of Joe Kuhel Wrinkles Barney's Brow," *The Atlanta Contitution*, May 21, 1931.

"**A Napoleonic figure**" James C. Isaminger, "Vangilder Blanks Mackmen and Browns Capture Second Contest of Series," *The Philadelphia Inquirer*, June 7, 1926.

"**It is unfortunate**" "Oscar Melillo," *The Sporting News*, July 6, 1933.

"**Late in March**" John B. Foster, "Vegetables Made Melillo Valuable," *Worcester Evening Gazette*, June 9, 1931.

"**The two men who have robbed**" "Rabbit Warstler," *The Sporting News*, June 13, 1964.

"**In cases where older patients**" "Melillo Will Be Cured On Quitting Local Hospital," *The St. Louis Star*, October 28, 1926.

"**There is no assurance**" "Dan Howley Leaves Least for Regrets," *The Sporting News*, March 31, 1927.

"**They told me**" "Oscar Melillo," *The Sporting News*, November 30, 1963. This obituary of Melillo places his dietary instructions as having been issued during the 1927 baseball season, after Melillo had become ill "in Cleveland," but, on July 21, 1927, the same paper reported that, "Illness forced Melillo to go on a vegetable diet.... For six months Melillo has not tasted meat," which pushes the switch to spinach back to the offseason after his initial diagnosis in 1926.

"**Don't spill that spinach**" "Oscar Melillo Declares Spinach Tale Bologney [sic]," *The Sporting News*, October 15, 1931.

"**I hate the damned stuff.**" "'Me Bat .330 Because I Eat Spinach?' Bah a Couple Times Says Melillo," *The Milwaukee Journal*, July 20, 1931.

"**I just stored away the vegetables**" Associated Press, "Spinach, Claims Oscar Melillo, Saved His Life," *Baton Rouge Morning Advocate*, April 6, 1938.

"**I hated it worse**" Fred Bailey. *The Knoxville News-Sentinel*, February 11, 1934

"**The daily and Sunday newspaper strip**" Kim Thompson ed. *Popeye Volume One*.

"**Segar was only interested**" Bill Blackbeard, "The First (Arf, Arf) Superhero of Them All," in *All in Color for a Dime*, ed. Dick Lupoff and Don Thompson.

"**The United States Food Administration**" Richard Pillsbury. *No Foreign Food: The American Diet in Time and Place*.

"**The social norm**" Laura Lovett. "The Popeye Principle: Selling Child Health in the First Nutrition Crisis," *Journal of Health Politics, Policy and Law* 30: 803-838.

"**It's broccoli, dear**" Carl Rose and E. B. White, *The New Yorker*, December 8, 1928.

"**Notice to the Mothers of Chil'ren**" E. C. Segar, *Thimble Theater*, February 28, 1932.

"In 1933 the Children's Bureau" Edward Robb Ellis, *A Nation in Torment: The Great American Depression 1929–1939*.

"I hired Ski Melillo" Associated Press, "Ruel, Melillo Die," *The Palm Beach Post*, November 15, 1963.

"Children are often slow" Lovett, "The Popeye Principle."

"I hate myskeries" E. C. Segar, syndicated ad for *Thimble Theater*, June 8, 1932.

"Heavy hitting by the Cardinals" "Giants Beaten Twice," *The New York Tribune*, May 24, 1908.

"You yellow dog" Andrew Goldblatt. *The Giants and The Dodgers: Four Cities, Two Teams, One Rivalry*.

"Found that his legs" "Old-Timers Being Trimmed Off The Boston Pilgrims," *The Birmingham News*, December 8, 1912.

"'Mac,' he said one night" Christy Mathewson. *Pitching in a Pinch*.

"I'll tell you one queer turn" Grantland Rice, "The Sportlight," *New York Herald Tribune*, April 25, 1916.

"Arthur Devlin suffered a strange fate" Harold Kaese, *The Boston Braves*.

"I'm not so sure" Rob Kirkpatrick. *Cecil Travis of the Washington Senators: The War-Torn Career of an All-Star Shortstop*.

"You don't have to be off" Ibid.

"There are a lot of players" Furman Bisher, "The All-Stars from Fayette County," *The Atlanta Journal-Constitution*, July 11, 2000.

"The black fans came" Brad Snyder. *Beyond the Shadow of the Senators*.

"The ball hit Hinton's head" "Hinton Has Concussion Will Be Out for Week," *The Evening Star*, September 6, 1963.

"It hurt!" James R. Hartley, *Washington's Expansion Senators*.

"Simply wasn't Hodges' type" Merrell Whittlesey, "Held and Chance Boost Senators' Power," *The Evening Star*, December 1, 1964.

"Then everybody got hurt" Mel Derrick, "Glib Hinton Was 'Scared' By Homer Output in July," *The Charlotte Observer*, August 14, 1966.

"I hit so many homers" Ibid.

"I got into the...well" Ibid.

"Hi Myers—an outfielder" Associated Press, "Stengel is Honored," *The York Dispatch*, October 8, 1949.

"Outshoot on the end of his bat" Rice, "Homer By Myers In First Inning; Smith Pitching," *The Brooklyn Daily Eagle*, October 9, 1916.

"His fielding twice saved the day" "Chill Winds Sweep Ebbets Field Today," *The Washington Times* October 10, 1916.

"For the simple reason" Jerry Sullivan, "Everyone in Brooklyn Knows New Tribe Pilot" *The Boston Globe*, June 24, 1951.

"Never did show much interest" Donald Honig. *Baseball Between the Lines*.

"Chunky" John Drohan, "Tommy Holmes Only Brave Using Willow with Effect," *Boston Traveler*, September 2, 1942; In "Tommy Holmes Clouts Way Into Fans' Hearts," *Springfield Republican*, July 4, 1945, he is described as a "chunky wrist-hitter"; there are many more.

"The greatest wrist hitter" Rich Westcott. *Masters of the Diamond*. Harold Burr credited a close variation on this remark to Clyde Sukeforth in his 1942 *Sporting News* profile of Holmes.

"Johnny watched me" Harold C. Burr, "Holmes, Braves' New Bingle Man, a Home-Run Hombre at Heart, Short-Circuited by Shortening of His Average," *The Sporting News*, February 19, 1942.

"The Phils apparently have heard" Arthur Sampson, "Javery Baffles Phils as Braves Win, 2–1," *Boston Herald*, April 15, 1942.

"Tommy got all" Drohan, "Tommy Holmes Only Brave Using Willow with Effect."

"This may sound a little odd" Ed Rumill, "Holmes Applies Pull at Platter to Push Average Close to .400," *The Sporting News*, May 10, 1945.

"Raving...quality of wood...The wood's as hard" "Si" Burick, "Tommy Holmes Hammers Those Hefty Hits With A Bat Broken In By Frederick 17 Years Ago," *The Dayton Daily News*, June 27, 1945.

"Ironwood" Bill King, "Holmes Loses Pet Bat But Continues to Hit," *Springfield Republican*, July 6, 1945.

"My own inclination" George C. Carens, "Holmes Plans Hitting Talk With Williams," *Boston Traveler*, March 19, 1946.

"How much Holmes will play" Bob Holbrook, "Tommy Holmes Straightens Out Marshall's Batting Defect," *The Boston Globe*, June 3, 1950.

"To be sure, in recent seasons" Bob Holbrook, "Marshall Rated Top Right Fielder In League by Rival Tommy Holmes," *The Boston Globe*, March 6, 1950.

"Never took a drink" Sullivan, "Everyone in Brooklyn Knows New Tribe Pilot."

"Fifteen hundred indignant fans" Al Hirshberg. *The Braves: The Pick and the Shovel*.

CHAPTER TEN

"The big, bald-pated catcher" Lou Smith, "Washington Senators Latest Victims of Rampaging Reds," *The Cincinnati Enquirer*, March 23, 1938.

"If you don't win" Newman, *The Birmingham News*, July 10, 1941.

"Retrade Winds" Leo Davi, "Sport Salad," *St. Louis Post-Dispatch*, November 17, 1933.

"The Cherokee Has No Regrets" Furman Bisher, "The Cherokee Has No Regrets," *Baseball Digest*, July 1954.

"That DiMaggio boy" Bob Ryan, "Sosa the new York, but don't forget the old one," *The Boston Globe*, June 26, 1998.

"Liable to get killed out there" Ira L. Smith. *Baseball's Famous First Basemen*.

"Half-Indian, half–first baseman" Bill Bryson, "Last Indian," *Des Moines Tribune*, July 29, 1966. Bryson credited Tom Meany for the expression.

"Rudy had good cause" Harold Kaese, "Rudolph Preston York" in *Famous American Athletes of Today* (Sixth Series).

"He studied pitchers" Ryan, "Sosa the new York."

"I don't know how many mattresses" Richard Bak. *Cobb Would Have Caught It*.

"My curtains were on fire" "Joe Coleman to Pitch Today Against Sox," *The Boston Globe*, April 27, 1947.

"RUDY YORK'S ROOM IN FLAMES" *The Idaho Statesman*, August 24, 1947.

"Don't be shortsighted." Furman Bisher. "Letter to My Son," *Sport*, 1954. Republished in Charles Einstein, ed. *The Fireside Book of Baseball*.

"Deep among the hot dogs" Red Smith, "Cards' Anti-Williams Defense Most Radical," *The Boston Globe*, October 7, 1946.

"A hell of a player" Ryan, "Sosa the new York."

"Sutherland makes the double play" Jim Hawkins, "Tigers 'Solve Their 2d-Base Problem," *Detroit Free Press*, December 4, 1973.

"The deal came as a complete surprise" "Carlisle Smith Sold to Boston Nationals," *The Brooklyn Daily Eagle*, August 9, 1914.

"**Long and new spikes**" "Doctors Say Smith Has Chance to Resume Playing Third Base," *The Brooklyn Daily Eagle*, October 7, 1914.

"Gave me just what I wanted" John McGraw. *My Thirty Years in Baseball.*

"Local baseball enthusiasts" "Brooklyn to Lose 'Bad Bill' Dahlen," *The Daily Standard Union*, December 14, 1903.

"Was within four feet" "Umpire Rigler Strikes Dahlen At Ball Game," *The Brooklyn Citizen*, April 21, 1912.

"The perturbed Dahlen" "Punched By Umpire Dahlen Hits Back," *The Brooklyn Daily Eagle*, April 21, 1912.

"Keeping Bill Dahlen in the game" "Manager Dahlen In Tilt With Umpire," *New York Times*, April 21, 1912.

"'Bill can't do it'" "Hanlon's Men Forfeit A Game to The Giants," *The Brooklyn Daily Times*, May 14, 1901.

"I've parted with Dahlen" "Fans Protest Over Loss Of Shortstop Dahlen," *The Brooklyn Times Union*, December 14, 1903.

"His ears go up" Lyle Spatz. *Bad Bill Dahlen: The Rollicking Life and Times of an Early Baseball Star.*

"It has always been my ambition" Noel Hynd. *The Giants of the Polo Grounds: The Glorious Times of Baseball's New York Giants.*

"You used to be Bad Bill Dahlen" William F. Kirk, "To Bill Dahlen," *The Salt Lake Herald-Republican*, October 4, 1911.

"My first time at bat" Casey Stengel, as told to John P. Carmichael, "My Biggest Baseball Day," *The Dayton Daily News*, April 29, 1945.

"Now, Manager Dahlen" "Dahlen in M'Graw's Class, Says Ebbets, Crediting Him With Success of Dodgers," *The Evening World*, May 17, 1913.

"Towards the end of Stengel's rookie year" Goldman, *Forging Genius.*

"The Braves were successful" Aaron with Wheeler, *I Had a Hammer.*

"Carty was a big guy" Ibid.

"The strange thing about Carty" Ibid.

"There are some of those" Alex Coffin and Sam Hopkins, "3 Policemen Suspended in Carty Fight," *The Atlanta Constitution*, August 26, 1971.

"Blatant brutality" Ibid.

"Worst case of misconduct" "Carty Case Called Unequal," *The Atlanta Constitution*, August 28, 1971.

"Carty was aided" Wayne Minshew, "Richards' Visit 'Shook' Rico Up," *The Atlanta Constitution*, January 9, 1971.

"Rico always played" Terry Pluto. *The Curse of Rocky Colavito*.

"We talk real funny down here" Randy Newman, "Rednecks," 1974.

"The big, grinning, good humored" Marshall Hunt, "Worse—And More Of It," *New York Daily News*, April 27, 1931.

"Lay on the ground writhing" Rud Rennie, "Senators Down Yankees, 9–7, as Lary's 'Boner' Costs Two Runs and Robs Gehrig of Homer," *New York Herald Tribune*, April 27, 1931.

"Displaced the outer end" Associated Press, "Cooke Hurt, Unable to Play Two Weeks," *The Post-Star*, April 27, 1931.

"Yesterday, it was learned" Marshall Hunt, "Cooke Alarms Yanks!" *New York Daily News* January 6, 1932.

"Allen Cooke's arm" Walter Trumbull, "Reserves Make Yanks Stronger," *The Boston Globe*, March 23, 1932.

"Ah was doin' all right" John Kieran, "The Forgotten Man," *The New York Times*, July 9, 1932.

"You have to look at the other side" Lawrence Ritter. *The Glory of Their Times*.

"McIntyre is now posed" "M'Intyre Getting Little Sympathy," *The Washington Times*, June 28, 1906.

"Matty McIntyre, erstwhile outfielder" "M'Intyre, 'Horrible Example,' Will Right Suspension Rather Than Make Jump To Outlaws," *The Detroit Free Press*, June 26, 1906.

"It's just not the way" Jim Murray, "The Rose Is Still the Rose," *Los Angeles Times*, October 15, 1931.

"Imagine getting $10,000 a day" Ibid.

"**Jail is no good**" "Home not so sweet," *The Pittsburgh Press*, January 12, 1985.

"**A sick man**" Michael Kay, "A Problem Called Pascual," *New York Daily News*, March 29, 1990.

"**This is like getting a front-line pitcher**" Gerry Fraley, "Perez's comeback appears complete," *The Atlanta Constitution*, March 29, 1986.

www.ingramcontent.com/pod-product-compliance
Lightning Source LLC
Chambersburg PA
CBHW051646040426
42446CB00009B/996